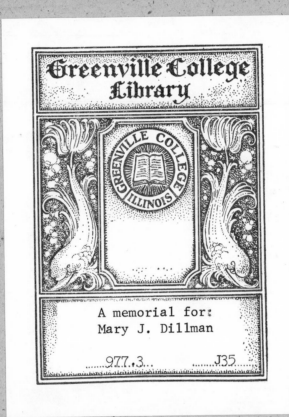

Center for Archaeological Investigations
Southern Illinois University at Carbondale

The Archaeology of Carrier Mills

10,000 Years in the Saline Valley of Illinois

Richard W. Jefferies

Illustrated by Thomas W. Gatlin

Southern Illinois University Press
Carbondale and Edwardsville

The publication of this volume was made possible by a grant in celebration of Peabody Coal Company's 100th anniversary.

Copyright © 1987 by the Board of Trustees, Southern Illinois University
All rights reserved
Edited by Barbara E. Cohen
Designed by Quentin Fiore
Production supervised by Natalia Nadraga

90 89 88 87   4 3 2 1

Library of Congress Cataloging-in-Publication Data

Jefferies, Richard W.
   The archaeology of Carrier Mills.

   Bibliography: p.
   Includes index.
     1. Carrier Mills Region (Ill.)—Antiquities.
2. Indians of North America—Illinois—Carrier Mills
Region—Antiquities.   3. Afro-Americans—Illinois—Carrier
Mills Region—Antiquities.   4. Illinois—Antiquities.
I. Southern Illinois University at Carbondale. Center
for Archaeological Investigations.   II. Title.
F549.C357J45   1987   977.3′992   86-4005
ISBN 0-8093-1309-X

Contents

Illustrations

Figures

Foreword

The genesis of Peabody's association with Southern Illinois University at Carbondale's Center for Archaeological Investigations took place in 1967 with the Black Mesa Archaeological Project in northeastern Arizona. This was one of our first, and probably most comprehensive, experiences with contract archaeology—studies that were mandated by legislation in the late 1960s and early 1970s. Whenever archaeological remains might be endangered by earth-moving activity such as mining, a thorough investigation must be made and detailed reports filed with government agencies before the activity can begin.

We proceeded cautiously at first because these new requirements represented significant costs. The archaeological community had to be involved in our mining plans for the first time, and we needed to develop procedures to fulfill the new regulations. As we experimented, we eventually achieved a mutual understanding and respect for one another, and Peabody's commitment to archaeological investigation was established.

Our long-term and continuing relationship on the Black Mesa project caused us to turn again to the Center for Archaeological Investigations when a project in Saline County in southern Illinois—closer to home and practically in SIU's backyard—presented itself in 1977. Although we have had mines in the area for many years, it was not until the Will Scarlet Mine near Carrier Mills was expanding eastward that we were confronted with potentially significant prehistoric and historic sites and the requirements of the new laws. Initial inspections revealed archaelogical sites that were large, complex, and promising in terms of information and artifacts covering a 10,000-year period. And so another cooperative effort between Peabody and SIU's Center for Archaeological Investigations was launched.

As the research progressed, SIU archaeologists became aware of a strong public interest in what was found at the sites and in what could be learned about their former inhabitants. The reports compiled by archaeologists for this type of project conform to specific government regulations. They are extremely detailed and technical, which makes them valuable to scientists and scholars but often dry and unpalatable for the layman. Recognizing that their official reports might not be read by a curious public, SIU approached Peabody to request financial support in writing and publishing a popular book about the Carrier Mills project.

The request came during 1983 when Peabody Coal Company was observing its one-hundredth anniversary. Since Peabody was founded in Illinois, it seemed appropriate to underwrite this historical book as a Centennial project that could be shared with people throughout the state and particularly with our neighbors in communities where we have operations.

Despite our somewhat cautious entry into the archaeological milieu, we look back with a great deal of pride on the results of our cooperative efforts with SIU archaeologists and hope that this work will generate an even greater enthusiasm for the study and support of archaeology.

Robert H. Quenon
President and Chief Executive Officer
Peabody Holding Company, Inc.

Acknowledgments

Preparation of this book would have been impossible without the interest, dedication, and hard work of many individuals, institutions, and organizations. Much of this effort focused on preparing the two-volume Carrier Mills technical report (Jefferies and Butler 1982) from which much of the information presented in this book was derived. More recent endeavors have been directed toward the actual writing, illustrating, editing, and publishing of this volume.

Peabody Coal Company, St. Louis, Missouri, supported field investigations, artifact analysis, and report writing associated with the Carrier Mills Archaeological Project (1977–1982). The additional funding provided by Peabody Coal Company for this book underscores their interest in supporting the study of Illinois' cultural heritage and making the resulting information available to as wide an audience as possible. Publication of this book would have been impossible without their continued interest and support.

Special thanks are given to those analysts who wrote the various technical reports that provided the data for this book. Sections discussing the prehistoric diet and paleoenvironmental conditions were based on the research of Dr. Neal H. Lopinot, project paleoethnobotanist. The investigations of Emanuel Breitburg and Jonathan A. Bloom, project faunal analysts, contributed data about prehistoric animal exploitation and paleoenvironmental conditions. Breitburg's detailed study of the Black Earth site bone tools supplied important new information about this aspect of prehistoric technology. William I. Woods's excellent study of soils and site formation processes proved invaluable for examining the nature of prehistoric activities at Carrier Mills. Michael L. Hargrave's innovative study of the Carrier Mills pottery and Ernest E. May's projectile point analysis provided the information on these areas of prehistoric technology. The information presented in the chapter on the Lakeview community is derived from the research of Dr. Brian M. Butler and James D. Merritt. Information presented on Archaic and Woodland period burial customs is based on the research of the late Dr. B. Mark Lynch. Everett J. Bassett's study of human skeletal remains provided information on the age, sex, and health characteristics of the prehistoric Carrier Mills residents. Other project specialists whose research results were incorporated in this book are Carol A. Morrow (analysis of Middle Archaic flaked stone tools), Gerald A. Oetelaar (Black Earth site microremains), George E. Avery (modern environmental conditions), and Peter T. Bobrowsky (Black Earth site gastropods).

Thanks are also given to the Center for Archaeological Investigations staff at Southern Illinois University at Carbondale for their encouragement and assistance. Special acknowledgment is given to Dr. George J. Gumerman, Director, for his support and assistance in the planning of the book and for presenting to Peabody Coal Company the idea of an archaeological book written for a more general audience. Drs. Brian M. Butler and David P. Braun, Carrier Mills Project Co-Principal Investigators, provided valuable ideas and suggestions concerning the planning and preparation of the book. Brian Butler's reading and commenting on the edited manuscript are especially appreciated. The assistance of Susan Wilson is gratefully acknowledged for her careful editing of the manuscript and for translating technical jargon into plain English. Thomas W. Gatlin prepared the illustrations and figures for the book. His attention to detail in the drawings reconstructing scenes from the daily routine of the Carrier Mills residents is gratefully appreciated. Brad H. Koldehoff, Michael L. Hargrave, Emanuel Breitburg, Dr. Lynne Peters Sullivan, Dr. Susan M. Ford, Dr. Edwin C. Galbreath, and Dr. Andrew L. Christenson were valuable sources of information in the preparation of the drawings. The long hours put in on the word processing equipment by Terri Mathews and Cam Rotramel are also acknowledged.

John Richardson and his staff at Scientific Photography, Southern Illinois University at Carbondale, are acknowledged for their assistance in preparing the photographic plates. I also thank the more than 100 people who served on the crew during the 1978 and 1979 field seasons and worked in the laboratory from 1978 to 1982.

The assistance of the staff at Southern Illinois University Press, especially that of W. Kenney Withers and Robert S. Phillips, is also greatly appreciated.

Finally, I acknowledge the assistance given by my colleagues at the University of Kentucky while I was completing the book. Without their patience, understanding, and cooperation, it might never have been finished.

The Archaeology of Carrier Mills

1 Introduction

The rolling hills, level grasslands, and tree-covered river valleys of Saline County have provided a home for southern Illinoisans for many years. During the nineteenth century, residents included the descendants of Euro- and Afro-Americans who ventured west to homestead and to settle the untamed Illinois wilderness. These adventurous people who left their more secure lives in the East for the challenges of frontier life were, however, not the first to live in Saline County. As early as 10,000 years ago, the prehistoric ancestors of modern American Indians hunted deer and collected acorns and hickory nuts in the nearby Shawnee Hills, fished the waters of the Saline River and nearby lakes, and anticipated the seasonal appearance of the wild geese and ducks that are still a favorite food of southern Illinois hunters.

The untrained observer often cannot detect evidence of prehistoric Indians. A few obvious signs still remain, such as the "stone forts" found scattered through the Shawnee Hills and the earth mounds that served as burial mounds and platforms for public buildings. Unfortunately, remains of this type are rare and are only associated with the late prehistoric inhabitants. Most of the evidence left behind by the thousands of years of prehistoric Indian activity consists of small concentrations of chert flakes and broken pottery scattered across the southern Illinois landscape.

Places where prehistoric people lived and performed the basic tasks of daily life are called sites by archaeologists. Literally hundreds of archaeological sites have been found in southern Illinois. Some appear to have been continuously occupied for thousands of years; others were used for a much shorter time. Sites occur in a wide range of topographic and environmental settings and vary in their size and character. Many other sites exist that have not been identified and recorded by archaeologists. Still others have been damaged or destroyed by agricultural, industrial, commercial, or residential development, leaving little or no record of their location or content.

An archaeological site can be quite small. It may consist of only two or three chert flakes, reflecting the very short time the site was used and the limited activities that took place there. An example of such a site might be the place where an Indian killed, skinned, and butchered a deer while on a hunting trip. The only evidence of that brief event would be a few flakes produced by the resharpening of a flaked stone knife or perhaps a piece of a broken stone hide scraper or spear point. Other kinds of special-purpose sites include fishing camps, nut collecting and processing camps, and quarry sites where the raw material to make stone tools was obtained.

Sites can also be very large, covering many acres and containing a wide assortment of artifacts (objects made or modified by people) associated with the numerous activities performed there. These complex sites usually represent a series of permanent occupations or encampments that may have spanned several seasons or perhaps were occupied year-round. Many of the basic tasks of daily living were carried out at such sites, including preparing food, making tools, building houses, and even burying the dead. These large sites may have also served as base camps from which small groups of Indians ventured forth to conduct the wider range of tasks that are represented at the smaller, special-purpose sites. Regardless of size, all sites help archaeologists understand how prehistoric peoples adapted to their environment.

In southern Illinois, intensively occupied sites tend to be located in areas that provided the quantity and variety of natural foods required to feed the group. Areas containing a number of different environmental zones offered a wider variety of edible plants and animals than those containing a single environmental zone. For example, the occupants of a site situated near both the uplands and a river or lake would have access to the acorns, hickory nuts, deer, and turkey of the uplands, as well as to the fish, waterfowl, and other plants and animals found in the wet areas.

One of the richest and most environmentally diverse areas in prehistoric southern Illinois was located along the South Fork of the Saline River, in southwest Saline County. These conditions still existed when the first Euro- and Afro-American settlers arrived in southern Illinois. Early land records indicate that this area, located approximately two miles south of the modern town of Carrier Mills, contained a mixture of low uplands, large areas of relatively shallow lakes and swamps, and a portion of the South Fork of the Saline River; the northern edge of the Shawnee Hills was located about three miles to the south. This area could provide a reliable, year-round food supply, so it is not surprising that it also contains some of the largest and most complex archaeological sites in the region. Research has demonstrated that these sites contained not only intensive prehistoric occupations but also an important early Historic one, the Lakeview community.

This book focuses on the results of five years of archaeological investigations at three sites located in a 143-acre area known as the Carrier Mills Archaeological District (Figure 1-1). The existence of these large, intensively occupied sites had been known for more than a hundred years. Excavation of mid-nineteenth-century trash pits by the Carrier Mills archaeologists yielded a number of Indian artifacts, such as stone axes, spear points, and large, decorated pieces of Indian pottery, scattered among the more modern trash. The presence of these discarded artifacts shows that the nineteenth-century Saline County residents collected Indian artifacts much in the same way that their descendants do today.

Finding these sites would have been easy. The soil in the sites is much darker than the surrounding buff-colored soil. It is so dark in one area that the site is locally known as the Black Earth site. The dark color is caused by the charcoal from thousands of fires that were built on the site during the millennia of prehistoric Indian occupation. These sites were also easily identified by the dense concentrations of pottery, stone tools, chert flakes, and rock associated with the wide range of tasks conducted at those locations.

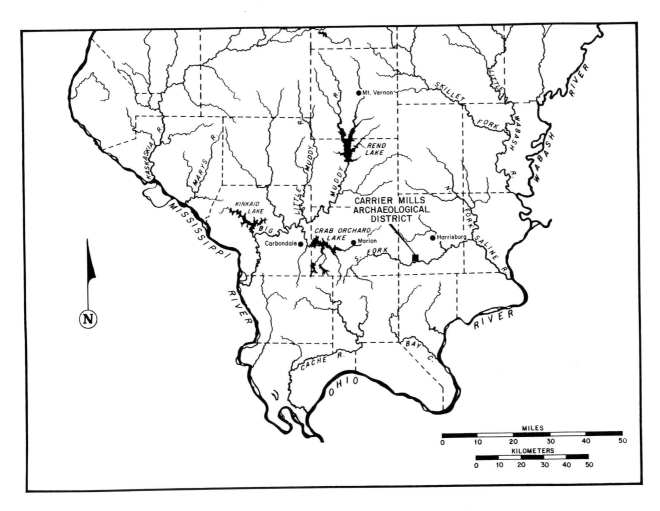

Figure 1-1. Location of the Carrier Mills Archaeological District.

Until the 1950s, we knew relatively little about the prehistoric people who inhabited what is now Saline County. Artifact collectors or amateur archaeologists performed most of the digging at the numerous sites in the area, including those sites at Carrier Mills. Unfortunately, most of this work added little to our knowledge of how people lived in the past because the diggers used improper excavation techniques and failed to keep detailed records of the work.

The earliest known work at Carrier Mills by professional archaeologists took place in 1957, when Bettye Broyles, an archaeologist from the Illinois State Museum in Springfield, conducted an archaeological survey—a procedure used by archaeologists to find previously unknown sites—of parts of Saline County. In a survey, archaeologists walk over an area looking for signs of prehistoric or historic activity. In areas of dense ground cover, such as grass or leaves, they use shovels to dig small holes and then examine the up-turned soil for indications (chert flakes, sherds, and charcoal, for example) of a site. If they find a site, the archaeologists collect artifacts from the ground surface and make a record of the site location and other pertinent information for future reference.

No additional archaeology was done in the area until 1972, when personnel from the Southern Illinois University Museum surveyed part of the Saline River valley. At that time, the locations of the Carrier Mills sites were more accurately plotted and the sites were assigned their current identification number, or site number. Encoded in the site numbers are three pieces of information. For example, in "11Sa-86," the "11" stands for the state of Illinois (derived from Illinois' eleventh position in an alphabetical listing of all states, exclud-

§ Archaeology at
Carrier Mills

ing Alaska and Hawaii); "Sa" is the abbreviation for Saline County; "86" signifies that the site was the eighty-sixth site recorded in Saline County. The numbers of the three Carrier Mills sites are 11Sa-86, 11Sa-87 (also known as the Black Earth site), and 11Sa-88. (Hereafter, for brevity, the state code has been dropped from the site numbers.)

In 1975, museum staff members collected additional information on the Carrier Mills sites for their nomination to the National Register of Historic Places, which was approved in 1978. The passage of the National Historic Preservation Act (NHPA) in 1966 established the legal and administrative framework for historic preservation in the United States. The NHPA authorized the Secretary of the Interior to maintain a national register of historic properties having local, state, or national significance. Although the National Register was originally established to identify important historical communities, areas, sites, structures, and objects, it lists prehistoric cultural resources as well (King et al. 1977). The listing of an archaeological site on the National Register does not guarantee that it will never be damaged or destroyed. Rather, it ensures that the effects of any potentially destructive activity will be carefully considered before that activity is begun.

§ The Coal Industry in Saline County

Although scientific investigation of the Carrier Mills sites has been a relatively recent, on-again off-again pursuit, another activity of much greater economic and social significance to area residents has had a longer and uninterrupted history—that of coal mining. The southern Illinois region contains some of the largest bituminous coalfields in the United States. The coal mining companies and their support industries have provided jobs for thousands of southern Illinoisans. Without the coal industry, the economic and social development of the region would have been quite different.

No official state records exist of coal mining in Saline County before 1880, but local stories and tradition indicate that at least two and perhaps many more small hillside mines operated in the county prior to that date. The first coal mine, owned by John Norman, was located about one mile south of Harrisburg. The Norman mine may have opened as early as 1856. In 1873, the first railroad shipping mine was opened near the community of Ledford, adjacent to the tracks of the Cairo and Vincennes Railroad. Between 1880 and 1910, the number of coal companies and mines operating in Saline County continued to grow. Most of these were shaft mines, but some were dug horizontally into the slopes of hills (Lindsey 1947:205–209).

In 1902, John Davenport and his associates formed the Egyptian Coal and Coke Company with a capital investment of $70,000. In 1906, the company opened two new mines about four miles southwest of Harrisburg. These mines, known as Mine A and Mine B, were eventually controlled by Big Creek Coals, Inc. In 1929, all of Big Creek Coals' Saline County holdings were purchased by Peabody Coal Company of Chicago. The purchase of these mines by Peabody Coal marked the beginning of a long-lasting relationship between that company and the people of Saline County. In that same year, Peabody Coal bought a mine in Brushy township, located north of Carrier Mills. The mine, commonly referred to as the Harco mine, produced an average of more than 5,000 tons of coal a day during the mid-1940s (Lindsey 1947:209–216).

During the late 1940s, Peabody Coal purchased additional land located about two miles west of the Harco mine. Peabody introduced new, innovative mining techniques at this mine. A conveyor belt system moved the coal out of the mine and loaded it in large-capacity trucks for transport to coal washing facilities. This new transport system was much more economical and efficient than the traditional method of using railroad cars on steel rails. It represented a major advancement for coal production (Lindsey 1947:219–220).

Major changes took place in the Illinois coal industry in the 1940s with the introduction and development of new surface mining technology. The new mining technique was generally safer and much less expensive than traditional shaft or underground mining, but it did have the disadvantage of disturbing more of the earth's surface.

Peabody Coal Company continued to expand its Saline County mining operations following World War II, eventually opening a new surface mine two miles south of Carrier Mills, known as the Will Scarlet mine. As mining at Will Scarlet progressed through the years, Peabody purchased the mineral rights on land located east of the mine to allow for future expansion. Unknown to any of the parties involved at that time, the Carrier Mills archaeological sites were located in this area.

The events that eventually led to the excavation of the three Carrier Mills sites had long and independent histories. First, the prehistoric Indians of modern Saline County found abundant food in the area, making it well suited for long-term settlement. Both artifact collectors and professional archaeologists recognized that these sites were not only large and contained many interesting artifacts but also that they were critically important for understanding how prehistoric people lived in southern Illinois.

§ The Cooperation of Science and Industry

Second, the economic well-being of the region was closely tied to the continued growth of the coal industry. Plans to mine the coal seams buried beneath the sites had been formulated years before their archaeological significance was fully realized.

A third important factor was the passage of federal legislation dealing with the protection and preservation of natural and cultural resources. Archaeological sites are considered to be a nonrenewable cultural resource, much in the same way coal or oil is considered to be a nonrenewable natural resource. Once they are used or destroyed, they are gone forever. These laws require federal agencies or private businesses using federal money to submit a report stating the effects of land modification on the environment and on cultural resources. Although it was unclear at the time whether the opening of the new section of the Will Scarlet mine was subject to these laws, Peabody Coal Company decided to fund the research required to fully evaluate the archaeological importance of the sites in the Carrier Mills Archaeological District.

In other parts of the United States, situations like the one at Carrier Mills have caused major disagreement between the groups favoring industrial or economic expansion and those favoring the preservation of a significant cultural resource. The history of this project, in marked contrast, is one of excellent cooperation between industry, represented by Peabody Coal Company, and science, represented by Southern Illinois University at Carbondale.

In September 1977, officials of Peabody Coal Company asked archaeologists from the Center for Archaeological Investigations, Southern Illinois University at Carbondale, to inspect some of the archaeological sites located in the Will Scarlet mine expansion area. When archaeologists Brian Butler and David Braun examined the sites, they realized that they were very large and complex and could reveal a tremendous amount of information about the past. After discussing the results of their inspection with Peabody officials, the archaeologists made plans to more thoroughly study the sites. A careful surface inspection was performed and small excavations were also conducted to collect more information. The field crew finished their work on the cold, snowy Christmas Eve of 1977. Their results were reviewed by Peabody officials who, after evaluating their mine development plans, gave the archaeologists permission to start full-scale excavations at the three Carrier Mills sites the following spring.

A Plan for the Past

In modern, scientific archaeology, the term "research design" describes a plan that helps ensure that the research will be conducted as efficiently as possible and that the results will be scientifically valid (Daniels 1972). Also, the research design specifies the topics or questions to be investigated, the kinds of information needed to address these topics, the techniques used to collect that information, the procedures that will be used for data analysis, and a variety of other important concerns that will help bring the research to a successful completion. It is impossible to do good archaeology without a well-conceived research design.

Before the 1978 field investigations, archaeologists formulated the research design for the Carrier Mills Archaeological Project based on the results of the 1977 testing. At Carrier Mills, primary research goals focused on examining the relationships between the prehistoric and early historic inhabitants and their environment. To accomplish this, the archaeologists had to collect a wide range of cultural and environmental information and to employ specialists from a variety of scientific disciplines to interpret it. The more specific goals of the project included the following: (1) to develop a better understanding of the ages of the various prehistoric occupations represented at the sites; (2) to understand more fully the technology and social organization of the prehistoric inhabitants; (3) to obtain a better understanding of the environment in which the prehistoric Indians lived; (4) to collect information about the diet, health, and physical characteristics of the prehistoric inhabitants by analyzing the numerous prehistoric human burials; and (5) to investigate the historical remains of the nineteenth-century Lakeview settlement. These five research topics were influential in determining the specific techniques used in excavation and the ways in which different kinds of information were recovered.

The Tools of the Trade

The archaeologists at Carrier Mills used a number of special techniques to collect information needed to address the topics defined in the research design. When excavation conditions called for very careful work, they used the more traditional tools of archaeology, such as the dental pick, trowel, and paintbrush. In other instances, large quantities of soil were moved by heavy construction equipment when more deeply buried deposits needed to be exposed.

The specific details of the field strategy were governed by three factors. First, the sites were known to be large, extremely complex, and very important from a historical and archaeological perspective. Second, fieldwork was scheduled to be completed within a six-month period extending from May 15 through November 30, 1978. It was not learned until later that a second field season would be possible during the summer of 1979. Third, the time available for fieldwork did not allow the use of a multistage field effort commonly employed in a project of this scale. In a multistage strategy, the results of each stage of work are used to plan the subsequent stages, permitting the alteration of research plans in the event that unexpected situations arise.

With these factors in mind, archaeologists investigated each of the three sites in a series of four phases. In some cases, because of time restrictions, more than one phase was conducted at a time. Phase One consisted of a controlled surface collection. Each site was first disced using a tractor and harrow to clear the vegetation and to improve surface visibility. Squares measuring 20 feet (6 m) on a side were laid out, with small flags on metal pins marking the corners of each. Artifacts on the surface were then collected. Diagnostic artifacts, those items associated with specific periods of time (such as certain kinds of projectile points [spear and arrow points] and potsherds [pieces of broken clay pots]), provide information about the age of prehistoric occupations. The quantity and types of artifacts found often help identify the parts of a site that were most intensively used and the kinds of activities that were performed there. This information is often used by archaeologists in deciding which parts of a site to excavate.

Phase Two consisted of the excavation of a series of squares called excavation units, roughly 10 feet by 10 feet (3 m by 3 m), that were placed at regular intervals across the sites (Figure 1-2). The soil in these units was carefully removed in layers (or levels) 4 inches (10 cm) thick using shovels and trowels. Dirt from each layer was screened through one-half-inch hardware cloth to ensure the systematic recovery of artifacts. The purpose of the Phase Two work was to recover a representative sample of artifacts and other materials from all parts of the sites with which to investigate the ways in which different areas were used.

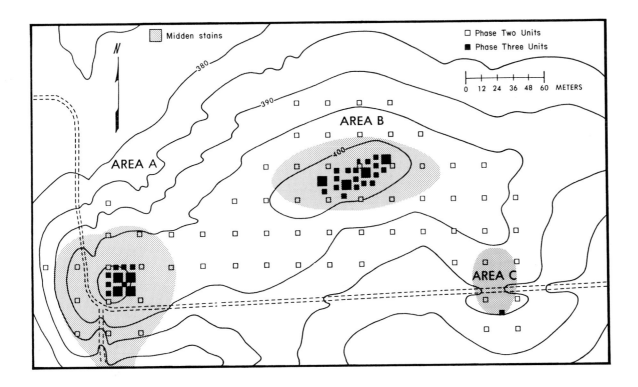

Figure 1-2. Location of excavation units at Areas A, B, and C of the Black Earth site.

Phase Three consisted of the excavation of deep middens, the dark, greasy, organically enriched soil containing the debris and by-products of thousands of years of prehistoric and historic occupation (Plate 1-1). The midden at the Black Earth site was at least 5 feet deep. Excavation techniques used in Phase Three were basically the same as those used in

PLATE 1-1. Excavation of a large Phase 3 unit at Area B of Sa-87.

Phase Two, except that the units were placed next to each other, forming larger excavation blocks. Emphasis was placed on recovering detailed information about the spatial distribution of artifacts, pits, burials, houses, and activity areas associated with different occupations, and examining how on-site activities changed through time.

The final phase of fieldwork, Phase Four, involved the use of mechanized equipment. After all hand-excavation was completed, the plowzone (the upper soil layers that had been repeatedly disturbed through the years by the farmer's plow) was removed. Mechanical pans, commonly used in highway construction, removed much of the plowzone, and backhoes were used for more localized areal stripping and for excavating deep exploratory trenches. This procedure exposed large areas for the mapping and excavation of subsurface prehistoric and historic features. In archaeology, a feature is a large, nonportable facility, such as food storage and processing pits, hearths, burials, and remains of buildings (Plate 1-2).

A number of different kinds of specialized collections or samples were taken during the various phases of excavation. One of the most common types collected by archaeologists was material for radiocarbon dating. Radiocarbon, or carbon-14, dating is the best known and most commonly used dating technique in the Midwest. Radiocarbon dates are obtained from a wide range of organic remains, including charcoal, wood, burned bone, and shell. Samples are carefully collected from those deposits for which precise chronological information is desired, then packed and submitted to a radiocarbon dating laboratory for analysis.

A second kind, a flotation sample, consists of soil collected from an excavation level or a pit. These soil samples are then processed, using water or chemicals, to separate seeds and other types of small plant remains from the soil. Plant remains recovered using the flotation process provide valuable new insights into the kinds of plant foods eaten by prehistoric people as well as data on past vegetation and climate.

Another kind of soil sample collected was used to analyze the chemical and textural characteristic of the soil itself. Many activities performed by prehistoric people resulted in the deposition of residues and by-products on the ground surface. Eventually, these materials decomposed and became part of the soil. The chemical decomposition of wood charcoal and ash introduced large quantities of calcium, potassium, and magnesium. Sandstone, used to make certain kinds of tools, gradually disintegrated through use and exposure to the elements. The deposition of sand grains produced by this process increased the soils' sand content. Collections of other types of specialized samples, such as snail shell and animal bone, provided additional information to assist archaeologists in the study of prehistoric cultures and past environments.

PLATE 1-2. Carrier Mills field crew shovel scraping the exposed features at Area 1 of Sa-86 after machine stripping of plowzone.

The demanding schedule faced by the archaeologists in charge of the Carrier Mills project required that a large number of workers with a wide range of archaeological expertise be quickly assembled. A search of anthropology departments and archaeology labs at colleges and universities in the East and Midwest produced personnel with the training needed to do this work. During the most intensive period of fieldwork in the summer of 1978, more than 50 people were employed by the project. Most were assigned to one of the three crews that performed the actual excavations. Others were assigned more specialized jobs, such as the operation of the flotation equipment located on the banks of the Saline River south of the site. Still others were on crews responsible for the recovery and preservation of human skeletal material or the washing, sorting, and analysis of artifacts (Plate 1-3). The successful completion of the Carrier Mills Archaeological Project would have been impossible without the dedication and hard work of these people.

PLATE 1-3. The project osteologist was responsible for the excavation and preservation of human skeletal remains.

Activities of the excavation crews were divided into three stages. During the first six weeks, extending from mid-May to the end of June, each crew consisted of a field supervisor, a crew chief, and five field workers. Phases One and Two of field investigations were completed during this period. The late spring and early summer of 1978 were exceptionally hot, and midday temperatures of over 100° F were not unusual. Despite these trying conditions, the crews succeeded in collecting artifacts from the surfaces of more than fifteen hundred 20 foot by 20 foot (6 m by 6 m) surface squares and excavating nearly one hundred fifty 10 foot by 10 foot (3 m by 3 m) units.

Phases Three and Four of fieldwork were started in July, and the size of each crew was doubled to meet the demands of the additional work. Many of the new crew members working during this stage were residents of the Carrier Mills–Harrisburg area. Although they had no previous archaeological experience, they contributed greatly to the success of the project. During the remaining two months of the 1978 season, crews gradually reverted to their pre-July size. Phase Three and Four work continued until the end of November 1978.

A number of specialists and consultants were hired by the project during the 1978 season. Many continued with the project in subsequent years. Included in this group were Neal Lopinot, ethnobotanical specialist responsible for analyzing the recovered plant remains; Emanuel Breitburg, the faunal analyst in charge of studying the nonhuman skeletal remains; William Woods, the soil scientist; and Peter Bobrowsky, an expert on land snails.

Field operations during May to August of 1979 were more limited than during the preceding year. Fieldwork focused on the completion of the Phase Three and Four work that was not finished in 1978. As a result of the two seasons of intensive excavation, the volume of hand-excavated soil amounted to more than 1,200 cubic yards (950 m³), and nearly 20,000 square yards (18,000 m²) of site area was exposed using mechanized equipment.

All excavated materials were washed, sorted, and stored for future analysis at the processing laboratory of the Center for Archaeological Investigations on the Southern Illinois University at Carbondale campus. One supervisor ran the laboratory, which was staffed by 5 to 10 student workers.

A team of experts at the Center for Archaeological Investigations analyzed the artifacts and other cultural materials. These specialists prepared reports on the many different kinds of remains recovered during the nine months of fieldwork. The expertise of these specialists covered the fields of human osteology (the study of bones), botany, zoology, geology, soil science, as well as many other specialized research areas, such as the analysis of pottery and flaked stone artifacts. Analysis was completed in July 1982.

§ The Inhabitants of Carrier Mills

Projectile points and potsherds excavated from the Carrier Mills sites indicate that prehistoric people visited and lived in the area for at least the past 10,000 years. They may have visited earlier, but no trace has yet been found.

Variation in the archaeological remains reflects the ways in which prehistoric societies changed through time. For example, differences in tools and in the materials of which they were made provide clues to changes in technology; variations in the way the dead were buried may reflect changes in the organization of prehistoric societies; and differences in the types of plant and animal remains may indicate changes in the diet of prehistoric peoples and in the environment in which they lived. By studying these and other complex technological and sociological processes, archaeologists can describe the various stages or periods of prehistoric cultural development in southern Illinois.

It is relatively unusual for one area, like the Carrier Mills Archaeological District, to provide enough information about past human behavior to explain how prehistoric people adapted to thousands of years of cultural and environmental change. Because of the lack of previous archaeological investigations in the Saline River valley, it is necessary to borrow examples from other portions of southern Illinois and adjacent parts of the Midwest to describe the different prehistoric periods. The following brief summary of the culture history of the Midwest will serve as a baseline with which to compare and contrast the findings from Carrier Mills. (Much of the cultural-historical information contained in the following synthesis and later sections of this book is adapted from Muller and Davy 1977 and Robison and Butler 1981.)

The Paleoindian Period (Pre-8000 B.C.)

The earliest known inhabitants of the Midwest were small bands of hunters and gatherers who lived on wild animals and plants. Archaeologists originally thought that they lived in migratory groups that pursued the large species of mammals, such as the mammoth and mastodon, which inhabited parts of North America 10,000 to 12,000 years ago at the end of the last Pleistocene glaciation. In more recent years, ideas about how Paleoindian peoples exploited the environment have changed. Although these large mammals may have formed a part of the Paleoindian diet, these groups probably also exploited a wide range of other plant and animal food sources.

Although rare, evidence of Paleoindian groups in southern Illinois has been found. Sites are generally small and appear to represent brief occupations by small groups of people. Sites are usually identified by the presence of a distinct kind of projectile point known as a Clovis or Clovis-like fluted point. They are called fluted points because of the channel, or flute, created by the removal of a flake from each of the points' two flat surfaces or faces. These points were mounted on the end of a javelin or spear used for hunting. Most of these projectile points and associated materials are found along the first terraces and uplands of major drainages, such as the Wabash, Cache, and Big Muddy rivers (Figure 1-1). If sites were present in the river valleys, they are now buried under more recent floodplain sediments. The scarcity of Paleoindian artifacts and sites probably reflects the low population density during this time. Although no Paleoindian artifacts were found at any of the Carrier Mills sites, Paleoindian groups probably occasionally visited this part of southern Illinois.

The Archaic Period (8000–1000 B.C.)

Since the Archaic period covers such a lengthy time span, it is usually divided into three subperiods, Early, Middle, and Late Archaic. Following the end of the Pleistocene, deciduous forests resembling those found in southern Illinois today gradually replaced the forests that grew in the glacial climate. This change had a significant impact on the way people lived, eventually leading to the development of specialized hunter-gatherer societies. Their primary sources of meat were deer and turkey, although they also ate a wide variety of fish, birds, and smaller mammals. Nuts, especially hickory, are one of the most common plant remains found on Archaic sites. A diverse assortment of other kinds of nuts, seeds, and miscellaneous plant parts supplemented the diet. Groups of hunters and gatherers moved across the landscape to take advantage of foods that were in season.

Different Archaic groups adapted to their environments in various ways. These different ways of living are reflected by their projectile point styles (Figure 1-3). As the Archaic-period Indians became more efficient in obtaining foods from their environment, their tools became more specialized—that is, they were created for a specific purpose. Many of the new tools were produced by grinding stone rather than by flaking and chipping it.

The population continued to grow during the Archaic, and in some areas more complex forms of social organization are echoed in the treatment of the dead. Burials containing a greater quantity of elaborate grave goods made from exotic materials (copper and marine shell) may represent higher status individuals than those containing few or no grave goods.

The Woodland Period (1000 B.C.–A.D. 1000)

The Woodland period is also divided into Early, Middle, and Late subperiods. The major characteristic that distinguishes the Early Woodland from the Late Archaic period is the appearance of ceramic vessels, or pottery. In southern Illinois, the first part of the Woodland period was basically a continuation of Late Archaic lifeways, with the very gradual adoption of pottery. The earliest pottery found in southern Illinois consisted of crude, heavy, thick-walled vessels. Differences in the vessel shapes and the way in which they

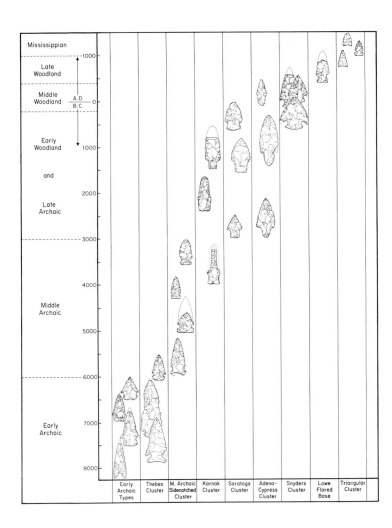

Figure 1-3. Chronological placement and cultural affiliations of the Carrier Mills projectile point types.

were made could reflect changes in the kinds of foods being cooked. This period was also characterized by the increasing importance of gardening, or horticulture, as a source of food. The earliest experiments in growing plants probably involved native varieties, such as sunflowers, marsh elder, and goosefoot. By the end of the Woodland period, an assortment of tropical plants from Mexico, including maize (corn) and squash, were being cultivated. Hunting and gathering, though, still accounted for most of the Woodland people's diet.

One of the major characteristics of the period was the development of an extensive exchange system known as the Hopewell Interaction Sphere (Caldwell 1964). The Hopewellian exchange network was responsible for the movement of an assortment of exotic items, like copper, obsidian, mica, and marine shell, throughout much of the East and Midwest. Many of the artifacts produced from these "foreign" materials are found in the graves of a few select individuals. These high-status people were often buried in specially prepared tombs in or under cone-shaped earthen mounds.

The population continued to grow during the Woodland period, and groups tended to live in one place for a longer time. The introduction of the bow and arrow during the last part of the period brought about changes in hunting strategies and made some kinds of game more accessible.

The Mississippian Period (A.D. 1000–1600)

The Mississippian period represents the highest level of sociopolitical development attained in prehistoric eastern North America. The period was characterized by the increased significance of cultivated foods, especially corn, beans, and squash. In spite of the increased importance of gardening as a food source, the Mississippian peoples still hunted and collected wild animals and plants. The period was also marked by a much more complex form of social and political organization, large communities consisting of a number of settlements, and the widespread exchange of exotic items.

Many Mississippian sites are located on the floodplains of major streams and rivers. Some sites are quite large, containing numerous earthen mounds and other public or ceremonial structures. Smaller Mississippian sites are located around the large ones; the smallest and most common consist of only one or two domestic structures, which operated as farmsteads in the complex settlement hierarchy.

Small, triangular-shaped projectile points that first appeared toward the end of the Woodland period became the predominant projectile point style during the Mississippian period (Figure 1-3). In many areas, Mississippian pottery was manufactured with particles of crushed mussel shell added to the clay paste to increase the strength of the vessel walls. This is commonly referred to as shell-tempered pottery. Finally, flat-topped earth mounds that served as substructures or foundations for ceremonial buildings were constructed at many of the large sites. Often, they were built at the edges of large public areas called plazas.

The Historic Period (A.D. 1600–Present)

The earliest known European contact with the southern Illinois Indians occurred when French explorers traveled through the Ohio Valley in the seventeenth century. By that time, the large Mississippian centers were largely unoccupied. The high level of social and political complexity had broken down and had been replaced by a much simpler way of life. The region had apparently undergone considerable depopulation and social disruption.

Just before the entry of the French into the region, much of Illinois was populated by the Miami tribe and by tribes of the Illinois Confederacy. The picture is very confusing due to the disruption and turmoil caused by the Iroquois tribes to the east and by the westward movement of other eastern tribes to avoid attack by the Iroquois. Eventually, many remnants of the displaced tribes, such as the Shawnee, Fox, and Kickapoo, ended up in Illinois (Fowler and Hall 1978:568). The unstable social conditions and the rapid and constant movement of the historic Indian tribes make it difficult, if not impossible, to establish any ties between Indian groups represented in the archaeological record and historic Indians.

The first large-scale Anglo-American settlement in southern Illinois took place near the end of the eighteenth century. One of the first permanent settlements was at Shawneetown in 1800. The number of settlers coming to Illinois sharply increased following the War of 1812. Early settlements in the Saline River valley were centered around the saline springs in Gallatin County. The subsequent development of the salt works eventually led to the first major industry in southern Illinois.

Saline County was formed from the western part of Gallatin County in 1847, but Anglo- and Afro-American settlers had been moving into this area during the previous 50 years. In 1818, approximately 90 families were living in the area, primarily along the road between Shawneetown and Kaskaskia. Many of the early Saline County residents came from Kentucky, North Carolina, and Tennessee. The earliest settlement was founded probably at Somerset, in the southeast part of the county. The Lakeview community, a small settlement of black freedmen located in and around the Carrier Mills Archaeological District, dates to the mid-1820s. According to local tradition, the community was founded by several families who moved to Illinois from North Carolina at the end of the War of 1812. Remnants of the community still exist, but most of the black population has moved to larger towns and cities because of better employment opportunities.

The Saline County economy has changed considerably since the county's formation in 1847. During the early years, salt production and tobacco cultivation were major economic activities. Timbering, grist mills, pottery manufacturing, and wood cording provided significant income during the last part of the nineteenth century. Coal mining became important around 1880, eventually becoming the county's major industry by the early twentieth century.

2 The Present and Past Environments

Artifacts and other cultural and environmental data from the Carrier Mills sites show that the prehistoric Indians depended on the plants, animals, water, minerals, and other natural resources found in their environment for their survival. They had few of the technological and economic benefits available to us today to modify natural conditions or to find alternate sources for the basic requirements of life.

We cannot assume that the environment was stable throughout the entire 10,000 years of prehistory represented at Carrier Mills. Information from other parts of the world indicates that the climate varied considerably following the end of the last glaciation, and southern Illinois was no exception. The modern landscape, with its trees, animals, streams, and lakes, may not accurately portray the conditions present 200, much less 10,000 years ago. We cannot hope to fully understand the way of life of the prehistoric people of the Saline unless we know something about the environment in which they lived and how it changed through time.

§ The Research Area

The Carrier Mills Archaeological District was located immediately north of the South Fork of the Saline River and approximately one and one-half miles south of the town of Carrier Mills (Figure 2-1). The District consisted of a roughly 143-acre area of low uplands that was divided into eastern and western sections by a small intermittent stream. The three sites, Sa-86, Sa-87, and Sa-88, plus a series of smaller sites and artifact scatters, were situated on adjacent upland ridges that overlooked larger expanses of lowlands to the south and west (Figure 2-2). Plate 2-1 is an aerial photograph taken by a Southern Illinois University Museum archaeologist in 1975 showing the location of the three major sites in the District. The dark areas identified in the photograph were midden stains marking the locations of the most intensive prehistoric and historic activity. Because of the size and complexity of the sites, two were further divided into "areas," representing discrete artifact concentrations within each site.

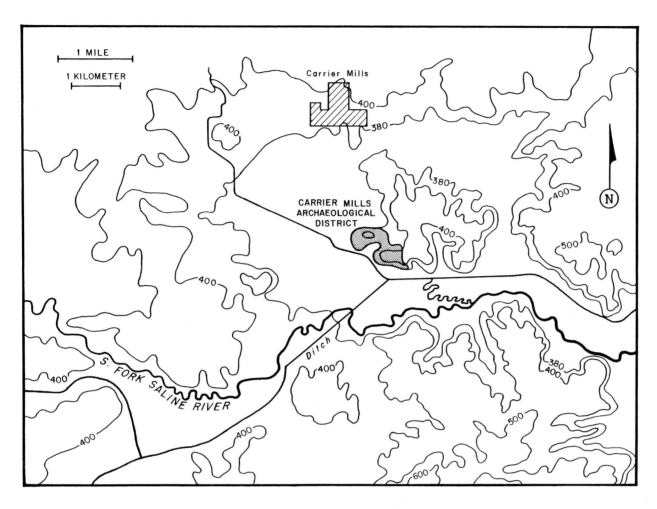

Figure 2-1. Topographic setting of the Carrier Mills Archaeological District.

The major site in the District's eastern section was Sa-86, which occupied the highest point in that part of the upland (Figure 2-2). Four artifact concentrations were identified during the surface collection and designated as Areas 1 through 4. Area 1 is the largest, covering more than 15,500 square yards (13,000 m). It had been intensively occupied pre-historically, but the artifact–bearing deposits were relatively shallow and were contained in the plow–disturbed soil, or plowzone. The removal of the plowzone during the final stage of fieldwork revealed many Middle and Late Woodland food storage and processing pits preserved in the undisturbed soil below the plowzone. Although artifacts dating from the Middle Archaic through the Mississippian period were found, the most significant information recovered from Area 1 concerned the Middle and Late Woodland and Mississippian occupations. Excavations at Area 2 revealed a similar situation as found at Area 1 but on a much smaller scale. Areas 3 and 4 were very small artifact scatters.

The largest and most complex site, Sa-87 (also known as the Black Earth site), was located in the western portion of the District (Figure 2-2). This site had three distinctly definable midden stains. Area A, covering about 20,000 square yards (17,000 m²), was at the extreme western end of the site, overlooking a large low area to the west. This part of the site was intensively excavated during both 1978 and 1979 and proved to be the most significant area in the District. Excavations in the center of Area A revealed an artifact-bearing midden deposit more than 5 feet (1.5 m) deep (Plate 2-2). The accumulation of the thick midden layer is directly attributable to the activities of the prehistoric inhabitants. The lowest and oldest portion of the midden deposit was a buff-colored soil that dated to the

PLATE 2-1. Aerial photograph of the District. View to the southeast.

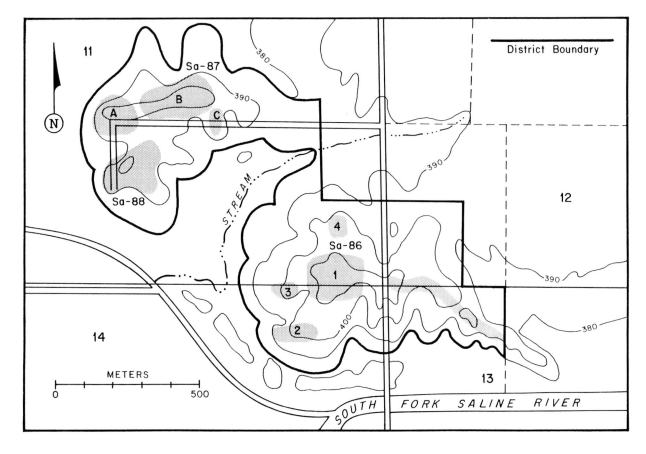

Figure 2-2. Location of sites in the District.

PLATE 2-2. Black Earth site field crew excavating Phase 2 and 3 units at Area A midden.

late Middle Archaic period (4000–3000 B.C.) (Figure 2-3). Many different kinds of artifacts, food remains, and other residues of daily life were contained in this cultural layer or zone. A large number of pits and other types of features were also present, along with more than 150 human burials.

The upper midden zones showed evidence of Late Archaic (3000–1000 B.C.) through Late Woodland (A.D. 400–1000) occupations. Archaeological remains from this portion of the midden include Late Archaic projectile points, Middle and Late Woodland pottery, and deep circular pits from the Middle Woodland occupation. Although fieldwork at Area A contributed information about many different aspects of prehistoric life at Carrier Mills, the large, relatively undisturbed Middle Archaic occupation zone yielded the most important data.

Area B was a roughly oval-shaped midden area located along a low ridge crest northeast of Area A (Figure 2-2). The artifact scatter covered roughly 31,000 square yards (26,000 m²), composing nearly half of the total surface area of Sa-87. Area B also had a midden deposit, but its maximum depth was only about 30 inches (80 cm), considerably less than found at Area A. Area B artifacts indicate that the site was occupied throughout the prehistoric period, but the size and intensity of those occupations varied considerably. The Area B Middle Archaic occupation was less intensive than Area A's, but Late Archaic activity was much greater. Without a doubt, the most significant aspect of Area B was the large Late Woodland occupation contained in the upper midden zones. The large quantities of Late Woodland pottery and projectile points recovered during excavation tell us that the site was intensively occupied during this period.

Area C was located about 330 yards (300 m) east of Area A and southeast of Area B on a low knoll formed by the southeastern extension of the ridge (Figure 2-2). Although a midden stain is visible in the aerial photograph, occupational intensity and midden depth

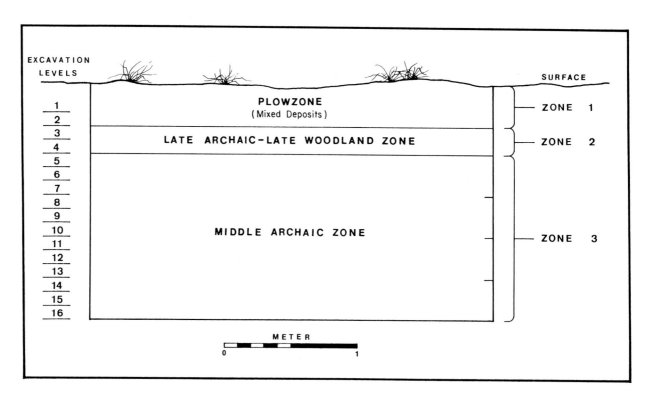

Figure 2-3. Diagram showing stratigraphic divisions of midden at Area A of the Black Earth site (Sa-87).

were much less than at either Area A or B. The shallow midden and extensive disturbance by plowing made it unlikely that much intact midden remained. Although artifacts dating from the Middle Archaic through the Late Woodland periods were found, their low frequency suggests that Area C was never an area of intensive prehistoric activity.

The second site in the western part of the District, Sa-88, was located on a low upland spur south of Sa-87 (Figure 2-2). The site's artifact scatter covered nearly 36,000 square yards (30,000 m²) and contained two distinct midden stains. The largest covered about 15,500 square yards (13,000 m²) along the ridgetop, and a second much smaller stain covered about 1,700 square yards (1,400 m²) on a small promontory along the site's southern edge. The Sa-88 midden had a maximum depth of about 24 inches (60 cm) and was similar in many respects to that at Area B. Middle Archaic through Late Woodland occupations were represented at the site. Excavation and large-scale stripping of the plowzone revealed hundreds of features attributable to these occupations. More than 200 human burials were also discovered during the two seasons of fieldwork.

This brief discussion of each of the Carrier Mills sites shows that they were not all used in the same way during the 10,000-year period. Many of the differences are closely tied to the location of the sites and the nature of the environment in which these prehistoric people lived. Before these relationships can be more thoroughly investigated, we must first examine the character of the environment and how it may have changed through time.

§ The Modern Environment

Our knowledge of the contemporary and Historic period environment of the Saline River valley region, and more specifically the Carrier Mills area, is based on a detailed study of nineteenth- and twentieth-century descriptions of the topography, geology, soil, climate, vegetation, and wildlife. These facts, combined with the information about the three archaeological sites presented in the previous section, will serve as a frame of reference from which to interpret the changing relationships between the prehistoric people and their natural surroundings.

Topography

The Carrier Mills Archaeological District is located near several distinct natural areas or divisions of Illinois (Schwegman 1975). The District is actually in the southern part of the Mt. Vernon Hill Country section of the Southern Till Plain division (Figure 2-4). The topography of this part of the state is hilly and rolling, with poorly drained river and creek bottoms. The northern edge of the more rugged Shawnee Hills division lies only three miles to the south. The topography of the Shawnee Hills is quite steep and cut by many small valleys and streams compared to that of the Mt. Vernon Hill Country. The western edge of the Wabash Border division is only three to six miles east of the District. This area is characterized by the dense forests, sloughs, marshes, oxbow lakes, and poorly drained bottomlands found in the Wabash River floodplain. Plants and animals common to the Shawnee Hills and the Wabash Border divisions are found in the area surrounding Carrier Mills, but those native to the Mt. Vernon Hill Country are the most represented.

The District is situated in the southwest corner of a low rolling ridge system that covers approximately two square miles (Figure 2-1). Until the early 1900s, it was nearly sur-

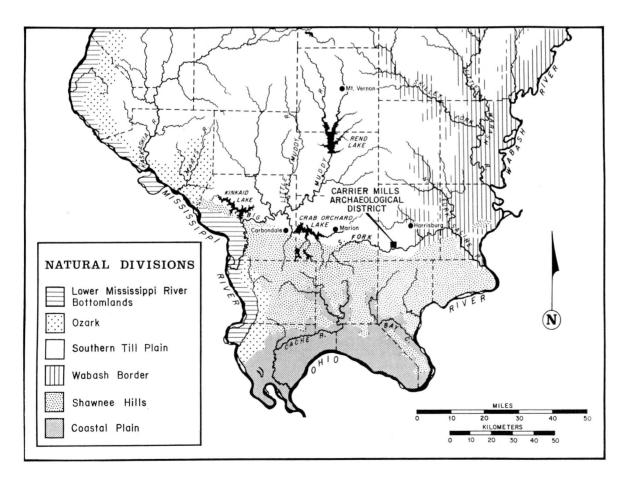

Figure 2-4. Natural divisions of southern Illinois.

rounded by shallow lakes, swamps, and low wet areas. The District was basically an island of uplands surrounded by a sea of wet lowlands (Figure 2-5). Eventually, the lowlands were drained by a series of man-made ditches so that the land could be cultivated. Today, some of this area is still farmed, but other sections have been allowed to lie fallow and are covered with brush, saplings, and other kinds of low vegetation.

The South Fork of the Saline River is located roughly 275 yards south of the District, but the position and character of the river were drastically altered when it was channelized and straightened to help improve drainage and control flooding. Before channelization, the river meandered through the Saline County countryside, roughly one-half mile south of its present course (Figure 2-1).

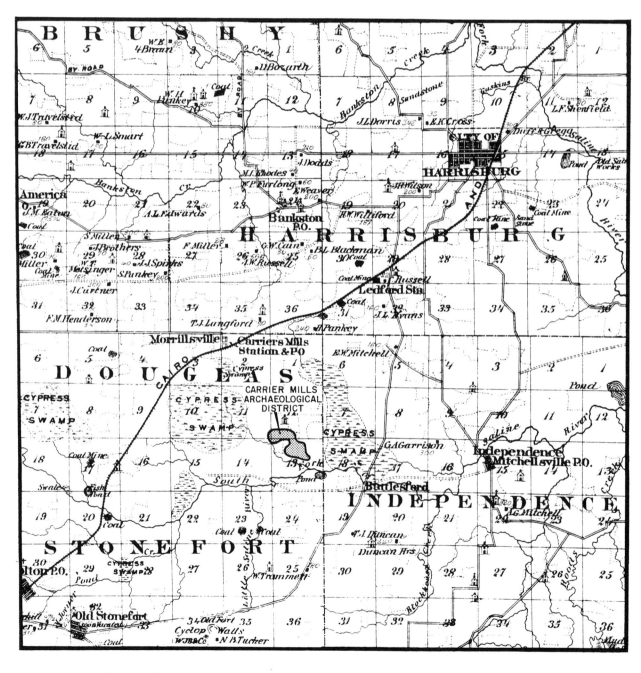

Figure 2-5. Outline of the District superimposed on an 1876 map of southwestern Saline County (from *Union Atlas of Illinois*).

Geology

The geology of the region is dominated by 300-million-year-old Pennsylvanian period bedrock largely consisting of sandstone, siltstone, and shale (Frye et al. 1972). Many of the landforms and associated geology of southern Illinois were shaped or modified by glaciers during the geologic period known as the Pleistocene (2 million–10,000 years ago). Geologic evidence indicates that only one glacier actually entered the area, occurring during the Illinoian glacial advance, the third of the four Pleistocene glaciations (200,000–130,000 years ago). Although evidence suggests that the Illinoian glacier extended as far south as the northern edge of the Shawnee Hills, geologic data from the Saline valley area indicate that the glacier came no closer than six miles north of Carrier Mills (Frye et al. 1972:2).

The Wisconsin glaciation, the fourth and last glacial advance of the Pleistocene (75,000–10,000 years ago), extended no further south than south-central Illinois, well to the north of Carrier Mills. Although it did not directly affect the Carrier Mills area, the melting Wisconsin glacier greatly increased the volume of water and sediments in the Wabash and Ohio rivers, effectively blocking the flow of tributary rivers, such as the Saline, and forming large slack-water lakes in many tributary river valleys. The lake formed by the back-up of the Saline River is known as Glacial Lake Saline and covered parts of five counties during its maximum extent about 20,000 years ago. The very fine sediments deposited on the lake bottom created large, flat, poorly drained plains once the lake drained. The lowlands situated to the south and west of the District mark areas that Glacial Lake Saline once inundated. The most recent indications of Glacial Lake Saline date to about 13,000 years ago (Frye et al. 1972), several thousand years before the first Indians entered the area. Although the early prehistoric people of southern Illinois were not directly affected by the glaciers, we will see that the ways the glaciers altered the landscape had a major impact on prehistoric life at Carrier Mills.

Soils

Soils in the Carrier Mills area are highly variable, with at least 23 kinds occurring within four miles of the District (Miles and Weiss 1978). Hosmer soils, characterized by high acidity, low levels of calcium, copper, iron, nitrogen, phosphorous, and potassium, and little organic material, are found on the ridges and upper slopes. The chemical and texture characteristics of these soils have been greatly altered in the vicinity of the sites by the thousands of years of prehistoric activity. The deposition (the laying down) of the materials that eventually created the middens produced a very alkaline soil having high concentrations of the chemicals just mentioned. The organic content of this soil is also quite high. Various kinds of silt loams are found in the low areas, and large expanses of silty clay loams occur in areas formerly occupied by the glacial lake. Other soils generally associated with prairie vegetation are found to the north of the District.

Climate

Southern Illinois has a humid continental climate with warm summers and cool winters. The influence of the nearby Shawnee Hills causes this part of southern Illinois to experience more rainfall than other parts of the state, especially during the summer (Illinois State Water Survey 1958). During an average year, about 42 inches of precipitation can be expected. The most severe part of the year generally occurs from December through February when temperatures are at their lowest and snowfall is heaviest. The period from March through May is marked by gradually increasing temperatures and precipitation, this being the wettest season of the year. Peak temperatures occur during June, July, and August, and rainfall becomes more erratic. Fall is the driest season. The average length of the growing season is 185 days. The earliest killing frost usually occurs in mid-to-late October, and the frost danger is generally over by the middle of April (Miles and Weiss 1978).

Vegetation

The proximity of the District to the three natural divisions and the geologic history of the area creates a very diverse environmental setting that includes forested uplands, wet floodplains, cypress swamps, prairie and grassy areas, and rivers and lakes. Because of these unique conditions, an extremely diverse assortment of vegetation is found in and around the District. As part of his research, Neal Lopinot, the Carrier Mills paleoethnobotanist, studied the modern vegetation and reconstructed the characteristics of native plant life before Europeans came to the area. To accomplish this task, he took a number of field trips during the summer and fall of 1978 and 1979 to study local vegetation.

The forests near Carrier Mills contain many different kinds of trees. The drier upland ridges and slopes are dominated by varieties of oaks and hickories, including black and shingle oaks and the mockernut and shagbark hickory. Post oak, blackjack oak, pin oak, and swamp white oak are commonly associated with areas of level, poorly drained uplands. The river floodplain forests are dominated by cottonwood, silver maple, willow, American elm, and sycamore. Drier parts of the floodplain support varieties of ash, hickory, and maple, as well as pin oak, white oak, honey locust, and hackberry. Cypress trees grow around the edges of some floodplain sloughs, ponds, and swamps (Schwegman 1975).

In addition to the forest trees mentioned above, many different kinds of smaller trees, shrubs, vines, grasses, and brambles are found in the woods and open areas. Common varieties include persimmon, mulberry, paw paw, sumac, blackberry, grape, may apple, greenbrier, pigweed, lamb's-quarters, and giant ragweed.

Wildlife

The wide array of plant communities in the vicinity of Carrier Mills provides homes for many different animals. Although no comprehensive study of the animal life of the Saline valley has been conducted, studies of parts of the valley and its tributaries were carried out in the mid-1970s (Rosso 1975; Urbanek 1976). Together, these two projects identified a minimum of 34 species of mammals, 155 species of birds, 19 species of reptiles, 15 species of amphibians, and 32 species of fish.

Animals commonly associated with forest or forest-edge habitats include the white-tailed deer, raccoon, opossum, skunk, rabbit, squirrel, and wild turkey. Aquatic habitats (rivers, lakes, ponds, sloughs, and swamps) also host a wide range of animal life, such as beaver, muskrat, mink, otter, ducks, geese, frogs, toads, and fish.

§ The Past
Environment

The information presented in the previous section gives us a fairly good idea of what the Carrier Mills area is like today. We have accurate information about the climate, we are familiar with the landscape and its wide range of habitats, we have studied the modern vegetation and animals, and we are aware of the geologic resources. Are we now ready to apply all of this knowledge toward our goal of determining how the prehistoric people interacted with the environment and how they used its resources? Unfortunately the answer is no! It would be very helpful if we could directly apply our knowledge of the modern environment to the study of prehistoric societies, but this cannot be done. The modern data, however, are useful for discussing general environmental characteristics, such as the presence or absence of certain plants or animals, but for certain species even this produces inaccurate results.

The errors produced by the misuse of modern environmental information can be traced to two sources. The first is long-term climatic change that has resulted in gradual or sometimes not-so-gradual changes in regional environmental conditions. In our rather short perspective of the climate, we are often unaware of the gradual, long-term fluctuations in temperature and precipitation that occurred in the past and are still ongoing today. A review of the paleoclimate data from the last 10,000 to 20,000 years shows that major changes have taken place that had a significant impact on local and regional vegetation. Changes in the composition and distribution of plant communities often affected the distribution of animals that fed on the plants and were hunted by the Indians.

A second problem is associated with the large-scale changes that have taken place as a consequence of historic landscape modification—those changes in vegetation, landforms, rivers and lakes, and other natural features that are the direct or indirect results of nineteenth- and twentieth-century agriculture, industry, urban expansion, and related activities.

The vegetation is perhaps the most severely affected part of the landscape. Many of the prehistoric forests were cut during the middle and late nineteenth century to make way for agricultural fields, homes, and towns, or for their lumber. Later, when some of the forests were replaced, the trees that were planted were different varieties than those originally present.

Also, many of the modern weeds and shrubs that grow near Carrier Mills today were recently introduced to the area from Europe, Africa, or other parts of the world and were not present during the prehistoric period. Because of the way that these non-native plants grew and spread, their areal coverage often increased at the expense of native plants.

Another aspect of recent change in the Carrier Mills area is the channelization and straightening of the South Fork of the Saline River. Before modification of the local drainage system in the early 1900s, the bottomlands along the south fork of the river contained numerous swampy lakes and ponds. These extensive wet areas were the remnants of Glacial Lake Saline. The lowlands immediately west and south of the District are all that remain of one of these shallow lakes.

Although their impact on the landscape was not as severe as that of the historic residents, prehistoric Indians also contributed to the modification of the southern Illinois area. They cleared areas of bottomlands for garden plots, cut trees to use for building houses and other kinds of structures, and moved quantities of soil to construct large earthen burial and platform mounds. In some parts of the East, open areas and the undergrowth in forests were burned to prevent abandoned fields from growing over and to make the tracking and hunting of game easier.

It is easy to see, based on the above examples, that the landscape of the Carrier Mills Archaeological District is quite different from that known to its prehistoric inhabitants. In view of the many changes that have occurred during the past 10,000 years, one might ask, Is it possible to reconstruct the environment that existed during a specific period of prehistory? The answer is a somewhat qualified yes. Although it is not possible to reconstruct all aspects of the environment for all time periods, different types of information exist, or can be collected, which provide indications of those conditions. This information comes from historic documents and maps made by early nineteenth-century travelers and explorers before the landscape was modified, from studies of plant pollen records that yield information about prehistoric climatic conditions, and from the analysis of prehistoric plant and animal remains from archaeological sites that provide information about the natural resources used by the Indians.

One of the most useful sources of information about local vegetation before widespread Euro-American settlement comes from the notes and records made by General Land Office (GLO) surveyors. Lopinot studied these notes during the course of his research. GLO surveyors covered much of the American frontier for the United States government during the early 1800s, laying out the section lines and township boundaries we use today. Most of the significant GLO information comes from the practice of using trees to mark the edges and corners of the surveyed tracts. Descriptions of these trees give us information about the variety, density, and size of trees along the survey lines. Section surveys near Carrier Mills were conducted from December 1806 to July 1807. Township plat maps, based on the GLO field notes, are useful for identifying major landscape features such as trails, roads, and boundaries between major vegetation areas (prairie versus forests).

The field notes of one of the surveyors, B. F. Stone, indicate that the swamps along the South Fork of the Saline River, near Carrier Mills, were extensive and deep and could not be crossed without great difficulty. Other descriptions of the swamp suggest that it was about 10 feet deep and was replenished with water when the river overflowed its banks. These areas were reported to be covered with water most of the year and could not be surveyed except during very dry years (Illinois General Land Office 1844, vol. 107, pp. 230–235). Areas slightly east of the Carrier Mills Archaeological District were described as "flat flooded land" and "flooded swamps" during the spring of 1807.

Analysis of GLO tree data indicates that several species of oak represented more than half of the trees in the Carrier Mills area. Hickory trees comprised an additional 15 percent. Trees other than oak and hickory were commonly found only in the floodplains and bottomlands.

The GLO information provides us with a picture of the Carrier Mills area that is quite unlike what we see today. The District was centered in an area of lakes, swamps, and marshes. These wet areas appear to have been concentrated in this part of the Saline drainage and were not common in other areas. The District was also situated near the juncture of the Shawnee Hills, the Southern Till Plain, and the Wabash Border Division. The area was centrally located with respect to a very diverse set of environmental conditions including low, wet floodplains; cypress swamps; prairie and grassy areas; open woods; savannas; and upland forests. Because of the wide range of conditions, many different plants and animals lived in or near the District. The intensive prehistoric occupation at Carrier Mills appears to have been largely attributable to the quantity, variety, and reliability of the natural food sources found in this area.

Additional information concerning prehistoric climate and vegetation comes from the study of pollen, or palynology. Most varieties of plants produce distinctively shaped pollen grains, so changes in vegetation can be detected and measured based on changes in the percentage of different kinds of pollen found in geological deposits.

The basic requirement for the analysis of prehistoric pollen is the discovery of a situation where pollen has been deposited and preserved for thousands of years. Such conditions are most commonly found in swamps and bogs. Pollen is produced and deposited annually, and through time layers of pollen-bearing sediments accumulate on the swamp's bottom, much in the same way archaeological deposits build up on sites. The newest pollen will be on the surface, and the age of the deposits will increase with depth. If a column of the pollen-bearing sediments is removed so that all the layers are represented, variation in the composition of the pollen samples can be studied and changes in the local and regional vegetation can be traced through time. No pollen studies were conducted at Carrier Mills, but several have been made of sites nearby and their findings can apply to this area.

Pollen records indicate that by approximately 14,000 years ago, the spruce and pine forests that covered southern Illinois during the late Pleistocene were gone (Gruger 1972). They were replaced by vegetation similar to that which we see today. Forests containing a mixture of oaks, hickories, and other deciduous trees covered much of the region, interspersed with isolated areas of prairie.

The period following the Pleistocene, known as the Holocene, was marked by a significant increase in temperature, and it was this climate that was encountered by the Paleoindian hunters of southern Illinois. The Middle Holocene, which extended from 9,000 to 5,000 years ago, was relatively drier and perhaps warmer than the preceding and subsequent parts of the Holocene. The Middle Holocene is sometimes referred to as the Hypsithermal interval (Deevey and Flint 1957). A significant characteristic of the Hypsithermal was the expansion of the prairies well to the north, east, and south of their present limits, perhaps extending as far east as Ohio and as far south as Tennessee.

Pollen preserved in a peat deposit at Old Field Swamp, located in southeast Missouri approximately 60 miles southwest of Carrier Mills, indicates that by about 8,700 years ago the Hypsithermal had started to affect local vegetation. The driest point apparently occurred around 7,000 years ago (5000 B.C.). The water level in the swamp was probably much lower during the Hypsithermal than during wetter periods. This period is marked in the pollen sample by an increase in the percentage of pollen from various grasses and herbs and a decrease in pollen from varieties of trees that are commonly found in moist areas. A return to wetter conditions occurred around 5,000 years ago and is marked in the pollen sample by a decrease in grass and herb pollen and an increase in bottomland forest species (King and Allen 1977). The intensive late Middle Archaic occupation at Carrier Mills took place during the last part of the Hypsithermal interval (4000–3000 B.C.).

The Late Holocene, from about 5,000 years ago until the present, experienced an increase in yearly precipitation. Pollen records from Old Field Swamp indicate that a brief cooling period took place from 400 to 100 years ago, but other than this brief interruption no other significant climatic changes occurred during the past 5,000 years.

§ Summary

The contemporary landscape does not accurately reflect what Carrier Mills was like before European settlers came to the area. In some cases, the same kinds of plants and animals are present today, but the abundance of certain species has been drastically altered. In other situations, major landscape features, such as the extensive lakes and swamps, have virtually disappeared, leaving little or no evidence of their existence.

Despite the major environmental alterations that have occurred, we can learn a lot about the prehistoric environment by using all available scientific and historic sources. We should keep in mind that changes in plant and animal life caused by the climatic fluctuations may not have always brought about big changes in human behavior. People are adaptive. They can adjust to environmental change by altering the way they perform certain activities. For example, Indians could compensate for a decrease in the availability of a resource, such as acorns or deer, by enlarging their collecting or hunting territory or simply by devoting more time each day to the search for that resource.

If we are to understand how prehistoric people adapted to their environment, we must view them as part of that environment and examine the relationships between the cultural remains, represented by the artifacts and other debris found at archaeological sites, and the landscape in which these people lived.

3

Hunters and Gatherers:
8000–1000 B.C.

Most Illinoisans share a common interest in learning about the Indian societies that lived in this region before European settlement. People want to know when the first Indians came to their area, who they were, and what their culture was like. The life-style of these early residents and the thousands of years that have passed since they first came to Illinois, unfortunately, prevent modern archaeologists from providing detailed answers to these questions. By studying the archaeological record, though, we can get some idea of the way prehistoric Indians lived thousands of years ago.

The earliest Indians to live in southern Illinois arrived during the Paleoindian period, sometime before 8000 B.C. Although no radiocarbon dates exist for Paleoindian sites in southern Illinois, dates from sites in other parts of the eastern United States indicate that they first came to this area much earlier, perhaps 12,000 to 15,000 years ago. These early people lived in small groups and obtained much of their food by hunting. Because they had to stay near the animals they hunted, they never remained in one place for very long. Their possessions were probably few in number and had to be portable. Obviously, this kind of life-style did not favor the formation of substantial archaeological sites. These early hunters left behind only a few isolated projectile points and chert flakes. Also, many small Paleoindian sites were reoccupied by later prehistoric people or were disturbed by a variety of natural processes, like soil erosion, making their identification difficult for archaeologists.

It is likely that Paleoindian groups visited and hunted in the vicinity of Carrier Mills, but the earliest traces of prehistoric people date somewhat later, to the Archaic period (8000–1000 B.C.). By the beginning of the Archaic, the environment of the Carrier Mills area was similar to that encountered by the first European settlers. Oak-hickory forests had replaced the spruce-and-pine-dominated forests that covered much of the region dur-

§ 8000–6000 B.C.:
The Early Archaic
Period

ing the late glacial period. Rainfall and temperature were roughly equivalent to that of today.

Carrier Mills archaeologists found several distinctive kinds of Early Archaic projectile points that resemble those found in contemporary sites in other parts of southern Illinois and in adjacent parts of the Midwest and Southeast. Archaeologists identify them by their unique shapes and call them by a variety of names. Early Archaic points found at Carrier Mills include examples of the Dalton, Thebes Notched, Cache Diagonal-Notched, Kirk, LeCroy, and Hardin Barbed types (Plates 3-1 and 3-2).

The most common Early Archaic projectile point was the Thebes point. Most of these points are large and thick. The body, or blade, of the point is triangular-shaped, and the bottom, or base, is characterized by deep, wide notches that converge toward the middle of the point. These notches were used to attach the point to the wooden shaft of a spear or lance or to the handle of a knife. The edges of the body are often steeply beveled, indicating that the point had been resharpened. These points were used by Early Archaic hunters for hunting and butchering.

Undoubtedly some of the other nondiagnostic artifacts recovered during fieldwork at Carrier Mills were made by the Early Archaic inhabitants. But because the Early Archaic materials were found in deposits that contained artifacts of later periods, these objects could not be distinguished from one another with any certainty.

PLATE 3-1. Early Archaic projectile points. Row 1, Dalton; Row 2, LeCroy; Row 3, Number 1, Hardin Barbed; Numbers 2 and 3, Kirk Stemmed; Row 4, Hidden Valley.

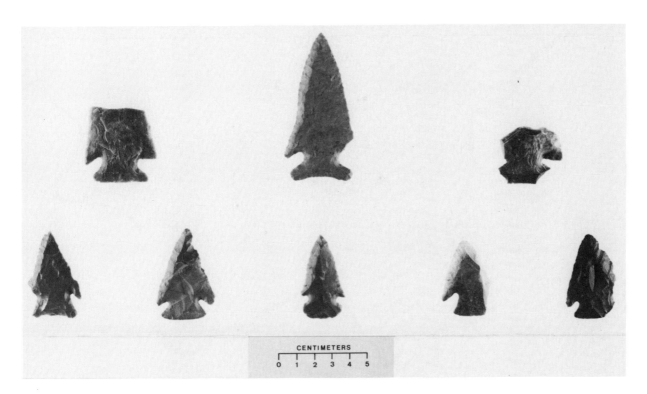

PLATE 3-2. Early Archaic projectile points. Row 1, Thebes Notched; Row 2, Cache Diagonal-Notched.

The number of Early Archaic projectile points found at Carrier Mills is quite small when compared to points attributable to later prehistoric occupations. Of the 1,970 projectile points that could be assigned to a specific cultural period, only 23, or 1 percent, were Early Archaic. The low number and percentage of Early Archaic points suggest that the Carrier Mills Archaeological District was not occupied by large groups of people for extended periods during the Early Archaic.

We can obtain information about the Early Archaic way of life by studying the types of raw materials used to make the projectile points. All of the Early Archaic points were made of chert, a flintlike, fine-grained stone associated with many of the limestone formations in southern Illinois and in adjacent states. Chert is commonly found in the beds of streams that pass through or near these formations or in soil formed by the weathering of the limestone. Chert occurs as round, ball-like lumps and as more irregularly shaped slabs and fragments. In parts of southern Illinois, the Indians obtained some kinds of high-quality cherts by quarrying.

The Early Archaic inhabitants used many different kinds of chert. Because of the unique color and texture of many of the southern Illinois cherts, archaeologists can often identify the specific geological formation or even the exact location from which they came. Among the different types of chert were examples of Cave-in-Rock and Kinkaid chert from the nearby eastern Shawnee Hills, examples of Cobden, Kaolin, and Mill Creek chert from the western Shawnee Hills, and examples of Burlington chert from west-central Illinois or east-central Missouri. The locations of many of these chert source areas are illustrated in Figure 3-1.

The chert source areas in the eastern Shawnee Hills are the closest to Carrier Mills, located some 19 miles to the southeast of the District, so it is not difficult to see why many of the points are made of these materials. But what about the cherts from the western Shawnee Hills and those from west-central Illinois or east-central Missouri? These source areas are located anywhere from 40 to 125 miles from Carrier Mills. Were these cherts of such

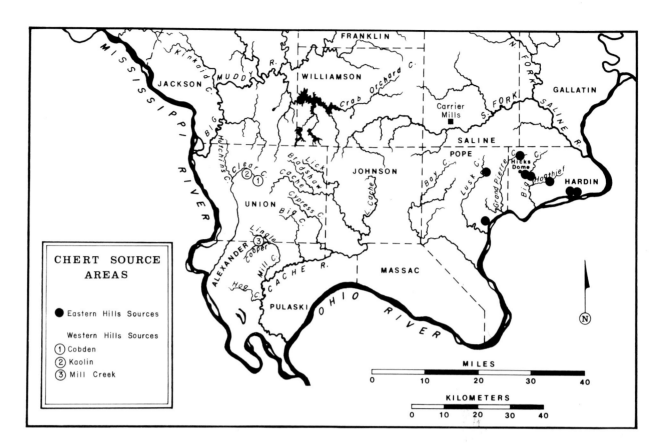

Figure 3-1. Location of eastern and western Shawnee Hills chert source areas.

fine quality that Early Archaic people would walk long distances to get them? Archaeologists believe that there is a simpler and more realistic explanation. Early Archaic groups may have obtained the raw material while they were in the vicinity of these distant source areas, perhaps while hunting. This possibility supports the idea that these people moved throughout a large area. They made tools from the chert and incorporated them into their tool kits. The tools would have been used and resharpened as the group traveled from place to place in search of game or other daily needs. Eventually, the tools would be completely worn out or broken and then discarded at some location far away from where the chert was originally collected. The Early Archaic projectile points from Carrier Mills made of chert from these distant chert sources may reflect the mobility of Early Archaic people who occasionally visited the District.

Summary

Although few Early Archaic artifacts were found at Carrier Mills, the information obtained from these objects contributes to our understanding of the Early Archaic way of life in southern Illinois. Life at Carrier Mills during this period was similar to that recorded in other parts of the region. Early Archaic groups were relatively small and highly mobile. They hunted and collected many of the animals and plants found in the forested, postglacial environment. The wide variety of chert used to make projectile points suggests that these groups moved over a relatively large geographic area, perhaps including most of southern Illinois and parts of adjacent states.

Changes in the way of life of the prehistoric Indians of southern Illinois occurred very slowly. The differences archaeologists perceive in artifacts are obvious only when a considerable amount of time separates the examples they are comparing. Because of this slow rate of change, there are few apparent differences in life-style between the last part of the Early Archaic and the beginning of the Middle Archaic. We can, however, identify a number of long-term trends that eventually made many aspects of Middle Archaic life in southern Illinois quite distinctive from those periods that came before it.

The Middle Archaic people of the Midwest were becoming increasingly more familiar with their environment and with its abundant natural resources. During the last half of the period, they tended to live in larger groups and to stay longer in one place. This tendency is reflected by larger, more complex sites that were occupied on a multiseasonal or perhaps year-round basis. Relatively large, late Middle Archaic cemeteries are associated with some of these sites, again suggesting that they were occupied for a long time. Certain kinds of artifacts, such as projectile points and carved and engraved bone pins, are very similar over a very large area of the Midwest during this time.

We do not know much about the early Middle Archaic (6000–4500 B.C.) in southern Illinois. Once again, this stems from our inability to locate sites containing undisturbed cultural deposits that date to this period. But years of research at the Koster site, located in the lower Illinois River valley near Kampsville in west-central Illinois, have produced considerable information (Figure 3-2). Although the Koster site is located approximately 150 miles northwest of Carrier Mills, the general characteristics of the early Middle Archaic occupations at Koster are applicable to the Carrier Mills area.

Archaeologists have described the early Middle Archaic occupation at Koster as a series of residential camps occupied by groups of relatively mobile hunters and gatherers. These occupations contain a wider variety of artifacts, pits, and other debris than the special purpose sites, such as hunting camps or plant-collecting stations. Residential camps were probably occupied by all or most of the group, but only for short periods of time. These people tended to move from place to place, taking advantage of the seasonally available foods, much like their Early Archaic predecessors. They ate a wide variety of wild plants and animals, including large and small mammals, fish, river mussels, nuts, fruits, and seeds. Their tool kit included corner-notched projectile points, chert hammers and choppers, drills, and groundstone pestles and milling stones (Brown and Vierra 1983).

By about 4500 B.C., many of the long-term trends that characterize the Middle Archaic were evident at many midwestern sites. At Koster, archaeologists found a series of late Middle Archaic occupations that have been radiocarbon dated to between 3770 and 2930 B.C. Collectively, these occupations are called the Helton phase. Phase is a term that archaeologists use to describe a series of occupations or sites that are fairly restricted in their distribution and limited to a relatively short period of time (Willey and Phillips 1958:22). We can think of a phase as being roughly analogous to a prehistoric cultural group. "Helton" is the last name of a landowner who lived in the vicinity of the Koster site. Archaeologists often name sites, projectile point types, pottery types, and other archaeological "things" after local landowners or nearby geographic landmarks.

The Helton phase inhabitants used the Koster site as a base camp. Base camps were more permanently occupied than residential camps and contain a wider range of tools, debris, and other archaeological features. Up to one meter of greasy, black midden containing artifacts, burned clay, mussel shell, and various features accumulated during a thousand years of Helton occupation.

These people used a variety of side-notched projectile points as well as several corner-

§ 6000–3000 B.C.:
The Middle Archaic
Period

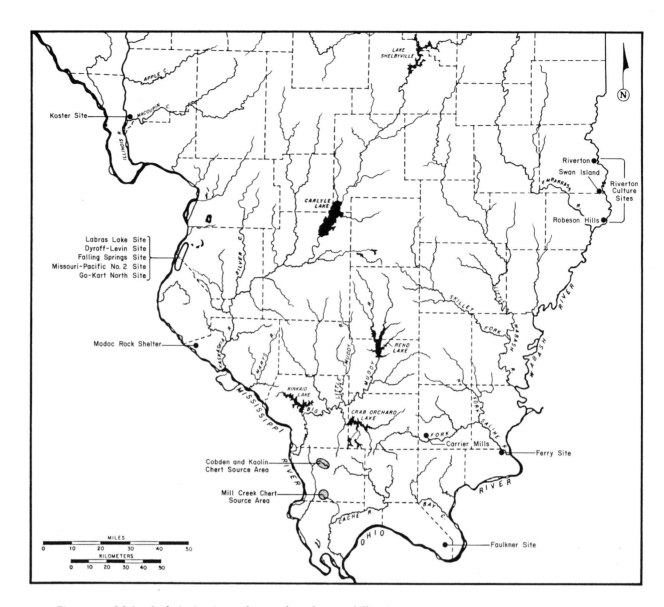

Figure 3-2. Major Archaic sites in southern and south-central Illinois.

notched and stemmed types. Their wide assortment of flaked stone, groundstone, and bone tools indicate that they pursued a wide range of activities at their base camp. A large number of pit features, reflecting an assortment of food preparation and storage activities, along with evidence of at least three houses, were uncovered during excavation. Two distinct burial plots containing the skeletal remains of 25 children, adolescents, and adults were also identified (Brown and Vierra 1983).

Indications of significant changes in diet and differences in the techniques used to obtain food appear during the Helton phase at Koster. Certain habitats, particularly the backwater swamps, were more intensively exploited than during earlier times. The increased importance of this aquatic habitat is marked by increased percentages of fish and migratory waterfowl remains from species that prefer these calm, shallow water areas. Deer, raccoon, and turkey were the primary land animal meat sources. The inhabitants also appear to have developed specialized techniques for collecting and processing nuts (Brown and Vierra 1983).

The Koster research has shown that, at least in the lower Illinois valley, there was a gradual shift away from a life-style in which people obtained their food by living in highly mobile groups that moved on a regular basis to take advantage of seasonally available foods toward a way of life in which people stayed in certain highly productive areas for much longer periods. The number, diversity, and organization of activities at Koster during the late Middle Archaic are those associated with a more sedentary base-camp situation (Brown and Vierra 1983).

Trends similar to those identified at Koster are also evident at late Middle Archaic occupations in other portions of Illinois and adjacent parts of the Midwest. At Modoc Rock Shelter, located in Randolph County in the Mississippi River valley of southwest Illinois (Figure 3-2) (Fowler 1959; Styles et al. 1981), archaeologists exposed deep deposits dating to the Middle Archaic period. These materials indicate that many different activities were conducted, including hunting, gathering, tool manufacturing, and food processing and preparation. Diagnostic artifacts include the same types of side-notched projectile points found with the Helton phase occupation at Koster. Human burials and evidences of structures, probably wind-breaks, were also found. Collectively, this information suggests that Modoc Rock Shelter also served as a general habitation site or base camp during the Middle Archaic period (Fowler 1959).

Finally, research conducted at nine sites located in the floodplain of the Ohio River, near Louisville, Kentucky, revealed intensive Archaic occupations that were dated from 3740 to 2230 B.C. This area is rich in natural resources, and sites appear to be located to minimize seasonal movements. The variety of food resources in this part of the Ohio valley probably allowed the inhabitants to remain in the same location throughout much of the year (Janzen 1977).

These examples illustrate the changes in life-style that took place in the Midwest during the Middle Archaic period. Obviously, not all sites were as large and complex as these examples, and many other smaller Middle Archaic sites existed that reflect occupation of shorter duration and more restricted activities. Although differences in the plants and animals living in the different parts of the Midwest produced subtle variations in the way Middle Archaic people adjusted or adapted to their immediate environment, the broader trends defined for the period apply to much of this region, including the Carrier Mills Archaeological District.

Life at Carrier Mills during the Middle Archaic

The Middle Archaic period was a time of significant change in the way the Carrier Mills area was used by its prehistoric inhabitants. During the first half of the period, from 6000 B.C. until roughly 4500 B.C., archaeological evidence indicates that the way of life was quite similar to that of the Early Archaic. The few diagnostic artifacts found at the site tell us that the District was used by a series of small groups of hunter-gatherers for short periods of time. By around 4500 B.C. or shortly thereafter, however, some major changes took place. The District was inhabited by larger, more sedentary groups of people who lived in the area for several seasons of the year or perhaps even on a year-round basis.

Evidence of a late Middle Archaic presence was found at all prehistoric activity areas identified in the District. The most common class of artifacts associated with this occupation was a series of projectile points having notches situated on both edges, near the base of the point. These artifacts are commonly referred to as "side-notched" projectile points and are known by a variety of type names, including Godar, Faulkner, Matanzas, Big Sandy, and Raddatz (Plate 3-3).

The clearest picture of what life was like during the Middle Archaic period comes from the excavation of Area A of site Sa-87, the Black Earth site. This site is important be-

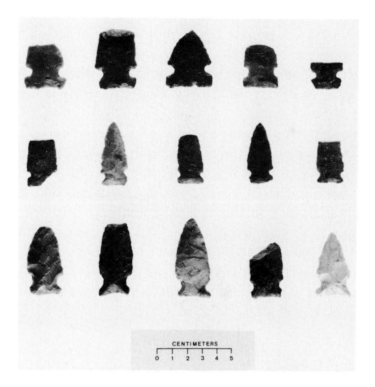

PLATE 3-3. Middle Archaic side-notched projectile points. Row 1, Godar; Row 2, Faulkner; Row 3, Matanzas.

cause of the one-meter-thick late Middle Archaic midden zone discovered there during archaeological testing in late 1977. The zone was buried below other midden zones containing the remains of later prehistoric occupations. It was relatively undisturbed by both the later prehistoric activity and by more recent plowing by nineteenth- and twentieth-century farmers (Figure 2-3). The fact that the zone was sealed from later disturbance allowed archaeologists to assume that all the artifacts and other cultural and natural remains found in the zone could be dated to the late Middle Archaic. Thanks to this situation at Area A, archaeologists were able to greatly expand their knowledge about how the Middle Archaic residents adapted to the local environment, which of the natural resources were most important to their survival, what types of tools they used to collect and process these resources, how living in that environment affected their health, and something about their social organization.

When trying to interpret the activities of the former inhabitants of archaeological sites, most of us immediately think of the artifacts these people left behind and the information they might reveal. While it is true that artifacts are very important to the study of past human behavior, sites contain many other kinds of useful information. At Carrier Mills, one of the most useful sources of information about past activities was the midden soil. The project soil scientist, William Woods, conducted a series of detailed studies to learn more about the cultural and natural processes responsible for the buildup of the deep midden deposits.

Visual inspection of the midden showed that it contained chert flakes, chunks of sandstone, broken tools, food residues (bones and charred plant remains), and other miscellaneous items. Analysis of the midden soil in which these materials were contained revealed two major color zones. A dark brown zone, extending to an average depth of 20 inches (50 cm) below surface near the center of the site (Plate 3-4), contained objects dating from the late Middle Archaic to the Late Woodland periods. Most of this zone had been

PLATE 3-4. Wall profile of Black Earth site excavation unit showing midden zone. Square dark area in center of wall is a Middle Woodland feature intruding into the older Middle Archaic zone.

disturbed by plowing and other recent activities. A second, lighter, yellowish brown midden zone was identified below the first, extending an additional 20 inches to 39 inches (50 to 100 cm) below surface. The color of the second zone tended to become lighter with increasing depth. The lower midden zone generally corresponded to the largely undisturbed late Middle Archaic occupation zone (Plate 3-4). Test excavations indicated an area about 250 feet in diameter, having midden greater than 1.5 feet deep.

Analysis of the chemical composition of the midden soils demonstrated that it was quite unlike the natural soils surrounding the site. The thousands of years of prehistoric activity at Area A extensively altered and enriched the midden soils. Compared to soil surrounding the site, midden soils contained very high levels of certain chemicals including calcium, iron, nitrogen, copper, phosphorous, potassium, and zinc. The midden was also characterized by high levels of organic material and a basic soil pH.

What does this information tell us about the late Middle Archaic people who lived at Area A? It tells us quite a lot. The soil at Area A was neutral to strongly alkaline. In contrast, soils off the site were extremely acidic. Analysis showed that the alkaline character of the soil was the result of the high concentration of calcium, magnesium, potassium, and sodium in the soil. These chemicals came from wood ash from the thousands of fires built by Middle Archaic people for cooking, heating, and illumination. The high level of organic matter in the Area A midden was created by large quantities of charcoal and burned plant remains, primarily nutshells (hickory nuts, walnuts, and acorns were important foods to the prehistoric people of southern Illinois).

The chemical alteration of the soil at Area A also had a hidden benefit for archaeologists. Under normal circumstances, the high level of acidity present in the local soils would have quickly destroyed all trace of bone. Because of the alkaline character of the Area A soil, however, bone was perfectly preserved. Thus, investigators could examine the bones of the animals that were hunted and trapped to provide food, clothing, and shelter and could study the skeletal remains of the Middle Archaic inhabitants buried at the site.

The texture of the midden soil was also quite different from the surrounding natural soils. Sand made up roughly half of its volume. Since sand represents only about 5 percent of the soil off the site, where did all the additional sand come from? The most likely explanation is that sandstone was the only rock available in the local area to make certain kinds of tools and to use in making fireplaces and hearths. When the sandstone deteriorated from heating, weathering, or trampling, grains of sand that formed the rocks were deposited in the midden. Another source of sand particles may be related to the burning and decomposition of certain plant materials, such as grasses and wood. The cells of these plants contain small silica particles known as opal phytoliths. When the organic portions of these plants deteriorate, the more durable phytoliths remain and are deposited in the soil.

The study of soils on archaeological sites can provide a wide range of information about past activities. We will later see how this information, when combined with other kinds of data, can even give us an indication of how many people lived at Area A during the late Middle Archaic period.

Dating Archaeological Remains

The Middle Archaic midden consisted of the trash deposited by many hundreds of years of prehistoric activity. Much of the organic matter that was discarded (such as most plant materials, residues from butchering, cooking, and eating animals, and many other perishable items) quickly decomposed, leaving little trace of its existence. Stone artifacts and bone appear today much as they did when they were discarded. Through the years of Middle Archaic activity, the surface of the ground increased in elevation as a result of the midden buildup. Artifacts, pits, and other debris from earlier occupations were buried by the discarded residues of later inhabitants. When the midden became deep enough, the Middle Archaic residents used the soft, well-drained soils as the final resting place for the remains of their dead.

Because of the way the midden formed, materials associated with the earliest Middle Archaic inhabitants are located near the bottom of the deposit and the more recent materials are located near the surface. By measuring the vertical position or depth below surface of a particular artifact, archaeologists can determine its relative age by comparing it to other materials in the midden. If it is positioned above another object, it is younger because it was deposited after the lower one. If it is located below another item, it is older. This dating technique provides the relative age of two objects, but it does not give us any idea of their actual or absolute age. An absolute date gives the age of an object in radiocarbon years, which can easily be converted to the calendar years with which people are more familiar.

Archaeologists use a number of techniques to obtain absolute dates, but in the Midwest, radiocarbon (carbon-14) dating is the most common. Radiocarbon dates can be obtained from a wide variety of organic materials, including charcoal, wood, leather, cloth, and bone. Samples of these materials are carefully collected from desired locations within the site, such as pit features or hearths. Carbon samples are submitted to special laboratories that have the facilities for processing and analyzing this material. When a laboratory analyzes the carbon sample, the readings used to calculate the age vary somewhat because of random variation in the process of radioactive decay. Radiocarbon dates consist of two parts. The first is the actual estimated age of the sample, represented in years before present (B.P.), a value that is converted to actual calendar years (A.D. or B.C.) using correction factors to account for sources of error. The second part of the date is a ± value, which reflects the statistical uncertainty of the age estimate. In statistical parlence, this error term (the ± value) is known as one standard deviation. For example, for a date given as 2000 B.C. ± 100, the ± 100 means that there is a 67 percent probability that the true age of the sample lies in the 200-year range from 1900 to 2100 B.C.

Analysis of the eight carbon samples taken from the midden at Area A indicated that the earliest major occupation of the site dates to about 3955 ± 85 B.C. Although this date is a good estimation of the earliest intensive occupation of Area A, it does not necessarily date the first occupation of the site. Earlier occupations were not sufficiently intensive for the deposition of cultural material to overcome the destructive effects of erosion, soil acidity, and other natural processes. These earlier occupations are represented only by scattered nonperishable items, such as stone tools and chert flakes. Seven additional carbon samples produced dates ranging between 3725 ± 70 and 2910 ± 85 B.C. The date of 2910 ± 85 B.C. was obtained from a charcoal sample collected from a hearth near the top or upper limits of the Middle Archaic midden zone. This final date appears to mark the approximate end of the most intensive segment of the Middle Archaic occupation. Most of the resulting midden appears to have been deposited during the roughly 1,000-year-period defined by the eight radiocarbon dates.

The Area A radiocarbon dates, combined with the information provided by the soil analysis, tell us that, starting around 6,000 years ago and continuing for approximately 1,000 years, the site experienced an increase in the frequency and duration of occupation by Middle Archaic Indians. These occupations involved relatively small groups living on the site throughout most or all of the year.

The Changing Environment

Some researchers have suggested that the increase in prehistoric people living in the District 6,000 years ago was linked to the changing environment. As we previously discussed, the period between 4500 and 3000 B.C. corresponds with the latter portion of the Hypsithermal interval. The effects of the Hypsithermal on regional and local environments would have included an increase in vegetation adapted to growing in dry conditions, primarily grasses and herbs, and a corresponding decrease in plants preferring more moist habitats. In general, the extent of the wet areas and their associated plant and animal life would have been reduced across the region. At the Old Field Swamp in southeast Missouri, pollen studies show that this period was characterized by a decrease in plant species found in open swamp and an increase in herbs and grasses. Bottomland forests and swamps that grew in periodically flooded areas were reduced in size. Although the specific effects of the Hypsithermal in the Saline valley are not well documented, they probably were not unlike those found in southeast Missouri. The recovery of the bones of a small rodent known as the plains pocket gopher, considered by zoologists to be an indicator of nearby prairie-grassland conditions, indicates the presence of grasslands in the Carrier Mills vicinity during the Middle Archaic period. Also, isolated areas of grassland/prairie observed by General Land Office surveyors near Carrier Mills in the early 1800s may have represented "relic" vegetation that had been more widespread during drier climatic periods. Because of the reduction in areal coverage of many types of vegetation, food resources may have been less abundant in the drier upland parts of the region during the peak of the Hypsithermal than they were during the preceding or subsequent wetter periods.

As the effects of the Hypsithermal increased their influence on the landscape, reducing the quantity, diversity, and reliability of certain food sources in the upland areas, the lake-swamp system and surrounding areas took on an increased significance to the prehistoric inhabitants of the Saline valley. Although climatic changes may have somewhat reduced the size of this wet area, archaeological evidence indicates that it existed throughout the Middle Archaic period. The abundant plant and animal resources found in and around the District served as a buffer against the effect of the Hypsithermal. The drier conditions probably brought about a greater emphasis on more scarce water resources, an increase in the number of people living in the vicinity of these resources, and occupations of longer duration. Although the drier uplands continued to be exploited, visits were probably conducted by fairly small groups of people and it does not appear that they occupied the uplands for very extended periods.

The People and Their Possessions

Literally thousands of objects play some technological role in our lives. These items include a large assortment of tools that are used to perform a very wide range of tasks. Some of the raw materials used to make these tools, like metal, wood, stone, clay, and fabric, have been used to make tools for thousands of years. If we examine the drawings and documents left by the early explorers and travelers who ventured into North America, we see that some of these same materials were employed by the native Indian cultures to make tools.

The most obvious raw material used by the prehistoric people of southern Illinois is stone. They used many different kinds of stone. Chert was selected to make the flaked stone tools used to kill, skin, and butcher the animals hunted for their meat and fur. Various kinds of sedimentary and metamorphic rocks were chosen to make the wide assortment of groundstone implements, such as axes for cutting wood and grinding and nutting stones for processing food. The main reason that stone tools are usually the first kind of Indian artifact people think of is because they are often the most common type found at archaeological sites. They are virtually indestructible compared to artifacts made of many other materials. Artifacts made of baked clay, such as pottery, and the few made of metal are also more likely to be represented in the archaeological record than are items made of less durable organic material like wood, leather, cloth, and at most sites, bone.

Undoubtedly, wooden tools also played an important role in the daily lives of southern Illinois Indians. They used wood to make many kinds of tools, containers, houses, boats, and ornaments. Baskets made from vines, grasses, or strips of wood were an indispensable part of the household. Fabrics woven from an assortment of vegetable fibers were probably also very important in many aspects of daily life. Unfortunately, except under ideal conditions, these more fragile, less durable materials are rarely preserved at archaeological sites in Illinois.

For the most part, archaeologists have to reconstruct the way of life of most prehistoric peoples using only a very small part of the total inventory of objects they used in their daily lives. As if this limitation were not enough, most artifacts that are recovered represent broken or worn-out tools or the discarded by-products of the many activities performed at the site. Nevertheless, the materials that have been preserved do tell us about the many activities conducted at a site. By studying the objects left by past cultures, we can learn a great deal about their technology, social organization, and even their beliefs.

The equipment used by the Middle Archaic residents of Carrier Mills included many kinds of small, portable objects that were probably owned by individuals. Some of these objects were used to obtain and process the natural resources found in the rich environment surrounding the District. Others were employed in some social capacity, perhaps as indicators of a person's social position.

Not all equipment could be easily moved. Examples of nonportable items include the many types of pits, fireplaces, and other types of food storage and processing facilities that are called features by archaeologists. A feature is any man made object or facility, the remains of which cannot be removed intact. Features include houses and other structures, clusters of rock, soil discolorations, or other anomalies that reflect some aspect of human activity.

Personal Equipment. The "Personal Equipment" category of artifacts consists of the utilitarian, ornamental, and ceremonial items used by the early inhabitants of Carrier Mills. Utilitarian equipment, as the name implies, was utilized for practical purposes—like stone tools, for example. Ornamental artifacts are those that were probably items of personal adornment, such as beads that were worn as necklaces or sewn on articles of clothing, pendants that were worn suspended from the neck, and carved bone pins that probably served as hair decorations. Ceremonial artifacts are often classified as such through a process of elimination. If an item is not clearly utilitarian or ornamental, then it may have had a ceremonial purpose. This category includes a large number of miscellaneous artifacts whose use cannot be determined by archaeologists. Many of the artifacts described as ceremonial at Carrier Mills were found in burials, and it is often this fact, along with the unusual nature of the artifacts, that results in their being labeled ceremonial. For example, a miniature axe, much too small to be useful for cutting wood, that was found with a Middle Archaic burial was classified as ceremonial despite the fact that axes served a very definite practical purpose in the daily lives of these people.

We cannot go back in time to see for ourselves how artifacts were used by prehistoric people. In the past, many archaeologists interpreted the ways artifacts were used by studying their shape and size, then comparing them to modern tools sharing similar characteristics. In some cases, the interpretations were probably fairly accurate. For example, most artifacts described as projectile points were probably placed on the tips of spears or arrows, although some artifacts put in this group may have actually been knives. It is also likely that some artifacts were used for a number of different tasks, not just the one their name implies.

In recent years, archaeologists have used new approaches for studying prehistoric artifact use. Some have tried to determine tool use by comparing prehistoric artifacts with those used by groups of hunters and gatherers still living in isolated parts of the world. Since these groups maintain a way of life similar to many prehistoric groups, these comparisons are probably more appropriate than those made between prehistoric groups and twentieth-century America.

Other archaeologists conduct experiments to determine the specific kinds of activities (cutting, scraping, drilling) for which stone tools were used. They do this by first making a stone tool, then using it for a specific task. The tool is then examined under a microscope to determine the effects of that activity on the tool. Once a specific activity is linked to the kind of damage it causes, prehistoric tools can be examined for similar damage. This technique, known as edge-wear analysis, is discussed in more detail later in this chapter. Interpretations of the uses of other kinds of artifacts, especially those classified as ceremonial, are less clear cut and more prone to error.

Utilitarian Artifacts. Utilitarian tools were the most common type of artifact used by the late Middle Archaic residents. They formed tool kits used by these people to meet the requirements of daily life—to collect the plants and hunt the animals that made up their diet, to prepare food for eating, to cut trees for firewood and various building requirements, to process animal hides for clothing and shelter covering, and to dig food processing and storage pits. Although we will discuss these various tool types, their uses, and their methods of manufacture independently, they were actually part of a complex technological system in which one tool or one activity must be considered with respect to other tools and activities. If we view the artifacts as unique items, independent of the system, we will not be able to see the complex interrelationships between the tools and the activities that ensured the survival of these Middle Archaic hunter-gatherers.

These tools were made from a variety of materials, but only the ones made of more durable inorganic materials, primarily stone, were preserved. The Black Earth site is very important to archaeologists because of the wide assortment of bone and antler tools (and the debris resulting from their production) that was preserved in the alkaline soil. At most other sites in southern Illinois, bone and antler tools have not been preserved, eliminating numerous kinds of tools from consideration in reconstructing how these people lived. We can only speculate about the kinds of wooden implements for which no archaeological record exists.

Flaked stone implements. Excavation of the Middle Archaic midden during the 1978 and 1979 field seasons produced more than 1,100 flaked stone tools. These artifacts are referred to as flaked stone tools because they are shaped and their edges are sharpened by the removal of flakes of stone. A tool can be made from a flake that is knocked off a larger piece of rock, called a core, or it can be made from a core by the removal of additional flakes until the desired shape is achieved. Tools made from flakes are commonly referred to as flake tools; tools made by the removal of flakes from a core are called core tools.

Some stone tools are very carefully flaked so that their shape matches some preconceived form in the mind of the maker. These are known as formal tools. A projectile point is a good example of a formal tool. Many of the Middle Archaic projectile points from Carrier Mills are quite similar in appearance (Plate 3-3). The points from Carrier Mills are very similar to points dating to the same period from sites in other parts of the Midwest. When people think of Indian artifacts, they are usually visualizing some kind of easily recognizable formal tool.

Other kinds of flaked stone tools are made simply by sharpening the edge of a flake (Plate 3-5, Row 3). These informal flake tools require much less time to produce than do formal tools. Many formal tools are hafted, or attached, to some type of handle, whereas most flake tools were apparently not hafted for use. The relative importance of formal and flake tools in a prehistoric tool kit depended on the kinds of activities being performed, the technology of the society, and the effort required to obtain more suitable raw material.

In addition to the tools themselves, archaeologists are also interested in the by-products of toolmaking. In most cases, the by-products are flakes and fragments of the raw material used for tool production. These waste products are often referred to as debitage—a French word meaning "throw-away waste." The application of different kinds of force during toolmaking produces distinctive kinds of flakes: (1) The first technique commonly used to remove a flake is to hit a piece of stone with another rock called a hammerstone. This technique is referred to as percussion flaking. These flakes produced by percussion (percussion flakes) are fairly thick and large. (2) Other flakes can be removed by the application of pressure to the edge of the tool. Pressure is applied to the edge of the stone tool by using a punch, a pointed object made of wood or antler. Flakes removed in this manner are called pressure flakes. The person making the tool can exert much more control over the removal of a flake using this technique, which is commonly done in the later stages of flaked stone tool manufacturing. Pressure flakes are generally smaller and thinner than percussion flakes. These flakes are removed either from one side of the tool only, to produce unifacial tools such as scrapers, or from both sides of the tool, to produce bifacial tools such as projectile points and knives. (3) A third type of flake found in the Middle Archaic debitage is a thinning flake. These flakes are produced during the finishing stages of bifacial tool production and are the result of reducing the thickness and straightening the cutting edges of the tool. Thinning flakes are commonly found on sites where projectile points were manufactured or resharpened. Many smaller flakes are also produced during resharpening of the dulled cutting edge of the projectile point. Since archaeologists have determined through experimentation that these flake types occur during certain stages of flaked stone tool manufacturing, they can get an idea of the kinds of tool-making activities that occurred on a site by studying the tools and debitage.

All of the Middle Archaic flaked stone tools found at Carrier Mills were made from chert. Like the Early Archaic flaked stone tools, the cherts used by the Middle Archaic people came from a variety of locations in southern Illinois and nearby parts of Missouri, but to a lesser extent. Fewer tools were made from cherts that came from the western Shawnee Hills and eastern Missouri. More tools were made from chert obtained from the nearby eastern Shawnee Hills. This observation may reflect the more sedentary life-style of the Middle Archaic groups compared to that of Early Archaic groups.

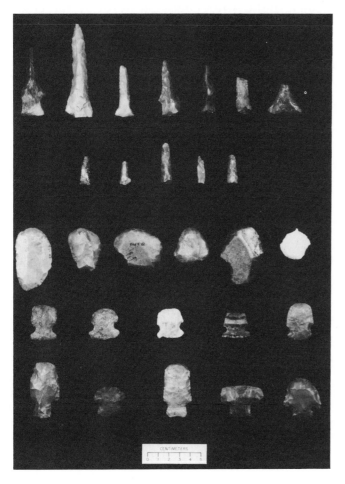

PLATE 3-5. Miscellaneous flaked stone tools. Rows 1 and 2, drills and drill bits; Row 3, Numbers 1–5, flake scrapers; Number 6, combination scraper and graver; Row 4, Middle Archaic hafted end-scrapers; Row 5, Numbers 1–4, Late Archaic or Early Woodland hafted end-scrapers; Number 5, Middle Woodland hafted end-scraper.

The cherts from sources both near and far were used in the same manner. Archaeologists assume that if the Indians obtained cherts from more distant areas through trade with other Middle Archaic groups to the west or if they acquired them by some other means that required more time or energy than needed to get the local chert, the nonlocal chert would have been more highly valued and perhaps used only for some special purpose. Since this was not the case at Carrier Mills, the nonlocal cherts were probably collected while Middle Archaic people were hunting in, or simply passing through, these distant areas. The presence of chert collected from areas 40 to 50 miles away from Carrier Mills gives us an idea of the size of the area that supplied the daily necessities of these people.

The Middle Archaic tool kit included formal tools as well as a wide variety of informal tools made from only slightly modified chert flakes. The most common formal tool was the projectile point. Although the term "projectile point" is an accurate description for many of the artifacts placed in this category, other tools grouped under this heading were probably knives or other kinds of implements. A microscopic examination of the damage to the edges of the tool can reveal how tools were used, and this helps in distinguishing between types of tools that are not otherwise distinguishable.

Many of the flaked stone artifacts left by the Middle Archaic people at Carrier Mills were produced during the manufacture of projectile points. Points were made in a series of steps. The first stage is the selection of a piece of chert of the proper size and texture. The chert block, the core, is then shaped using a hammerstone, producing large percussion flakes. This stage of manufacture produces a relatively thick biface having an irregular margin or outline, known as a blank. The second stage of production also uses percussion to shape the biface, but instead of a hammerstone, a piece of antler is used to remove the flakes. Because the bone is softer than the hammerstone, the force from the blow to the blank is more diffused, resulting in the removal of thinner flakes. This type of flaking is called "soft hammer" percussion flaking because of the softer character of the antler, compared to a hammerstone used for "hard hammer" percussion flaking. Application of the soft hammer technique produces a thinner biface, called a preform, having straighter or more regular edges. Bifacial thinning flakes are commonly produced during this stage of production. During the final production stage, final shaping of the edge takes place and the notches for hafting are placed on both edges near the bottom, or base, of the projectile point. Pressure flaking is used to do much of the final shaping. Examples of the various stages of projectile point manufacture are shown in Plate 3-6.

Middle Archaic Indians extended the life of their projectile points by resharpening and recycling as their edges became dull. Resharpening the tools involved removing a series of small flakes along the cutting edge, thus making the tools slightly smaller each time. Broken projectile points were often recycled into a totally new type of tool. The recycling of broken artifacts during the Middle Archaic was an attempt to salvage the raw material and the time and energy of the toolmaker by extending the usefulness of the implement.

Examination of the blanks, preforms, and projectile points, and of the flakes or debitage produced during their manufacture, indicates that the early stages of projectile point production were not done at Area A. The making of blanks from chert cores probably took place near where the chert was collected. The Carrier Mills inhabitants then produced projectile points from preforms and resharpened and repaired damaged points at their base camp at Area A.

Because of the excellent craftsmanship of many prehistoric toolmakers and the beauty of some projectile points, many artifact collectors believe that hours of work were invested in making one point. Experiments conducted by modern chert toolmakers (called chert knappers) have shown that a well-made projectile point can be produced in less than 30 minutes. The job of firmly attaching (hafting) the projectile point to a wooden shaft probably required more time and energy than making the point.

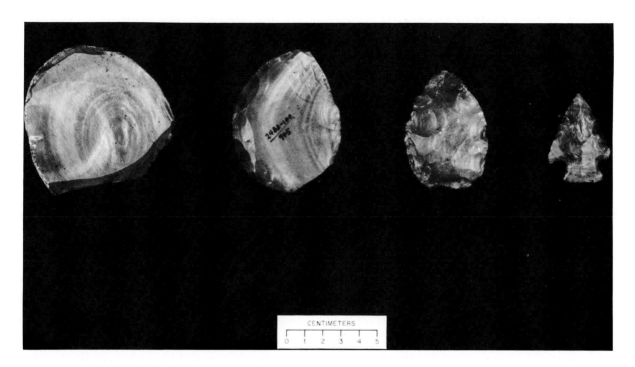

PLATE 3-6. Stages of projectile point manufacture. Number 1, unmodified Cobden chert; Number 2, blank; Number 3, preform; Number 4, finished projectile point.

Most of the Middle Archaic projectile points and the tools made from broken points have distinctive side-notching (Plate 3-3). Archaeologists divide this large group of side-notched artifacts into three projectile point types. A type is a group of artifacts that share certain physical characteristics. Artifacts are grouped in types so that they can be easily compared. The names of the three side-notched point types found at Carrier Mills are Matanzas, Godar, and Faulkner.

Nearly three-quarters of side-notched points were classified as Matanzas points. These points are quite similar to others dating to this period found throughout much of the Midwest. The examples from Carrier Mills vary in size, although they average about 2 inches (5 cm) long. The body of the point is generally lanceolate-shaped, and the tip is usually rounded. The notches on some specimens are very shallow, but others are deep. Several examples of Matanzas projectile points are shown in Plate 3-3.

Godar projectile points comprised about one-fifth of the Middle Archaic side-notched points. The primary distinction between Godar and Matanzas points occurs in the notching. Godar notches are perpendicular to the long axis of the point and are deeper than those on most Matanzas points. The notch openings usually form a 90-degree angle where they intersect the edge of the tool (Plate 3-3).

Faulkner points represent only about 6 percent of the side-notched points found at Area A. They closely resemble Godar points, except that they are somewhat smaller. Faulkner projectile points from Carrier Mills were rarely any longer than 1.5 inches (4 cm) (Plate 3-3).

Although these three projectile point types were used to describe and compare the Carrier Mills projectile points with those from contemporary sites, the significance of these distinctions to the Middle Archaic chert knapper and hunters is not known. It is entirely possible that the differences in the side-notched points observed, measured, and recorded by the archaeologists may only reflect the quality of the chert and the abilities of the prehistoric toolmakers. On the other hand, some archaeologists have indicated that Godar projectile points may predate the Matanzas and Faulkner types. Although this may be the case in some parts of the Midwest, all three point types occurred throughout the Middle Archaic occupation zone, suggesting that all were made and used contemporaneously. The Godar points were slightly more common in the lower levels, possibly indicating that they were relatively more popular during the earlier part of the Middle Archaic occupation than during the latter.

A second group of flaked stone tools that were very important to Middle Archaic Indians are called scrapers. Scrapers were probably used to process various plant and animal materials. Some scrapers were used to prepare deer hides so they could be used to make clothing and shelter coverings. Other kinds of scrapers may have been used to shred plant materials and to shape wood.

Scrapers are usually identified by a steeply chipped area along the edge of a flake (Plate 3-5, Rows 3 and 4). They were often made from recycled projectile points that were broken or otherwise unsuitable for their original purpose (these are called hafted end-scrapers). Scrapers are classified as either sidescrapers or end scrapers depending on which part of the implement the scraping edge was located.

An artifact was classified as a scraper because of its shape and the type of flaking used to shape the tool and because of its working edge (Plate 3-7). The working edge is that portion of a tool used to perform the task (like cutting, drilling, or scraping) for which the tool was designed. In recent years, a growing number of archaeologists have started examining the working edges of many types of tools under a microscope and studying the marks left from doing those tasks. This kind of study is called edge-wear analysis. In order to do a study of this nature, archaeologists carry out numerous experiments to find out the specific kinds of damage (crushing, polishing, or abrading) produced by certain activities. For example, an archaeologist would first make chert tools. Then he or she would use them to butcher a deer. Butchering would involve cutting and scraping meat, cutting through bone, and many other tasks. The archaeologist would then examine the tools' edges under a microscope and measure, describe, and photograph the tiny scars produced by butchering. Later, the edges of tools made and used by prehistoric people would be compared with the experimental tools. The archaeologist could then find out for what tasks the prehistoric tools might have been used.

Carrier Mills archaeologists selected 20 Middle Archaic hafted end-scrapers for an edge-wear analysis conducted by Dr. Lawrence Keeley of the University of Illinois at Chicago Circle. Examination of their edges and flat surfaces revealed many different kinds of wear and damage. On most specimens, the scraping edge, located on the end of the tool where the tip of the projectile point was formerly located, had a "polished" or "rounded" appearance when viewed under the microscope. Experiments have shown that this kind of polish is produced by scraping dry hide. These tools were probably used to "curry" deer hides during the final stages of preparation so they could be used to make clothing, robes, or other products. A few of the scrapers did not show any damage on the scraping edge, indicating that they had been sharpened for use but were probably never used. Several of the scrapers also showed evidence of woodworking, perhaps as a result of planing or smoothing wood.

PLATE 3-7. Close-up of the working edge of a Middle Archaic hafted end-scraper.

Edge-wear studies are time-consuming and expensive, but they are usually a good investment. They enable archaeologists to make accurate statements about how the people who made the tools used them. Perhaps more importantly, these studies clearly demonstrate that one tool could be used to perform a wide range of tasks.

Other types of flaked stone implements comprise a small but nevertheless important part of the Middle Archaic tool kit. The most common of these are drills, or more correctly, drill bits (Plate 3-5, Rows 1 and 2). These tools were probably used to make holes in wood. Some Middle Archaic drills were no doubt fastened to a wooden shaft in the same manner as spear points were attached to a spear shaft. These tools could have been rotated by hand or by using some type of bow mechanism.

Still other types of flaked stone tools were used to perform a wide variety of additional jobs, such as engraving bone or shell and shredding plant fibers. Most of these tools were made with flakes that were not extensively modified, except on the actual working edge. Still other tools are represented by flakes that were not modified before they were used. The only indication of these flakes being used as tools occurs as damage on the working edge resulting from that activity. In other words, these flake tools were modified *by* use rather than *for* use.

A topic of special interest to the Carrier Mills archaeologists was whether any changes occurred in the activities performed at Area A during the roughly 1,000-year-long Middle Archaic occupation. A major change in the kinds of activities that took place at the site should show up in differences in the kinds of tools needed to do those tasks. The percentage of the various types of flaked stone tools found in different excavation levels was first calculated, then levels dating to different parts of the Middle Archaic occupation were compared. The study showed that there was relatively little difference from the lower or oldest levels (about 4000 B.C.) to the upper or youngest levels (about 2900 B.C.). These results support the idea that, at least as far as the flaked stone artifacts indicate, similar activities were performed at Area A throughout the Middle Archaic occupation.

Groundstone implements. Although flaked stone tools represent a significant portion of the Middle Archaic tool kit, a wide variety of groundstone implements also played important roles in the daily activities conducted at Carrier Mills. Unlike most flaked stone tools, many groundstone tools are shaped by pecking on the stone with another rock until the general shape of the tool is achieved, then the final shaping is performed by grinding the unfinished tool on the surface of a larger, harder stone until the desired form is produced. Like flaked stone implements, some groundstone tools are classified as formal tools, while many other types are referred to as informal tools. Formal groundstone tools require considerably more time and effort to complete. Examples of formal Middle Archaic groundstone tools include axes, atlatl weights, and plummets. Many types of informal groundstone tools required very little modification before use and include such implements as grinding stones, hammerstones, pitted stones, and abraders.

Middle Archaic groundstone tools were manufactured from a wide variety of sedimentary and metamorphic rocks. In general, formal tools were made from metamorphic material and informal implements were made from sedimentary rock, primarily sandstone. Metamorphic rock was probably collected from glacial till deposits located north of Carrier Mills. Sandstone could be collected along the banks of the Saline River, south of the Black Earth site.

Informal groundstone tools were much more common at Area A than the formal varieties. More than half of these tools were used to prepare or process food, primarily nuts and seeds. Implements used for these tasks include grinding stones, grinding slabs, and pitted stones. Grinding slabs and grinding stones were used together. The grinding slab was made from a large rock with flat or slightly concave surfaces that could serve as a base for grinding. The seeds or nuts to be processed were placed on the flat surface so that they could be ground with a grinding stone, which was held in the hand of the person doing the grinding (Plate 3-8).

PLATE 3-8. Grinding stone resting in the concave depression of a grinding slab.

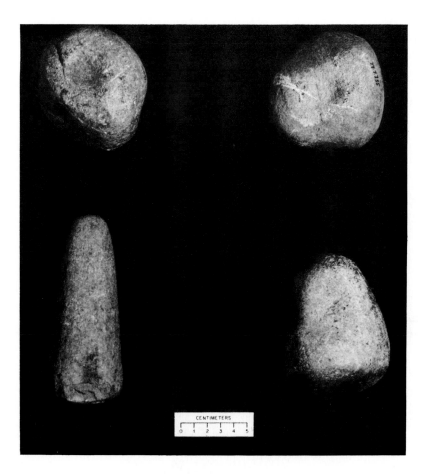

PLATE 3-9. Row 1, pitted stones; Row 2, pestles.

Pitted stones were probably also used to process plant foods, in this case, nuts. These implements generally have a flat surface into which have been pecked one or more small, circular depressions (Plate 3-9, Row 1). According to some archaeologists, hard-shelled nuts, like hickory nuts and walnuts, were placed in the small depressions, or pits, so they could be easily cracked by hitting them with another stone. Experiments have shown that they are useful for this activity. The large number of grinding stones, grinding slabs, and pitted stones recovered from the Middle Archaic zone demonstrates the importance of plant foods in the diet of these people.

Some groundstone tools appear to have been used to manufacture certain kinds of flaked stone and bone tools. Groundstone abraders played an important role in the production of bone awls and pins. Abraders consisted of a piece of sandstone against which a long piece of bone could be rubbed or abraded to smooth and polish its surface.

Hammerstones were probably used to perform many different tasks, much in the same way a modern hammer purchased at the hardware store can be used to accomplish tasks ranging from hammering a nail to cracking a nut. Hammerstones vary in size but are usually smaller than a softball. The stone is rounded, and evidence of crushing or hammering is present on most surfaces and edges.

Formal tools require more time to manufacture, and most examples of a specific kind of formal tool, such as an axe, have a similar shape. Many of the Middle Archaic formal groundstone tools found at Carrier Mills were used for the procurement of plants and animals.

The most common formal tool found at Area A was the grooved axe. This implement gets its name from the relatively deep groove present just below the butt of the axe (Plate 3-10).

PLATE 3-10. Rows 1, 2, and 3, Number 1, assorted grooved axes; Row 3, Numbers 2 and 3, grooved adzes.

Since the groove completely encircles the axe butt, this type of axe is referred to as a fully grooved axe. In other parts of the Midwest, axes dating to this time have the groove on only three of the four sides. These axes are known as three-quarter grooved axes. In both cases, the groove served as the means of attaching a wooden handle to the axe. The end of the wooden handle was first split, then the axe head was inserted between the two sections and secured by wrapping the ends with some type of bindings, much in the way a projectile point was hafted to the tip of a spear shaft. The size of these tools vary. Grooved axes were probably used for a variety of heavy-duty woodworking activities, including cutting trees for use as firewood or as building materials. Tools called grooved adzes were also used for woodworking (Plate 3-10). Many of the examples from Area A appear to have been near the end of their use-life and were discarded because they could no longer be efficiently re-sharpened. Other examples appear to have been broken during use and discarded because they could not be repaired.

A second kind of formal groundstone tool made by the Area A Middle Archaic people is known as an atlatl weight (Plate 3-11, Row 1). The term atlatl is an Aztec word meaning "spear thrower." These artifacts are sometimes referred to as bannerstones. Atlatl weights from Area A, as well as those from other parts of the Midwest, greatly vary in size and shape, but all have a hole drilled through the center of the artifact. Atlatl weights appear to have been part of an implement known as an atlatl, which basically consisted of a wooden shaft, the weight, and a hook carved from bone or antler attached to one end of the shaft. The end of a spear (the end without the projectile point) was placed in the atlatl hook and the other end of the atlatl and the shaft of the spear held in the throwing hand of the hunter (Figure 3-3). When the throwing arm and the atlatl and spear were brought forward, the spear was propelled through the air. The atlatl served to extend the length of the hunter's arm, increasing the speed with which the spear was propelled and the distance it could be thrown. The atlatl greatly increased the "killing range" of the hunter.

PLATE 3-11. Row 1, examples of finished atlatl weights; Row 2, unfinished atlatl weight; and Row 3, grooved plummets.

One example of an unfinished atlatl weight was found in the Area A Middle Archaic midden zone (Plate 3-11, Row 2). The weight had been roughly shaped and the hole through the center started but not completed. Evidence from other sites in the Midwest and Southeast suggest that the hole may have been drilled using an implement made from a dried reed (Webb 1974:268). Some type of abrasive material, such as sand, may have been placed in the hole during drilling to help speed up the process, but undoubtedly it still took a long time to penetrate the hard stone.

One example of an artifact known as a plummet was found in the Middle Archaic midden deposit. The precise function of this object is still unclear to archaeologists. This tear-drop-shaped object was made from diorite, a very dense, heavy stone that was probably collected from a deposit of glacial cobbles (Plate 3-11, Row 3). The plummet had a groove near one end that may have been used to attach a leather thong or cord of some kind. Some archaeologists have suggested that plummets were used in a manner similar to a bola. Several plummets, each attached to a long leather strap or cord, could be twirled

Figure 3-3. Archaic hunter throwing a spear using an atlatl.

over a hunter's head, then let go to tangle in the legs of an animal. Plummets probably also served a variety of other purposes.

    Bone and antler implements. Perhaps one of the most significant aspects of the Carrier Mills Archaeological Project was the recovery of more than 2,400 artifacts made from the skeletal remains of various mammals, birds, and reptiles. Relatively little is known about the technology of making and using bone artifacts because this material is not often preserved in the highly acidic soils of the region.

    Many of the bone and antler artifacts found at Carrier Mills were manufactured by the Middle Archaic residents of Area A. Thanks to the soil's alkalinity, archaeologists have been able to identify many types of bone and antler tools that composed part of the Middle Archaic tool kit, to determine which animals and which bones of those animals were selected to make these tools, and to collect information concerning how these tools were made and used.

The faunal analyst, a person highly trained in the field of animal anatomy, analyzed the nonhuman Middle Archaic bone artifacts. He had to identify the bones and determine what part that animal played in the prehistoric economy. By carefully examining the characteristics of many bone tools, analyst Emanuel Breitburg could sometimes identify the specific animal and bone from which the tool was made. In other cases, the bone tools had been altered to such an extent during manufacture and use that it was impossible to determine the bone or animal they originally came from.

The specific bone selected to produce a certain tool depended on the size, shape, and intended purpose of the implement being manufactured. Based on the results of the very detailed faunal analysis, the white-tailed deer was the most extensively exploited animal in terms of the parts of the animal used and the variety of tools made from its bones. Items made from deer bone and antler represent nearly one-third of all Middle Archaic bone artifacts. Deer was the largest mammal commonly available to the Middle Archaic hunters in southern Illinois. Tools made from deer antler and bone include awls, hide-scrapers, cutting tools, chert-knapping implements, and fishhooks.

A wide variety of small mammal skeletal parts were also used to manufacture bone tools. Although the bones of many species of these mammals were used, the number of tools made from them was relatively small. Awls were made from the long bones (leg bones) of bobcat and dog, and the dental elements (teeth and jaws) of squirrel, woodchuck, and beaver may have been used as engraving, chiseling, or abrading tools.

Aquatic and terrestrial birds represented an additional source of bones for tool production. Turkey bones were used to make awls and fishhooks. Turtles were a major source of raw material for making cups, bowls, and rattles. The eastern box turtle was the most frequently used, but the modified remains of other land and water turtles were also recovered.

One of the most common Middle Archaic bone tools found at Area A was the awl (Plate 3-12). The size and shape of these tools vary, but most examples were made from the shaft portion of the long bones of deer or other large mammals. One end of the awl was sharpened to a point by grinding the bone on a rough stone. A grooved sandstone abrader may have been used for this purpose. Awls were probably used for many different jobs, such as making and enlarging holes in leather hides and skins, sewing, and skewing meat. The surfaces of the bone awls were highly polished as a consequence of their use for these activities.

Middle Archaic bone pins were also relatively common. Although some may have been used to perform utilitarian activities, the majority of pins are highly decorated and considered by the Carrier Mills archaeologists to be ornamental items. A detailed discussion of these interesting artifacts is presented in the next section.

Other interesting, although relatively rare, bone tools were also part of the Middle Archaic tool kit. Several bone needles, each with an eye drilled at one end, were recovered (Plate 3-13, Row 1). Fishhooks and bone scraps attributable to manufacturing fishhooks were also found (Plate 3-13, Row 2). Although finished fishhooks were relatively rare in the Middle Archaic occupation zone, the by-products of fishhook-making were more common, suggesting that these artifacts may have played a more significant role in the economy than indicated by the finished artifacts. As with other types of tools, the amount of by-products or waste attributable to making the tool may be a more accurate indicator of their importance than the number of finished artifacts recovered at a site.

Bowls and cups were made from the shells of land and water turtles, the shell of the eastern box turtle apparently being the one most commonly selected for their production. No unbroken examples of turtle-shell cups or bowls were recovered, but numerous fragments of broken turtle shell on which the interior had been smoothed and polished prob-

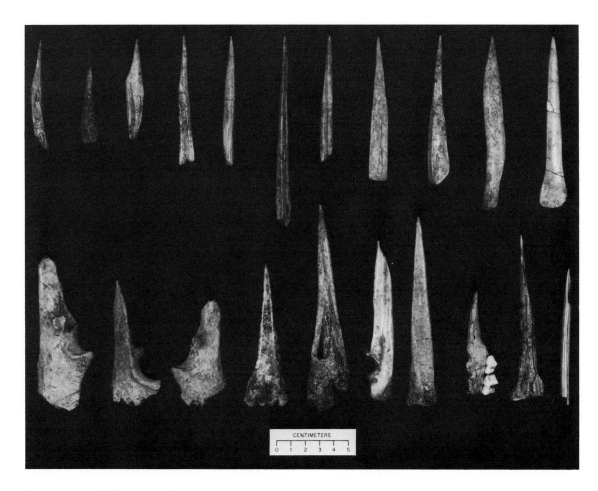

PLATE 3-12. Middle Archaic bone awls.

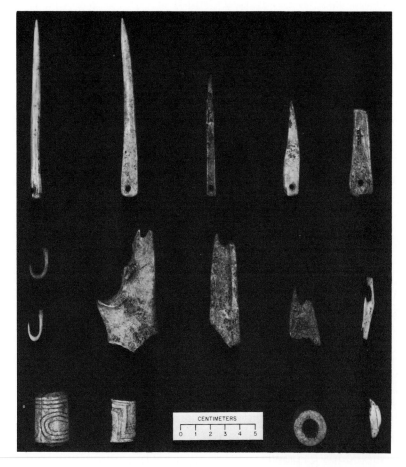

PLATE 3-13. Row 1, bone needles; Row 2, bone fishhooks and fishhook manufacturing residue; Row 3, Numbers 1–3, bone beads; Row 3, Number 4, possible pendant made from the canine tooth of a carnivore.

ably represent pieces of these containers. The exterior surface of some shell fragments were polished, possibly as a result of handling the bowl or cup. A reconstructed cup or bowl made from a box turtle shell is shown in Plate 3-14.

In addition to the more diagnostic bone tools discussed above, the faunal analyst identified many other bones and bone fragments that had been substantially modified for or by different domestic activities. Based on present information, it is difficult to determine the specific job for which many of these bone tools were used. Undoubtedly, these miscellaneous implements represent a wide range of scraping, cutting, and drilling-perforating tasks conducted by the Middle Archaic people.

Antler is a special kind of bone that is only found on certain mammals in southern Illinois. The most common source of antler was the white-tailed deer, but elk may have also provided a limited quantity. Tools were made from all portions of the antlers. The desired part of the antler was separated from the remainder by a process known as score and snap (Plate 3-15). This procedure involved cutting the dense outer bone of the antler until the softer inner bone was reached. The desired piece could then be broken off with ease.

The antler tips (tines) were used to make chert-working tools (pressure flakers), projectile points, awls, and atlatl hooks (Plates 3-15 and 3-16). The antler atlatl hook would have fitted on the end of the wooden spear-thrower shaft, opposite the end held in the hand of the hunter (Figure 3-3). The hook served to hold the spear in the atlatl until it was released by the hunter. The atlatl example shows how tools were made using different raw materials (chert, wood, metamorphic rock, and bone) and employing different technologies (flaking, stone grinding, bone carving and abrading) to produce a single weapon (spear and spear thrower).

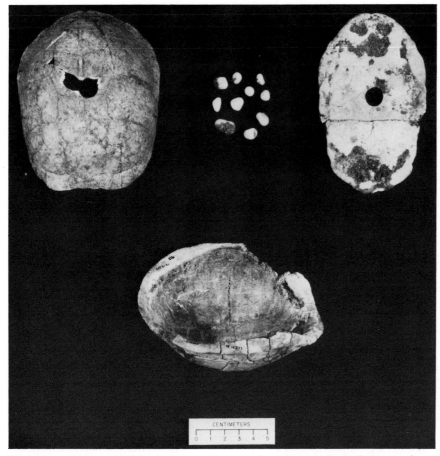

PLATE 3-14. Row 1, Middle Archaic rattle made from box turtle shell; Row 2, box turtle shell cup.

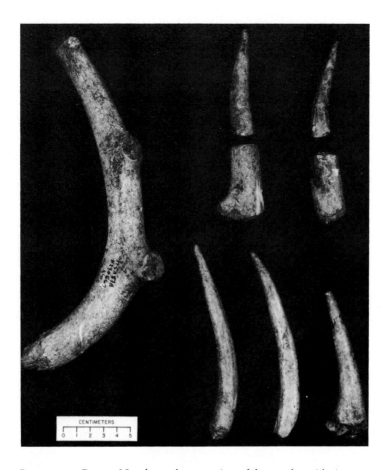

PLATE 3-15. Row 1, Number 1, large section of deer antler with tips removed using score and snap technique; Row 1, Numbers 2 and 3, sections of antler cut using score and snap technique; Row 2, antler tip pressure flakers.

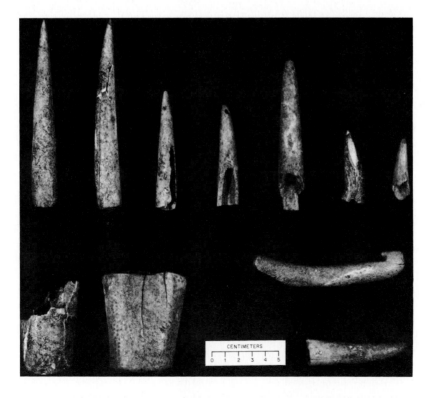

PLATE 3-16. Miscellaneous deer antler artifacts. Row 1, probable antler projectile points; Row 2, Numbers 1 and 2, antler cups; Row 2, Number 3, atlatl hook; Row 2, Number 4, probable atlatl hook.

Ornaments. Ornamental artifacts were probably items worn for personal adornment. Some types of ornamental items were made or decorated in such a way that they may have conveyed information about an individual to others who saw the object (like a diamond engagement ring today signals impending marriage). The information transmitted by the ornament may have related to an office or position held by that person or to his or her membership in a particular social or kin group. Archaeologists base the identification of an object as "ornamental" on the role similar artifacts play in past or modern societies and by largely depending on their own judgment. Middle Archaic ornamental artifacts from Carrier Mills were usually made from shell, bone, or antler. These raw materials were probably more suitable for making ornaments because they could be shaped and decorated more easily than could most kinds of stone.

The Middle Archaic inhabitants made a variety of pins and beads out of bone and antler. Bone pins were the most common type of Middle Archaic ornamental artifact (Plate 3-17). Some of these highly decorated and stylized objects were found in burials. Careful examination of the pins revealed that some were probably made from parts of long bones of white-tailed deer. Someone wanting to make a bone pin probably did so by splitting a bone lengthwise, selecting a bone splinter, carving it to the desired shape, and then finally shaping and polishing it by grinding and abrading.

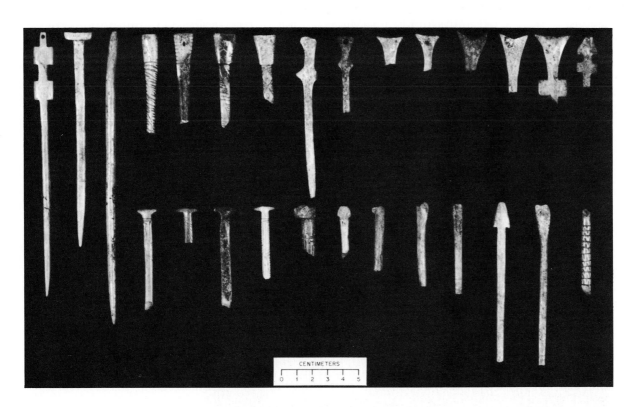

PLATE 3-17. Middle Archaic carved and engraved bone pins.

The shafts of many of the Middle Archaic bone pins are decorated with very detailed engraving or incising. A variety of different designs are represented, including parallel lines, zigzags, diamonds, and various combinations of these designs. Designs were probably engraved into the surface of the pins using a flaked stone tool known as a graver (Plate

3-5, Row 3, No. 6). A graver has a small projection on its edge that is suitable for scratching the surface of the bone, producing the fine lines that form the intricate designs. Residents at Carrier Mills may have also used the lower jaw (mandible) and teeth of certain small mammals, particularly squirrel and woodchuck, for engraving designs on pins.

The exact manner in which the Middle Archaic people used these pins is uncertain. Some pins may have been worn to hold hair arrangements in place, while others may have served more utilitarian purposes, such as fastening articles of clothing.

The shapes of the bone pins and the designs engraved on them provide archaeologists with a means of looking at Middle Archaic life at a regional level instead of just at the site level. Middle Archaic sites in the Illinois River valley (Koster) and Mississippi River valley (Modoc Rock Shelter) in Illinois, and sites in Missouri (Graham Cave and Arnold Research Cave), Kentucky (several sites in the Louisville area), and southern Indiana (Crib Shell Mound) have yielded bone pins with similar shapes and engraved designs. The similarity of these artifacts from such distant locations suggests that there must have been some degree of interaction or communication among the people living in this region 5,000 to 6,000 years ago.

Bone and antler were also used to make beads, fashioned by drilling a hole through the center of the bone. A number of beads could then be strung together to make a necklace. An example of an engraved antler bead found with an Area A Middle Archaic burial is shown in Plate 3-13, Row 3, No. 1.

Examples of ornaments made from shell are illustrated in Plate 3-18. Most of the shell used to make the pendants and beads comes from a type of shellfish commonly referred to

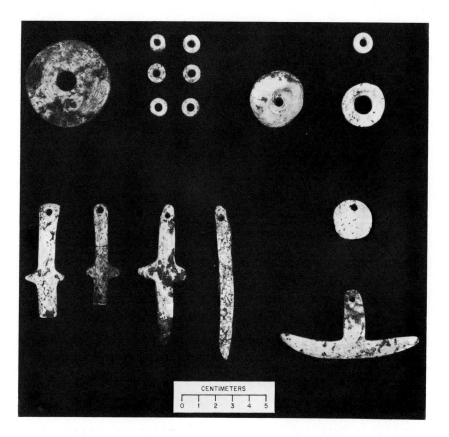

PLATE 3-18. Row 1, shell beads and miscellaneous ornaments; Row 2, shell pendants. The large shell disc (Row 1, Number 1) may have been made from a conch shell collected from the Atlantic or Gulf coasts. Other examples are made from river mussel shells.

as a river mussel, which was probably collected from the Saline River or other nearby streams or rivers. Artifacts produced from mussel shells were manufactured by cutting the design out of the shell. Smaller beads were made from small freshwater snail shells. Archaeologists found some of these small shell beads in the neck area of a Middle Archaic infant burial; they are probably the remains of a necklace or perhaps were sewn to a piece of clothing or to a blanket.

A number of Middle Archaic adult burials included several shell pendants. Most of the pendants were shaped to form some type of cross, but some were circular (Plate 3-18). These ornaments were suspended by a cord or string that passed through a small hole at the top of the pendant. Archaeologists also found another shell artifact that also may have been worn in some way under the chin of an infant (Plate 3-18, Row 1, No. 1). The disclike object was probably made from marine shell that originally came from the Atlantic or Gulf coasts. Marine shell was a popular trade item in parts of the Southeast and Midwest during the Late Archaic period (3000–1000 B.C.).

Ceremonial/Miscellaneous Artifacts. Ceremonial/miscellaneous artifacts represent the final category of personal equipment. Artifacts in this group were usually made from exotic or nonlocal raw mateials and are unusual in appearance. They are often found in special contexts, such as in a burial. In most cases, we cannot determine if these artifacts were associated with a specific type of ceremony.

One of the more unusual collections of ceremonial objects was found in a Middle Archaic burial of an approximately 43-year-old male (Burial 137) (Plate 3-19). Forty-five

PLATE 3-19. Middle Archaic burial containing a cache of artifacts near right shoulder.

items were found in a small concentration near his right shoulder. The position of these artifacts suggests that they were originally placed in some kind of container, perhaps in a bag or in a bundle. Many of the objects were not found with any other Carrier Mills burials. These unique items included eagle talons, sections of bones from a bear's paw, a miniature grooved axe, pieces of slate, side-notched projectile points, opossum jaws, a bone awl, pieces of hematite (a mineral used to produce red paint pigment), pieces of limestone with ground and polished areas, and a dog's tooth that had a groove around one end (Plates 3-20 through 3-22). The artifacts may have been some type of kit used by the individual to perform special ceremonies, similar to a medicine bundle used by curers, shamans, or "medicine men." If this interpretation is correct, then this man probably occupied a special position in his society.

PLATE 3-20. Projectile points from artifact cache (see Plate 3-19).

PLATE 3-21. Groundstone and unmodified stone artifacts from artifact cache (see Plate 3-19).

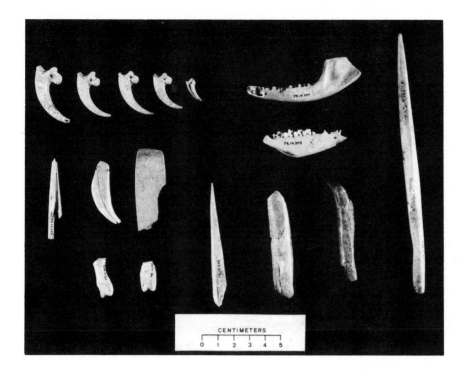

PLATE 3-22. Bone artifacts from artifact cache (see Plate 3-19).

A rattle made from the shell of an eastern box turtle may have also been used in a ritual (Plate 3-14). The rattle was made by drilling a one-half-inch (13 mm) hole in the center of the top and bottom portions of the turtle shell so that a handle could be attached. Ten small white quartz pebbles were still inside the rattle when archaeologists uncovered it at Area A. Howard Winters's research on the use of turtle-shell rattles by Historic period eastern North American Indians indicates that they were usually items of personal equipment and that they were used in some of the most important sacred ceremonies. Larger turtle-shell rattles made from the box turtle were the preferred type for sacred ceremonies, and smaller rattles, made from the shells of other kinds of turtles, were preferred for more secular individual dances (Winters 1969:78).

Archaeologists found a second Middle Archaic burial containing what might be described as a ceremonial item at site Sa-88, located on the ridge immediately south of the Black Earth site. This approximately 27-year-old male (Burial 190B) was placed in the burial pit with a number of utilitarian items in the chest area: a bone awl, a chert scraper, a side-notched projectile point, and an antler tine flaker (Figure 3-4). In addition, a copper wedgelike artifact was placed where the base of the skull should have been; the skull itself was missing (Plate 3-23). The skeleton of an approximately nine-year-old child (Burial 190A) accompanied the adult male.

The "blade" of the wedge is thickest at the butt, gradually decreasing in thickness toward the beveled working edge, or "bit." Notches are located on each side of the blade, immediately below the butt, and may have been used for attaching the object to a handle. The butt is battered and flattened, probably as a result of hammering. The wedge was made by heating and hammering a nugget of pure copper into the desired shape (the technology of smelting metals was unknown to the prehistoric people of the Midwest). Similar artifacts dating to the Late Archaic period have been found in Wisconsin, Michigan, and Minnesota. A few copper artifacts were also found at some late Middle Archaic Helton phase sites in the lower Illinois valley (Cook 1976).

PLATE 3-23. Artifacts from Middle Archaic burial at site Sa-88.

Figure 3-4. Burial 190A and B and associated artifacts.

BURIAL 190
(A and B)

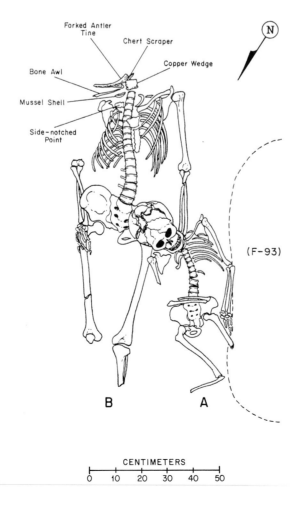

Two cups made from elk antler were found at Carrier Mills (Plate 3-16, Row 2, Nos. 1 and 2). One was with an Area A Middle Archaic burial. The second cup was found in a burial at Sa-88, which could not be precisely dated. Both cups were made from a short section of elk antler from which the soft inner bone had been removed. The exterior of the Area A cup was decorated by a series of "dots" that were drilled or engraved in the surface, forming a linear arrangement connecting the top and bottom of the cup.

Features. Archaeologists can learn a great deal about a prehistoric occupation by examining its associated features. Since excavating a feature destroys it, archaeologists must make detailed records of the size, method of construction, and contents of the feature during excavation. These records include precise measurements, a detailed description, drawings of different views of the feature, and black-and-white and color photographs. Collecting all of this information enables the archaeologists to later reconstruct what the feature looked like and where it was located at the site.

Excavation of a site may yield hundreds of features. Most of these can be assigned to one of several feature categories or types, based on their size, shape, and contents. Features having similar characteristics, or attributes, were probably used for similar activities. It is usually quite difficult to assign a specific function to each feature, and undoubtedly some features were used for a variety of different purposes. With these limitations in mind, we can start to discuss the kinds of features used by the Area A Middle Archaic people.

Excavation of the Middle Archaic midden zone uncovered over 200 features, including two kinds of pit features, as well as areas of charcoal, ash, and clay, and a baked clay hearth. (Although human burials and burial pits are often labeled as features by archaeologists, they were not designated as such at Carrier Mills.) Nearly two-thirds of the Middle Archaic features were pits dug by the people who lived at the site. At any one time, a number of pits would have been in use. Some of these were probably used to prepare food or process other resources, and others may have been used for underground food storage. Eventually, old pits would be abandoned and new ones dug. Abandoned pits may have been used for trash disposal or may have been slowly filled by natural processes. Through the years, the gradual buildup of midden soil buried the ground surface on which the older pits originated. Many years later, when excavated by archaeologists, these filled-in pits appeared as dark circular or oval stains on the newly cleaned surfaces of excavation units. Sometimes, the features' edges were difficult for the archaeologists to define since the soil in the pit, or pit fill, was often the same color as the surrounding midden soil into which the pit was dug. Many times, the distinction between pit fill and midden was based on differences in soil texture rather than color. Some features contained higher densities of artifacts than the surrounding midden soil, suggesting that they may have been used for trash disposal.

The most common Middle Archaic features were small, shallow, basin-shaped depressions known as Type 2 features. These shallow pits averaged about 6 inches (16 cm) deep and 28 inches (70 cm) in diameter. They were circular to oval in outline. The inhabitants at the site used many of the Type 2 features to prepare various plant and animal foods with both direct and indirect heat. Direct heat involved building a fire in the pit; indirect heating was done by heating rocks in a fire built outside the pit, then placing the hot rocks in the pit and using the heat from the rocks for cooking.

Type 1 features, also used by the Area A Middle Archaic people, had circular to oval outlines, flat to slightly rounded bottoms, and straight to slightly tapering walls or sides. They averaged about 35 inches (90 cm) in diameter and 14 inches (35 cm) deep. Their specific purpose is unclear. They may have been used for underground food storage. The soft, well-drained soils found at Area A made this area highly suitable for underground storage of certain kinds of foods, unlike other parts of the District where pits tended to collect water during periods of heavy rain.

Small concentrations of burned plant material or charcoal (Type 3 features) were often found during excavation of the Middle Archaic zone. These features were generally circular in outline and basin-shaped in cross section. Although the average depth was similar to that of Type 2 features, they had a much smaller diameter. Type 3 features contained fine charcoal, pieces of burned wood and bark, and fragments of charred nutshell. Very few artifacts or other objects were found in them. These features probably represent some kind of fire pit or hearth. Small fires would have provided a limited amount of heat and light with which to conduct a wide variety of domestic activities. Archaeologists were puzzled by the lack of oxidized or burned soil associated with these features, but some experiments done at the site revealed that these midden soils rarely show any color change from burning. Type 3 features also indicate that many Middle Archaic activities conducted at Area A involved burning large quantities of wood and other plant materials.

The rest of the features consisted of an assortment of irregularly shaped clay and ash concentrations, one baked clay hearth, and clay burial caps. The purposes of the clay and ash concentrations are unclear, but they too may have been the remains of fires or hearths. The one example of a baked clay hearth may have been an isolated example of this feature type that had not been destroyed by the daily activities of the Middle Archaic residents. The clay burial caps will be discussed in a later section.

Postmolds are features that appear as small, dark, circular stains in the soil, which mark the spot where wooden posts were placed in the ground. Posts were used to build houses, shelters, walls, or other kinds of structures. Eventually, the portion of the posts below ground rotted away, leaving stains created by the decomposed wood. The presence of postmolds on an archaeological site is usually associated with a long-term or permanent occupation. Short-term encampments of several days or weeks might result in the construction of a light-weight windbreak or a small temporary shelter; few indications of the temporary structures would be visible today. In contrast, more substantial structures built to last for several seasons or years would require stronger, more durable materials that would be more likely to leave a permanent record of their construction. If enough of the structure is exposed during excavation, the pattern of postmolds may reveal the size and shape of the structure that once stood on that spot.

Four concentrations of postmolds were found with the Middle Archaic occupation. The largest of the concentrations, containing a minimum of 26 postmolds, was located in the southwest part of Area A (Plate 3-24). The outline of a structure is not readily apparent in this area, but the number and density of postmolds suggest that considerable building of some sort took place. This above-ground architecture was constructed in the area of maximum midden accumulation, the location of the most intensive activity during this occupation.

Food Habits

Plant Food Sources. In parts of the Southeast and Midwest, some late Middle Archaic or early Late Archaic groups were starting to experiment with plants and may have been involved in the very early stages of gardening (Asch and Asch 1982; Crawford 1982). However, archaeologists did not find any evidence of this at Carrier Mills. Their detailed

PLATE 3-24. Small circular holes are excavated postmolds at base of Middle Archaic zone in the southwest part of Area A.

studies of Area A plant and animal remains show that the Middle Archaic people ate only those foods that grew naturally in the Saline River valley and adjacent areas.

The archaeologists studying prehistoric eating habits had several goals in mind: to find out how important the different habitats (riverine, upland, forest, and so on) were in providing food; to determine what portion of the diet was represented by the various plants and animals found in those habitats; and to analyze how those resources were collected or hunted and prepared for human consumption. Neal Lopinot, the Carrier Mills paleoethnobotanist (a scientist who studies prehistoric plant remains), analyzed samples of charred (carbonized) seeds, stems, nutshell, nutmeat, and other plant parts from 46 Middle Archaic features and nearly 50 excavation levels. He carefully examined and identified the plant remains by using a low-power binocular microscope.

Nuts. Nuts were probably the most important plant food to the Middle Archaic people. Many different kinds of nuts were available in the forests of southern Illinois, and large quantities could be collected with the expenditure of little time or energy. Nuts were collected during the fall and early winter and with proper preparation could be stored for a long time. The nuts were no doubt "put up" in order to be eaten during late winter and early spring, a time when most other food sources were not available.

Hickory nuts appear to have been the most popular nut with the Middle Archaic residents of the Black Earth site. Many different varieties of hickory trees can now be found in the Carrier Mills area, including bitternut, mockernut, kingnut, pignut, and pecan hickories; the Middle Archaic people used all of these hickories to some extent. Most of these grow in the upland forests found on the drier hilltops and slopes, but some prefer the more moist soils near streams and swamps.

According to reports of early travelers and explorers, Indians in the Southeast and Midwest collected hickory nuts for their oil. The oil could be extracted from the nuts by cracking the nutshell and dumping the shell and the nutmeat in a pot of boiling water. The oil would float to the surface and the shell would sink to the bottom. Walnuts were also collected for their oil (Smith 1966:26).

Acorns were another important and nutritious food source. Many different varieties of oaks grew in the vicinity of Carrier Mills, including white, black, pin, post, and red oaks. Only small amounts of acorn shell were recovered from most Middle Archaic features, no doubt due to its very fragile nature (acorn shell does not usually survive carbonization). We must remember that, although it is the *nutshell* that is preserved, it was the *nutmeat* that was important to the Indians. Experiments comparing the relationship between the weights of hickory and acorn shell and the weights of the nutmeat contained in the nuts revealed that 1 g (gram) of carbonized acorn shell may represent the same quantity of meat as 12 to 56 g of charred hickory nutshell, depending on the specific kind of hickory nut (Lopinot 1984). This indicates that acorns were probably a much more important part of the Middle Archaic diet than suggested by their shells.

Unlike hickory nuts and walnuts, most acorns cannot be eaten without first removing the tannic acid in the nutmeat, usually by parching the acorns. The meat was used to make acorn mush or bread or was added to porridge. Although oil was sometimes extracted from acorns, this practice was not common among the southern Illinois Indians (Lopinot 1982:720).

Seeds. Over 6,000 seeds and seed fragments were recovered from Middle Archaic features. Some seeds that could be identified came from plants like the hackberry, hawthorn, persimmon, honey locust, American plum, wild black cherry, black raspberry or blackberry, greenbrier, and grape. Many of these plants produce fruits that can be eaten when picked or dried and stored. The starchy roots of the greenbrier may have been consumed on occasion.

Several examples of weed seeds (giant ragweed, sunflower, and lamb's-quarters or goosefoot) were found in one Middle Archaic feature and in a number of levels. Although weed seeds became a much more important part of the diet during later times, they apparently were not a favorite food in this part of southern Illinois during the late Middle Archaic period. Seeds from other plants include tick trefoil, bedstraw, and wild bean.

Archaeologists also found examples of carbonized subterranean plant parts (roots, tubers, rhizomes, bulbs, and so on). The one Middle Archaic specimen was a carbonized tuber from the groundnut. The tubers of this plant were regularly eaten by historic American Indians. Tubers could be eaten raw, roasted, or dried for eating at a later time.

Analyzing seeds tells us when a site was occupied. Middle Archaic plant remains indicate a late summer and fall occupation of Area A. However, this picture could be misleading because the seeds and nuts available during these seasons are much more durable and have a much higher potential to be carbonized and preserved than edible plant parts available during the spring and early summer (greens, syrups, tubers, and so on). In addition, seeds and nuts can be stored for use during the less bountiful seasons of the year.

Analysis of plant remains can also provide considerable insight on environmental conditions in and around the site. The Middle Archaic Indians obtained food from the forests and forest edges, lakes and river edges, and areas modified by human activity (like forest clearings). Oak-hickory forests on upland ridgetops and slopes were intensively exploited during the fall for nut collection. Seeds from fruit trees and from the hazelnut, wild grape, wild bean, and bedstraw indicate the existence of open or disturbed forests, forest edges, or thickets. Giant ragweed and sunflowers are commonly found in open, disturbed areas, and bulrush grows in shallow standing water along the edges of ponds or lakes.

Animals. Plant foods formed only part of the Middle Archaic peoples' diet. A very wide assortment of mammals, birds, reptiles, amphibians, and fish provided much of the necessary protein and fat in their diet. As we have already seen, animals contributed other important resources besides food, such as bone to make many kinds of tools and ornaments and skins and furs for clothing.

Because of the excellent preservation conditions at Area A, archaeologists recovered nearly 57,000 pieces of bone from the Middle Archaic midden zone and features. This material, combined with faunal remains from a number of flotation samples, allowed the detailed study of the animals hunted, fished, and trapped at Carrier Mills.

One of the project's faunal analysts, Emanuel Breitburg, discovered that virtually all of the animals living in the forests, lakes, rivers, and fields of southern Illinois were used by the Area A Middle Archaic inhabitants. It appears that the most intensively exploited animals were found in three ecological zones or habitats: forest edges, forest, and aquatic/riverine. The forest-edge zone consisted of all those areas where forests bordered on swampy or grassy areas. Because of the diverse selection of plant foods available, many different animal species were attracted to these areas. The forest zone comprises all those areas covered by mature stands of trees. Aquatic/riverine areas include all of the wet areas, such as lakes, rivers, creeks, sloughs, and swamps.

Animals found in the forest-edge zone were the primary source of meat during the late Middle Archaic period. The most important animals hunted in this zone, based on the amount of meat they provided, were the white-tailed deer, elk, bobcat, woodchuck, rabbit, skunk, fox squirrel, turkey, and quail. Box turtles and snakes were also collected from this zone.

The white-tailed deer was by far the most important source of meat. In addition to meat, the deer also supplied bone and antler to make tools and ornaments. The stage of antler development and the age of the deer at death indicate the season in which the deer was killed. This determination is possible because deer shed their antlers in late winter or early spring, then grow new ones during late spring and summer. Also, most fawns are born in late May or early June, so the time of death can be easily determined on the basis of age. The Middle Archaic inhabitants hunted deer throughout the year, but especially during the fall and winter months.

The raccoon, opossum, gray squirrel, gray fox, and the now-extinct passenger pigeon were the most important meat sources hunted in the forest zone. Collectively, these animals provided roughly 6 percent to 8 percent of the meat in the Middle Archaic diet. The aquatic/riverine zone served as home for many species of mammals, birds, reptiles, and fish that were hunted, trapped, and fished by Area A residents. Beaver, mink, otter, and muskrat could be hunted or trapped year-round. Many species of ducks, geese, and swans were present during the spring and fall migrations, and others were available primarily during the summer. Turtles, fish, and numerous amphibians were most easily caught during the warmer months of late spring through early fall.

The beaver appears to have been the primary meat source in the aquatic/riverine zone. Resident and migratory waterfowl, turtles, and amphibians contributed a small but consistent amount of meat to the Middle Archaic diet.

The role that fish played in the Middle Archaic diet is still open to question. Although a large lake-swamp area was located near Area A at that time, archaeologists found relatively few fish remains. Most of the fish that could be identified are the kind that live in heavily vegetated, slow-moving bodies of water (like catfish and bowfin).

It is also possible that the Middle Archaic people ate large quantities of very small fish—their tiny bones would have passed undetected through the archaeologists' wire mesh used to sift soil removed by excavation. However, flotation samples yielded the bones of many small fish, amphibians, and mammals. Archaeologists do not know just how much food is represented by these small fish. They do suspect, though, that they were caught in a seine or some other kind of net, probably during the drier months of late summer and fall when water levels dropped and fish became trapped in shallow pools. Only two bone fishhooks were found in the entire Middle Archaic zone.

Each of the natural habitats near the Carrier Mills Archaeological District provided important resources. Some of these foods were available all year; others were available only during certain months or seasons. Plant foods that were produced in large quantities and could be stored, such as hickory nuts and acorns, and animals that were available year-round formed the mainstay of the diet. Other plants and animals that were only seasonally available supplemented other food sources. The plant and animal remains reflect a multiseasonal pattern of hunting, fishing, and collecting, providing additional support for a year-round occupation of Area A during the late Middle Archaic period.

Burial Customs

The treatment of a dead person varies greatly from culture to culture. Most societies bury their dead, sometimes cremating or burning the remains before burial. Others place the body on a scaffold exposed to the elements, allowing the flesh and organs to decompose; after a designated period, the bones are then collected, bundled, and buried. Sometimes burial goods or other items are placed in the grave; other times they are not. There are probably just about as many variations in the procedures for disposing of the dead as there are societies in the world.

There can also be considerable variation in the treatment of the dead even within a culture. The way a person is treated at the time of death reflects his or her status or social position while living. For example, a high-status individual, such as a king or a chief, may receive a very elaborate funeral involving rituals, a large grave, and many burial offerings; in contrast, a lower-status person or commoner may simply be placed in an ordinary burial pit with little or no special treatment. At other times, differences in burial treatment may simply be based on the sex or age of the deceased. The treatment of the dead often provides archaeologists with information about the organization and complexity of the society of the deceased. Archaeologists refer to the set of rules and procedures that govern how an individual is treated at death as the mortuary program of a society.

Excavations of Area A produced 223 burials, of which 154 were identified as being from the late Middle Archaic period. Since only about one-third of the central part of the site was excavated, as many as 400 to 500 Middle Archaic persons may have been interred at the site. Human skeletal material was very well preserved because of the high alkalinity of the Area A midden soil. Even the fragile bones of a human fetus were recovered. Some of the Middle Archaic burials were disturbed by pits dug by later prehistoric people who lived at Area A or by twentieth-century artifact collectors, resulting in the loss of many of the skeletal elements (Plate 3-25). In spite of the disturbance, the Area A skeletal material is particularly important because there are very few well-documented Middle Archaic burials from the Midwest; the Area A collection is one of the largest and best preserved.

PLATE 3-25. Middle Archaic burial cut by Middle Woodland storage pit. Feet of burial are in foreground.

Archaeologists recorded many different kinds of information during the excavation and analysis of burials, including the individual's age and sex; orientation (which direction the head was pointing); position (legs flexed or extended); side on which the person had been placed (right, left, back, or face-down); and the presence or absence of grave goods. Most of these burial characteristics have proven to be useful for analyzing other prehistoric and historic mortuary programs.

To learn more about the Middle Archaic people buried here, archaeologist Mark Lynch divided the age of individuals at the time of death into six categories: infant, 0–3 years; child, 3–12 years; adolescent, 12–18 years; young adult, 18–35 years; middle adult, 35–50 years, and old adult, 50 + years. Infants accounted for a relatively high percentage of the burials (21 percent), but infant mortality is usually quite high in hunter-gatherer groups. The number of deaths falling in the child and adolescent age groups (3–18 years) is very low, followed by an increase in the young adult and middle adult categories, reflecting the increasing age of those individuals. Males slightly outnumbered females 53 percent to 47 percent.

Over one-third of all individuals were interred with the head pointed toward the west, which tells archaeologists that these people preferred that burial orientation. The reason for their preference is unknown. Sex of the individuals apparently did not play a role in determining burial orientation.

The position of the dead person was evenly divided between the extended and flexed positions. In the extended position, the legs are set straight out from the body (Plate 3-26); in the flexed, the legs are bent with the knees brought up to the chest (Plate 3-27). Burial position apparently depended on the age of the person. Infants, adolescents, and young adults were usually buried in an extended position, and middle and old adults were normally flexed. Archaeologists found no obvious correlation between an individual's burial position, orientation, or sex.

Four Middle Archaic persons were placed in other burial positions. The most unusual of these was that of a 38-year-old male (Burial 182) placed in a seated position, with the right leg extended and the left leg bent at a 90-degree angle (Figure 3-5). The upper part of the body was bent forward over the legs. The left arm was extended beside the upper body,

PLATE 3-26. Middle Archaic burial placed in an extended position.

PLATE 3-27. Middle Archaic burial placed in a flexed position.

and the right arm extended from the body at a 90-degree angle. The lower part of the right arm was bent back at a 90-degree angle at the elbow. This person was certainly not buried in a natural position. The body would not have stayed in such a pose during burial unless some type of pressure was applied to keep the upper body down. No objects were buried with him.

Figure 3-5. Position of Burial 182.

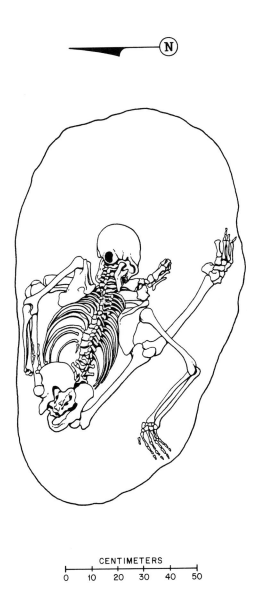

The quantity and variety of artifacts buried with an individual (called grave goods) can provide information about the status of that person in his or her society. Anthropologists often find that individuals who occupied a high social position are buried with very elaborate objects made from exotic raw materials not obtained locally. The time, energy, and expense invested in obtaining these raw materials and in manufacturing the objects reflect the importance of the deceased individual to the other members of the group. Artifacts were found with only 27 percent of the Area A Middle Archaic burials. Archaeologists found that grave goods were placed with people buried in extended positions more often than with those in flexed positions, but there did not appear to be a relationship between the presence of grave goods and the sex of the individual.

Utilitarian artifacts were mainly buried with adults. Items found only with males included flaked stone drills, chert cores, projectile points, and grooved axes. Utilitarian artifacts associated with (but not necessarily restricted to) females consisted of flaked stone scrapers, bone awls, modified pieces of deer antler, bone needles, and an unfinished chert biface. Perhaps we can detect a division of labor among these Middle Archaic peoples. In general, utilitarian artifacts found with male burials are associated with hunting and other ways of obtaining natural resources. Most artifacts found with females were used to process or prepare those resources. Plates 3-28 and 3-29 show the placement and kinds of artifacts interred with a Middle Archaic male at the Black Earth site.

Ornamental and ceremonial/miscellaneous objects were buried with both adults and subadults. The largest number of ceremonial/miscellaneous artifacts was found in the medicine bundle located near the right shoulder of the Middle Archaic adult male burial (Burial 137) discussed earlier in this chapter.

PLATE 3-28. Middle Archaic burial and associated burial artifacts.

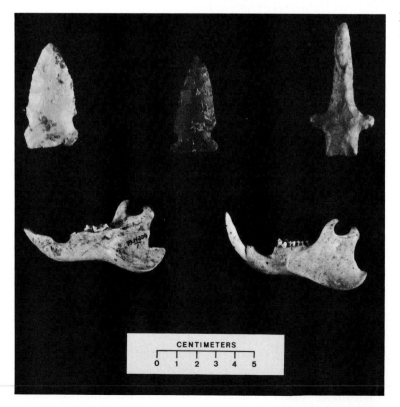

PLATE 3-29. Artifacts associated with burial in Plate 3-28.

Eight persons had been placed in burial pits capped with a layer of clay. These clay layers, ranging from 4 inches to 16 inches (9 cm to 40 cm) thick, were limited to adult burials, with one exception. Most were males buried in an extended position. The greater effort invested in the burial of these individuals suggests that they may have occupied a special position in the society generally reserved for adults. Nearly two-thirds of the clay-capped burials contained associated grave goods, many of an ornamental or ceremonial nature.

Although most Middle Archaic people were buried individually, archaeologists found nine burials containing two or more skeletons at Area A (Plate 3-30). Six of the multiple burials contained two people, two had three people, and one consisted of four individuals. The age and sex of the people in multiple burials varied. Of the 22 individuals interred with another person, 11 were females, 8 were juveniles, but only 3 were males, which suggests that men were generally interred alone. Few multiple burials contained burial goods.

PLATE 3-30. Middle Archaic multiple burial.

From studying Middle Archaic burial practices, we have learned something of how these people were organized in their society. The way in which they were treated at the time of their death depended on their age, sex, and personal abilities. Although we observed some differences (for example, the presence of a medicine bundle), they were not major when compared to the elaborate burial mounds and grave goods of later periods. The leaders of the Carrier Mills Indians probably earned their position by virtue of their sex or age, or perhaps by possessing certain physical or mental capabilities (for example, great strength or skill in hunting). On the whole, there was probably little social difference between members of the group.

Health and Disease

As we have seen, we can learn a great deal about the social organization of prehistoric groups by studying their burial customs. The bones of the Area A burials contained many other kinds of information that we can use to explore the Middle Archaic way of life.

Archaeologists have been interested in human skeletal remains for many years, but until the past few decades most of their research involved simply recording the physical characteristics of individual skeletons. Now, archaeologists use this information to study the paleodemography—biological and population characteristics—of the whole group.

Many of the advances of the past decade are the results of archaeologists using new research techniques (X-rays, for example) borrowed from the physical and life sciences. These techniques enable archaeologists to investigate many physical and chemical properties of bone not possible in the past. They use this information to explore the kinds of diseases that afflicted the people and their effects on long-term health, the importance of various foods in the diet, the types of injuries most commonly incurred, and many other topics concerning nutrition and health.

Before any detailed study of the Middle Archaic skeletal material could take place, archaeologists first had to identify the age and sex of all individuals. A number of skeletal characteristics assist scientists in determining the age of an individual, most of which are based on the stage of growth reached by certain bones. These stages of growth and development occur at specific ages, on the average. Various characteristics of the pelvic bones were the most useful indicators for distinguishing males from females.

From the age and sex data, archaeologists could then study life expectancy. The average life expectancy for a newborn Middle Archaic child was about 24 years, but this figure is somewhat distorted by the very high infant death rate; at least 27 percent of the population died during the first year of life. If the individual managed to survive that first year, a male could expect to live an average of about 32 more years, and a female about 38 more years. The oldest individual at Area A was a 58-year-old female.

Infant mortality rates are generally high among most hunter-gatherer groups, but those of the Area A Middle Archaic people were unusually high. One possible explanation for the numerous infant burials may have been the excellent preservation of bone at Area A. Since more infant remains were preserved, it may only appear that the infant death rate was higher. Death rates decrease radically following the first year. Only 7 percent of all Area A Middle Archaic people died between the ages of 1 and 15 years of age.

Relatively few Middle Archaic women appeared to have died as a result of childbirth, but several burials contained both a female and an infant, suggesting that it did occasionally happen. The percentage of women dying during the peak childbirth period of 15 to 30 years was lower than for men in the same age range.

Information about the rate of growth and development of the skeleton provides archaeologists with a means of studying various kinds of stress experienced by Middle Archaic people. The most common type of stress is a result of a poor diet. An insufficient or improper diet can cause an interruption in an individual's normal development. It is particularly noticeable in children and adolescents who are experiencing periods of rapid growth. These interruptions are often marked by lines extending across long bones that are visible in X-rays. Examination of various stress indicators revealed that the Area A Middle Archaic people did not experience long periods of nutritional stress attributed to food shortages or improper diet. Although these conditions probably periodically existed, they apparently did not continue long enough to affect bone growth and development.

Scientists can also calculate the height of individuals based on the length of the long bones of the legs and arms. The average height of an adult Middle Archaic male was 5 feet, 6 inches (167 cm). Adult females were slightly shorter at 5 feet, 2 inches (158 cm).

Signs of Injury and Illness

The bones of many Middle Archaic individuals were damaged or marked by a variety of lesions or abnormalities, including those caused by fractures, infections, and birth defects. Some of these reflect violent encounters between people or between a person and the environment. Others are the result of various diseases. Although few of these conditions were fatal, many, such as arthritis, undoubtedly restricted movement and participation in many activities. Others, such as severe head injuries, reflect more serious health conditions that may have been the actual cause of death.

Fractured bones were a common type of injury at Middle Archaic Carrier Mills. In many cases, particularly among younger individuals, fractures had completely healed and the location of the break was barely visible. The rate of bone growth is much slower in adults, making it more likely that fractures occurring later in life would be more visible and perhaps less completely healed. Often, the extent to which the healing process progressed can help scientists determine how long before death the injury occurred.

Although fractures were common for both males and females, males experienced more fractures than females. Some archaeologists suggest that this is because males performed more high-risk tasks, such as hunting and warfare, than did females (Blakely 1971). One kind of fracture commonly found in males is known as a "parry fracture" (Plate 3-31). This kind occurs in the forearms and may have been caused by warding off blows with the arm (Armelagos 1969). Males showed the only indication of fractures to the large, flat bones of the skull, shoulder blade, and pelvis. One particular male had a fractured lower arm, cheek bone, upper jaw, and the front part of the skull. His extensive injuries may have been caused by falling out of a tree or off a cliff. All rib fractures on males occurred as multiple breaks of two, three, or four ribs. Rib fractures in females occurred singly. Females had more fractures of the lower limbs than did males.

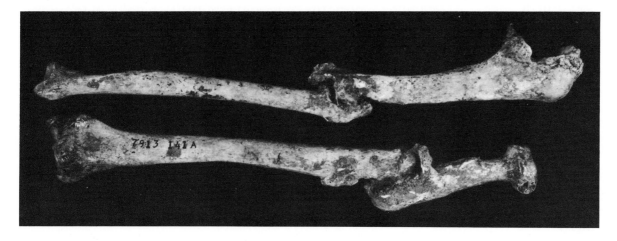

PLATE 3-31. Parry fracture of the forearm.

The bones of many of the Middle Archaic people showed signs of infection. Some infections may have been located in the muscle tissue near the bone. Other infections existed in the marrow inside the bone. Both types resulted in the formation of abscesses, pus-

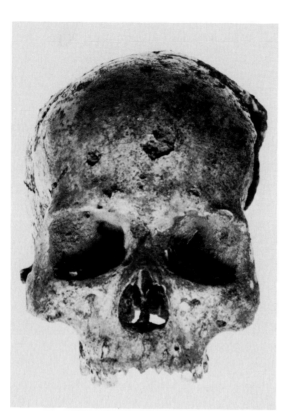

PLATE 3-32. Lesions on cranium associated with some type of severe infection.

draining sinuses, and areas of dead bone (Plate 3-32). If the infection reached an advanced stage, it could cause death.

One of the more interesting Middle Archaic skeletons was that of a 45-year-old man who had crushed vertebrae in his lower back resulting in damage to his spinal column. All of the skeleton below the neck displayed bony growths that are commonly found on the bones of paralyzed individuals. The upper leg bones (femurs) were dislocated from their sockets in the pelvis, resulting in the formation of new sockets nearby. The bony growths suggest that this person lived for many years after suffering a major injury. The survival of a person in this physical condition supports the archaeologists' belief that this man's group lived permanently at Area A.

Another health problem common among older Middle Archaic people is one still with us today—arthritis. Virtually all individuals over the age of 35 suffered from the disease, which became worse with age. Arthritis affected different joints in men and women. Males tended to have more serious joint degeneration in the upper part of the vertebrae than females; the joints of females degenerated more quickly in the lower back. This pattern detected in women could be the result of pregnancy and childbirth. Certain strenuous activities, such as digging, also may have contributed to the problem. The higher degree of degeneration in the upper bodies of men may be from certain hunting activities or from carrying heavy objects. In several cases, vertebrae became fused, severely reducing movement.

Dental Problems

Archaeologists have devoted considerable time to the study of teeth in recent years, and much of what they have learned has to do with the eating habits of prehistoric people. The kinds of food that people eat and the ways they prepare it often have a direct impact on their dental health. For example, individuals who eat lots of starchy foods, such as corn, tend to have more dental caries (cavities) than people who consume less starch. People who prepare much of their food by grinding with stone tools have a much higher rate of tooth attrition (wear) than those who process food in other ways (Plate 3-33).

The Area A Middle Archaic people suffered from two kinds of painful abscessing, apical and alveolar. Apical abscessing is caused by pus collecting around the tip of the tooth root and is usually associated with decay in the interior part of the tooth. In extreme cases, the abscess burrows out of the root area and drains into the mouth. Alveolar abscesses are similar to apical, except that they form at the gum line and usually are caused by a piece of grit or fiber trapped between the tooth and gum. The trapped particle causes the gum to become infected (Plate 3-33).

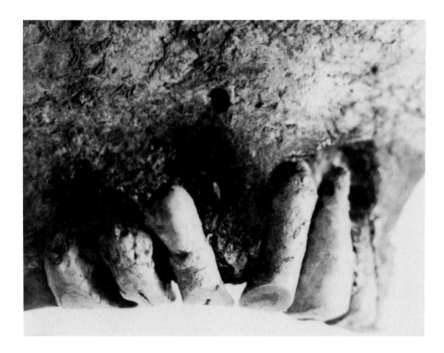

PLATE 3-33. Excessive tooth attrition (wear) and extensive alveolar abscessing.

Cavities were not a major problem for the Middle Archaic people, but unfortunately this was one of these "good news-bad news" situations. The good news was the scarcity of cavities; the bad news was that their absence was a result of the chewing surfaces being ground away (by eating gritty food) faster than the caries could form. Caries that did occur formed in the soft interior pulp of the tooth exposed by the tooth wear. Wear was so severe in some cases that the teeth were worn down to the root, below the gum line. The abscessing caused by excessive tooth wear undoubtedly kept many of the Middle Archaic people in pain much of the time.

No doubt most of the wear seen on adult teeth resulted from the inhabitants' use of friable, grainy sandstone to make many of their food processing implements. Small particles of stone or grit broke off the grinding slabs and grinding stones during processing and became mixed with the food. The tooth wear evident in very young children who had not yet been weaned before they died may have been caused by the high sand (grit) content of the Area A soil that probably covered most objects they touched. They probably placed grit-covered objects in their mouths during teething.

Trade and Exchange

Archaeologists occasionally find artifacts made of nonlocal raw materials (such as copper, mica, silver, or obsidian). One explanation for their presence on sites is that the people who lived there traded with groups living near the source of that material. Trading with other groups also presented an opportunity to exchange ideas and information relating to a variety of matters.

Archaeologists at Carrier Mills found little evidence for long-distance exchange of either raw materials or finished goods during the late Middle Archaic period. One of the few objects that may have been brought to the site from outside the southern Illinois region is the copper wedge found with a Middle Archaic burial (Plate 3-23). All of the copper used to make artifacts came from pure copper nuggets that could be shaped by heating and hammering. Although small amounts of copper may have come from deposits pushed south by the glaciers, the most likely source of the ore is the Lake Superior area. Many prehistoric copper pits or mines have been identified in that region (Griffin 1961). Also, copper wedges similar to the Carrier Mills specimen have been found at Late Archaic sites in Wisconsin (Ritzenthaler et al. 1957:308). A few late Middle Archaic copper artifacts have been reported from Helton phase sites in the lower Illinois valley (Cook 1976).

How did the copper wedge come to Carrier Mills? Was it brought by an outsider who traded it for something else, or was it brought by a local Carrier Mills resident who obtained it directly from the source while on a trip? Did the wedge arrive in its finished shape, or did the copper arrive as a nugget that was made into a wedge at a later time? These are questions archaeologists cannot yet answer.

Marine shells from the Gulf of Mexico and the Atlantic Ocean were major exchange items in parts of the Midwest and Southeast during the Late Archaic period (Webb 1974; Winters 1968). These shells were used to make many kinds of ornamental objects. However, most of the Middle Archaic shell artifacts found at Carrier Mills appear to be made from mussel shell collected from nearby rivers and lakes. One shell ornament found with an Area A burial may have been made from a conch shell collected from the Atlantic or Gulf coasts (Plate 3-18). If this identification is correct, it would serve as additional evidence for some type of long-distance Middle Archaic trading system.

A portion of the chert used to make Middle Archaic projectile points was obtained from chert deposits in southwest Illinois. Some of these cherts, particularly the kinds known as Cobden and Mill Creek, were widely traded during the later Woodland and Mississippian periods. Archaeologists thought, at first, that the presence of these cherts at Carrier Mills might indicate some type of Middle Archaic trade or exchange. But artifacts made from southwest Illinois cherts were used in the same manner as tools made from local cherts, suggesting that they were no more valuable or special to the Carrier Mills people than were artifacts made from locally available materials. Perhaps people from Carrier Mills picked up the southwest Illinois cherts while they were in the vicinity hunting or collecting.

The best evidence for Middle Archaic exchange, although not necessarily the exchange of material goods, is the presence of intricately carved bone pins (Plate 3-17). The similarity of the pin shapes and the engraved designs throughout much of eastern Missouri, southern Illinois, and southern Indiana suggests that late Middle Archaic people in the Midwest were communicating and exchanging information; they were not totally isolated or oblivious of each other's existence.

On the whole, though, archaeologists found few indications of long-distance trade of material goods at Carrier Mills during the Middle Archaic period. Those few examples that were recovered came from burials or other special contexts. This situation is not unusual. Artifacts indicating long-distance exchange are also rare at other Middle Archaic sites throughout the Midwest.

Summary

Archaeological investigations at Carrier Mills have provided a wealth of artifacts and other cultural materials that were made, used, or discarded by the Middle Archaic residents in daily life. Although some of these items are very interesting, their real significance is found not in themselves but in what they can tell us about the way people lived and behaved in the past. The many different kinds of information collected in the field or derived from the analysis of data in the laboratory represent the pieces of a puzzle that we must put together if we are to get the whole picture. We cannot understand one part of the archaeological record without understanding how it relates to all other parts.

The increased activity at Carrier Mills during the late Middle Archaic may be partially attributable to the long-term effects of the drier and possibly warmer Hypsithermal interval (see Chapter 2). The decreased moisture would have directly influenced the regional vegetation as well as the animals that fed on it. Upland forests receded and portions covered by grassland and prairie increased. The extent of bottomland forests also decreased, and many smaller wet areas were reduced in size or dried up. These changes in the climate reduced the variety and reliability of food in some areas. Large wet areas, like those at Carrier Mills, may have been reduced in size but still continued to exist. The environmental diversity of the Carrier Mills area ensured that food sources were more plentiful, predictable, and reliable than in many other areas and was largely responsible for the concentration of people in this area during the late Middle Archaic period.

The analyses of artifacts, features, burials, soils, and environmental data suggest that the Middle Archaic residents performed many different kinds of activities or tasks at Carrier Mills. For ease of discussion, we can divide these Middle Archaic activities into three groups: extractive, maintenance, and social.

Extractive activities include all those tasks that focused on obtaining food or other resources from the environment, such as hunting, fowling, fishing, and nut collecting. One of the most important extractive tasks performed by the Middle Archaic people was hunting. Hunting is indicated by a large number of flaked stone and antler projectile points, atlatl hooks and weights, and the bones of literally thousands of animals that were killed and brought to the site to be butchered, cooked, and eaten. Hunting represented a primary means of getting the food necessary for the group to survive, as well as providing skins for clothing and bones to make tools and ornaments.

Maintenance activities include all of those tasks that were required for the normal daily operation of the group. Many maintenance tasks involved processing the food that was obtained through various extractive activities or manufacturing the tools, clothing, and shelter needed to survive in the rugged environment. The most obvious Middle Archaic maintenance activity at Area A was the production, repair, and resharpening of flaked stone tools. Evidence of these activities occurred as unfinished projectile points (preforms and blanks), different kinds of waste flakes reflecting the various stages of tool production, hammerstones, and antler pressure flakers. Chert from many parts of southern Illinois were used to make these tools.

The final group of activities identified for the Middle Archaic occupation are social tasks, which include all those activities associated with the social life or organization of the group. Many of these activities consisted of ceremonies or rituals that required little durable equipment and that would have left little evidence of their performance.

One of the few obvious social activities performed at Area A was burial of the dead. Archaeologists uncovered more than 150 Middle Archaic burials during excavation of the site; projections of the total number of Middle Archaic individuals buried at Area A approach 500. Some of the burials found at Sa-88, located just to the south of Area A, also were attributable to the Middle Archaic occupation. Treatment of the dead indicates that no major distinction existed between the Middle Archaic residents of Carrier Mills, other than those based on the individual's age, sex, and personal abilities.

In view of what we know about the Middle Archaic people of Carrier Mills, we can characterize their general way of life (Figure 3-6). They lived in an environmentally rich area, adjacent to several distinctly unique environmental zones or habitats. Upland resources, such as deer, turkey, and many kinds of hickory nuts and acorns, formed the core of the Middle Archaic diet and could easily be reached from the site. The numerous and varied plants and animals living in and around the lake-swamp areas provided many additional foods to supplement those obtained elsewhere. Some kind of food was available through most of the year. Certainly, the availability and reliability of food in the Carrier Mills area was much greater than in many parts of southern Illinois at that time.

Although the site was occupied throughout much or all of the year, the size and composition of the group living at Area A must have varied. Permanent residents probably included the children, those individuals too old or too sick to participate in the full range of adult activities, and those people who took care of the first two groups. Most of the other group members were engaged in many activities that required their leaving the Carrier Mills area for a period of days or weeks. For example, groups of hunters and gatherers in the late summer and fall scattered over the landscape to hunt and collect the many kinds of foods that were available. During these trips, they may have collected other kinds of resources or raw materials, like chert used for toolmaking. Eventually, they brought back most of the items obtained on these trips to Carrier Mills for processing, storage, or consumption. Area A appears to have operated as a permanently occupied base camp. If someone was killed or died while away from Carrier Mills, his or her body was probably brought back and buried with the other members of his or her kin group. Because of the very favorable conditions found in the Carrier Mills area for groups following the hunter-gatherer way of life, Area A served as "home" for many generations of Middle Archaic people.

How many Indians lived at Carrier Mills during the Middle Archaic period? This question is very difficult to answer. However, we can get some idea by studying the soil at Area A. Soil scientists have found that the amount of certain chemicals in the soil is closely related to the number of people living at that location. Phosphorus is a particularly useful chemical for looking at the intensity of prehistoric occupations; once deposited in the soil, it dissipates very slowly. Most of the phosphorus in the Area A soil is from plant and animal residues deposited by the Middle Archaic people, such as wood ash, human urine, and plant and animal tissues.

By calculating the amount of phosphorus in the midden at Area A and knowing the length of time over which it was deposited, the project soil scientist, William Woods, determined that 24 pounds (11.1 kg) would have been annually deposited. The results of experiments indicate that about 273 pounds (124 kg) of phosphorus are annually deposited by a group of 100 individuals (Cook and Heizer 1965:8). Using this figure, a population of nine people living at Area A during the late Middle Archaic period could account for the phosphorus. Of course, Area A was not continuously occupied by nine people; sometimes it was inhabited by more people or perhaps by none at all. Also, more phosphorus was deposited at Area A than could be measured by the technique used in the analysis. Collectively, these factors suggest that the actual size of the Middle Archaic group averaged about 15 to

20 people. This is a year-round average, and for some portions of the year the size of the resident group may have been much larger.

Archaeologists estimate the death rate for similar hunter-gatherer groups to be about 3 percent of the group each year (Cook and Heizer 1965:8). Using this rate, a permanent population of 15 people would produce about 350 burials during this time, assuming all the deceased were buried at Area A. The 350 burials is not far from the 500 burials predicted by archaeologists based on the number of burials found in the excavated portion of the site. These population predictions provide a ballpark figure for estimating the average number of people living at Area A during the late Middle Archaic period.

§ 3000–1000 B.C.: The Late Archaic Period

Late Archaic inhabitants of southern Illinois lived in much the same way as their Middle Archaic ancestors. During this period, the number of prehistoric people living in the region increased, as indicated by a greater number of sites found by archaeologists. Although Late Archaic sites are more common than Middle Archaic ones, they are usually smaller, less intensively occupied, and more widely scattered over the landscape. These changes may be the result of shifts in the size of the territory used by Late Archaic people. Increased population may have reduced the territory size of individual groups, forcing an adjustment in settlement strategy. Groups would then have to make more extensive use of food resources in all parts of their territory rather than concentrating on a few rich areas. Environmental factors may also have played a major role in these changes.

The Late Archaic was significant for the beginning of horticulture in the region. People who grow a portion of the plant foods they consumed are called horticulturalists or gardeners. Unlike the hunter-gatherers, who relied on naturally available wild plants, the early gardeners grew domesticated plants in small garden plots. At first, food produced in gardens was not a very important part of the diet, but through the years gardening became an increasingly more significant food source. Successful gardeners produced a surplus of food that could be traded or stored for future use. On the other hand, preparing the fields and tending the crops required considerable effort, and crop failure could cause hardship. Eventually, by either choice or necessity, most midwestern prehistoric groups adopted gardening as part of their way of life. Archaeologists are very interested in finding out how, when, and why gardening was adopted in the prehistoric Midwest. People living in the Midwest started to experiment with plant cultivation during the Late Archaic period. Many of the plants grown by Late Archaic and Woodland gardeners were native to the local environment, although squash was probably introduced from Mesoamerica. Domesticated squash occurs at some Illinois Late Archaic sites (Asch and Asch 1982). Other local plants that may have been cultivated by Late Archaic gardeners include sunflowers, sumpweed, and maygrass.

In many parts of the region, Late Archaic sites located along major river systems include shell middens, very large piles of discarded mussel shell. The size of the shell middens indicates that these riverine food sources were collected and eaten in great quantities by some Late Archaic people.

Studies of some Late Archaic cemeteries indicate that there were greater social differences between individuals than during the Middle Archaic period. Burials of apparently high-status Late Archaic persons were often accompanied by exotic grave goods made from marine shell from the Atlantic or Gulf coasts and native copper from the Great Lakes area. Archaeologists have not found evidence of these burial customs in the immediate southern Illinois area, but large Late Archaic cemeteries occur along some western Kentucky rivers, especially the Green River.

Figure 3-6. This reconstruction of Middle Archaic life at the Black Earth site shows a number of food procurement activities. Indians in the background are fishing and collecting aquatic plants and animals from the shallow lake west of the site. Hunters in the foreground are returning to camp with a deer that they killed using their spears and atlatls.

Most of what we know about the Late Archaic hunters and gatherers of southern Illinois comes from the excavation of rockshelters or from surface collections. Very few sites having intact Late Archaic occupation zones have been identified and even fewer have been excavated. Recent work in the American Bottom, east of St. Louis, and in the lower Illinois River valley has greatly expanded our understanding of Late Archaic lifeways in those parts of Illinois.

Research in many parts of the Midwest suggests that substantial changes took place around the end of the Middle Archaic and the beginning of the Late Archaic in the way the people were distributed over the land. The Late Archaic occupation of Modoc Rock Shelter is very different from that during the late Middle Archaic. The Late Archaic occupation left behind fewer tools, debitage, postmolds, and burials and more animal bone and projectile points. Manufacturing and domestic tools virtually disappeared. During the Middle Archaic, Modoc was a general habitation site where many different activities were performed. In sharp contrast, the Late Archaic remains suggest that the site served only as a fall- or winter-occupied hunting camp (Fowler 1959; Styles et al. 1981).

Late Archaic projectile points at Modoc Rock Shelter include a variety of stemmed types commonly found on many Late Archaic sites in southern Illinois. A stemmed projectile point has an expanding-, contracting-, or straight-sided projection (stem) that extends from the base of the point. The stem is used to fasten the point to a shaft or handle (Figure 1-3).

Large-scale archaeological investigations associated with the construction of Interstate Highway 270 around East St. Louis have identified four Late Archaic phases in that area. The earliest of these is the Falling Springs phase (3500–2300 B.C.), followed by the Titterington (2300–1900 B.C.), Labras Lake (1900–1000 B.C.), and Prairie Lake (1000–600 B.C.) phases. Each of these phases is identified by distinctive kinds of notched or stemmed projectile points. Excavation has revealed groups of processing and cooking pits and possible structures representing a number of distinct Late Archaic communities. As in other parts of the Midwest, the size of the American Bottom population appears to have increased during this time. The Late Archaic residents of the bottom were very well adapted to the rich environment in which they lived, and their way of life focused on exploiting the abundant plant and animal life that lived in the creeks, lakes, swamps, and forests of the Mississippi River floodplain and adjacent areas. Occupations appear to have been relatively permanent, and diverse tool kits reflect the many different activities that were performed (McElrath et al. 1984).

The final Late Archaic phase pertaining to the Carrier Mills area is known as the Riverton culture, dating to between 2000 and 1000 B.C. The Riverton culture was identified in the central Wabash River valley of eastern Illinois based on the excavation by Howard D. Winters of three deep shell middens. The sites are distributed along the west edge of the Wabash River, with 10-mile intervals separating adjacent sites. Winters has proposed that the Riverton people occupied several different kinds of sites during the year, reflecting seasonal differences in the activities they conducted. Riverton sites are identified by the presence of small side-notched and stemmed projectile points known as Merom and Trimble points (Winters 1969).

Life at Carrier Mills during the Late Archaic

Fewer people apparently lived at Carrier Mills during the Late Archaic than during the Middle Archaic, and, as a consequence, fewer artifacts remained for archaeologists to find. Also, the Late Archaic inhabitants did not add substantially to the midden. Most Late Archaic artifacts were found in the upper soil layers disturbed by plowing. These artifacts were often mixed with the remains of later prehistoric occupations. The only Late Archaic artifacts that archaeologists could identify with certainty were diagnostic projectile points and a few other miscellaneous items. Unfortunately for the archaeologists, several of these point types were made well into the Woodland period.

The Carrier Mills Late Archaic projectile points are called Saratoga, Adena-Cypress, and Karnak points (Plates 3-34 through 3-36). Points similar to these have been found in Late Archaic sites throughout much of the eastern United States. The Late Archaic points look quite different from Middle Archaic ones. The later points have long stems rather than side notches.

Archaeologists found evidence of Late Archaic occupation at all seven activity areas at Carrier Mills (Figure 2-2). Yet the low number of Late Archaic projectile points per cubic meter of excavated midden led them to believe that some major changes took place during the Late Archaic period. Not only were there fewer people living at Carrier Mills during the Late Archaic, but they also tended to concentrate in different areas than their Middle Archaic ancestors. The most intensive Middle Archaic occupations occurred at Area A of Sa-87 and Sa-88, near the large lake and swamp region at the western end of the Carrier Mills Archaeological District. In contrast, many Late Archaic people chose to live away from the lake edge and more evenly distributed over the District. They apparently did not prefer one part of the District over another.

Archaeological survey of the area surrounding the Carrier Mills District did not reveal any large, intensively occupied Late Archaic sites that compared with the intensive Middle Archaic occupations at Area A or Sa-88. In general, Late Archaic sites in this part of the Saline River valley are characterized by a few artifacts and little or no midden accumulation. Most Late Archaic sites in this part of southern Illinois do not have the long-term, intensive, multiseasonal occupations found at some Middle Archaic sites.

PLATE 3-34. Late Archaic–Early Woodland Saratoga projectile points. Row 1, Saratoga Straight Stemmed; Row 2, Saratoga Broad Bladed; Row 3, Saratoga Expanding Stem.

PLATE 3-35. Late Archaic–Early Woodland Adena-Cypress projectile points. Row 1, Adena; Row 2, Cypress Constricting Stem; Row 3, Cypress Straight Stemmed.

PLATE 3-36. Late Archaic–Early Woodland Karnak projectile points. Row 1, Shouldered Karnak; Row 2, Karnak; Row 3, Karnak Stemmed.

The Changing Environment

The changes in the living patterns at Carrier Mills during the Late Archaic coincide with the end of the Hypsithermal and a return to cooler, wetter weather. As a result of these climatic changes, the areal coverage of upland and bottomland forests gradually increased and the area covered by grasslands and prairies decreased. Greater forest coverage in the uplands effectively increased the quantity and variety of animals that could be supported by the vegetation in a given area, as well as raised the potential for edible plant foods.

The decrease in the intensity of activity at Carrier Mills in general, and Area A in particular, may be tied to these environmental changes. The expansion of upland forests increased the availability and reliability of food in the uplands, producing a more uniform distribution of food sources throughout the region. The decreased activity at Carrier Mills may reflect a more general distribution of Late Archaic people over the landscape, reflecting the more general distribution of food. In other words, Late Archaic people were spending less time at Carrier Mills and more time hunting and gathering food in other parts of the region.

Environmental conditions in the Carrier Mills area probably did not change much following the Late Archaic period. Although minor climatic fluctuation occurred between then and now, these slight variations in temperature and precipitation did not have any long-term effects on people, animals, or vegetation. The types of plants and animals and their distribution during the Late Archaic period were probably similar to those observed by the first pioneers who came to the Saline valley 5,000 years later.

The People and Their Possessions

It is difficult to say much about the Late Archaic way of life at Carrier Mills because of the absence of undisturbed Late Archaic midden deposits or features. Nondiagnostic Late Archaic artifacts, such as many types of flaked stone and groundstone tools, chert debitage, and bone artifacts, were mixed with the debris from other periods.

Projectile points are one kind of Late Archaic artifact that can be recognized, but even these are something of a problem since some types of points made during the Late Archaic period continued to be made in the subsequent Woodland period. Saratoga points were the most common Late Archaic artifact found at Carrier Mills. These hafted bifaces have triangular-shaped bodies and either straight or expanding stems (Plate 3-34). The significance of the different stem shapes is not known. The straight-stemmed variety was the most common at Carrier Mills. The Adena-Cypress group contains a variety of straight- and constricting-stem points, including the Adena, Cypress Constricting Stem, and Cypress Straight Stemmed point types (Plate 3-35). Distinctions among the three types are based on size and precision of manufacture. Adena points are the largest and appear to have been the most carefully made of the three. They were also the least common. The two Cypress types are generally smaller, less carefully made, and much more common at Carrier Mills than the Adena points. Cypress projectile points appear to have been manufactured from the Late Archaic to well into the Woodland period. Other types of Carrier Mills Late Archaic projectile points include Karnak and Karnak Stemmed (Plate 3-36). Karnak Shouldered points are similar but were more often found with the late Middle Archaic occupation. Examples of Merom and Trimble projectile points, similar to those found at Riverton culture Late Archaic sites along the central Wabash River, were also found, but they were not common at Carrier Mills. Merom and Trimble points date to the terminal part of the Late Archaic period.

A few Late Archaic end scrapers and drills were identified because they were made from recycled broken Late Archaic projectile points (Plate 3-5). Fewer broken projectile points were recycled into these hafted tools than during the Middle Archaic period. The low number of Late Archaic hafted end-scapers may simply indicate a preference for using unhafted tools, or it may reflect a change in the types of material that were being scraped. Unfortunately, no edge-wear studies have been performed on the Late Archaic scrapers, so we cannot compare the kinds of materials that were processed.

Chert used to make the Late Archaic flaked stone tools came from at least 10 areas. These include cherts from a number of areas in the eastern Shawnee Hills, located relatively close to Carrier Mills, as well as material from the Cobden, Kaolin, and Mill Creek sources in the western Shawnee Hills and the Burlington source area in eastern Missouri and west-central Illinois (Figure 3-1). The relative proportion of tools made from chert from these sources is similar to that for the Middle Archaic period.

Food Habits

Archaeologists did not find unmixed midden and feature deposits dating to this period, so we can only generalize about the eating habits of the Late Archaic Carrier Mills people. Their diet was probably similar to that of the late Middle Archaic residents, but they may have preferred certain kinds of starchy weed seeds more than their predecessors. Hickory nuts and acorns continued to be very important, as did deer, turkey, and most of the other animals hunted by Middle Archaic people.

We can get a general idea of Late Archaic food habits by looking at the findings of other research projects in nearby parts of southern Illinois. Late Archaic people living in the American Bottom collected plant foods and hunted animals living in a wide variety of habitats. They gathered many kinds of nuts, such as pecans, hazelnuts, walnuts, acorns, and chestnuts, but seemed to prefer hickory nuts. Carbonized plant remains from Late Archaic features indicate that various berries, seeds, fruits, and legumes were also popular (Johannessen 1984). They also consumed many kinds of mammals, birds, and fish which they took from the wide range of natural habitats found in the American Bottom and surrounding areas (Kelly and Cross 1984). Scientists have not found any signs of plant cultivation at any of the American Bottom Late Archaic sites (Johannessen 1984).

Summary

The Late Archaic period at Carrier Mills witnessed a reduction in activity compared to the Middle Archaic. Changes in the ways the Late Archaic residents used the area are reflected by a much lower rate of midden buildup and a reduction in the number of artifacts attributable to their occupation. No undisturbed Late Archaic occupation zone was found at any of the Carrier Mills sites, making it difficult to study most aspects of their way of life. These changes may have several possible explanations. First, fewer people may have lived at Carrier Mills during the Late Archaic than during the Middle Archaic period. The people who did live there may have been doing the same basic tasks as their Middle Archaic ancestors, but at a much reduced rate. Second, the kinds of activities performed at Carrier Mills during the Late Archaic may have been significantly different from those of the Middle Archaic period. Third, the sites may have been occupied only on a seasonal basis during the Late Archaic period, with other seasons being spent at other sites in the region.

It seems likely that any one, or a combination, of these factors could be responsible for the changes in the Carrier Mills archaeological record. What seems certain is that Late Archaic life at Carrier Mills was different from that of the late Middle Archaic period.

The
Woodland People:
1000 B.C.–
A.D. 1000

In many parts of the Midwest and Southeast, the appearance of thick, crudely made clay pots marks the beginning of the Early Woodland period. The earliest dated occurrence of pottery in southern Illinois comes from the Landreth No. 1 site, located in the Cedar Creek area of Jackson County, Illinois (Figure 4-1). The radiocarbon date of 540 ± 60 B.C. obtained from this site suggests that pottery was not present in southern Illinois until well into the Early Woodland period, and even then it may not have been very common (McNerney 1975). The spread of pot-making technology and its adoption by the Early Woodland people was a very gradual process. In many ways, the Early Woodland way of life in much of southern Illinois represents a continuation of that of the Late Archaic, with the very gradual addition of ceramics.

Very few Early Woodland sites have been identified in southern Illinois. The difficulty in identifying these sites stems from three problems. First, since the projectile points made by Early Woodland chert knappers are virtually identical to Late Archaic ones, they cannot be used to distinguish occupations dating to these periods (Plates 3-34 through 3-36). Second, pottery made by the Early Woodland people, locally known by archaeologists as Crab Orchard ceramics, continued to be made throughout the subsequent Middle Woodland period (200 B.C.–A.D. 400). The way in which Crab Orchard vessels were made and decorated changed very little during the roughly 1,000 years they were produced, making it difficult to distinguish the pottery manufactured during the two periods. Third, many of the sites occupied by Early Woodland peoples were also inhabited by later Woodland groups. The Early Woodland vessels made, used, broken, and discarded at these sites were few in number, and their fragments would have been widely scattered. Most of the indications of the Early Woodland occupations would have been obscured by the more intensive Middle or Late Woodland activity.

In some parts of the Midwest, the harvesting and/or cultivation of certain native seed-producing plants became increasingly more common, but no evidence of this has been found at Carrier Mills. The widespread use of pottery also coincides with the appearance of large, cylindrical storage pits. Although the relationship between pots and pits is not clear, it may reflect changes in the kinds of plant foods that were being harvested or the way they were being prepared and stored (Butler and Jefferies 1986).

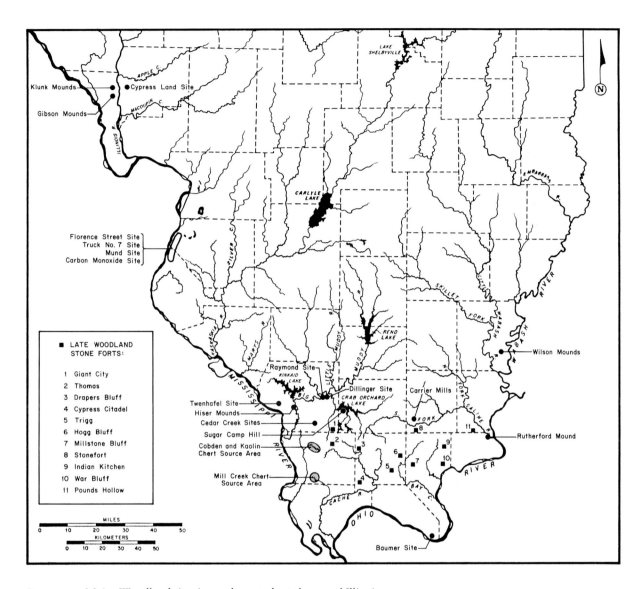

Figure 4-1. Major Woodland sites in southern and south-central Illinois.

Relatively little is known about Early Woodland life in much of southern Illinois, but recent archaeological investigations in the American Bottom have produced new information about Early Woodland life in that area. As mentioned in Chapter 3, some Late Archaic occupations in the American Bottom appear to have been relatively permanent and contained a wide variety of tools that were used to perform many different tasks. In contrast, Early Woodland occupations consisted of small encampments containing a limited variety of artifacts and were located along marsh and lake edges and creek banks and near river channels. Archaeological remains suggest that more specialized activities took place at these sites than at most Late Archaic sites. Flaked stone artifacts found at Early Woodland sites include a variety of straight- and contracting-stemmed projectile points (Fortier et al. 1984).

Several Early Woodland phases have been identified in the American Bottom. The earliest of these is the Marion phase, which dates from about 600 to 300 B.C. Marion phase sites are identified by the presence of Marion Thick pottery and straight-stemmed Kramer projectile points. Typical Marion Thick pots have flat bottoms (bases) and thick walls (sides); pieces of crushed granite or igneous rock were added to the clay paste to give the pot additional strength and durability (Fortier et al. 1984). Material that is added to the clay by the potter is referred to as temper. The inside and outside of the vessel wall were marked by cord impressions produced by striking the wall with a cord-wrapped paddle while the clay was still soft. The potter used the paddle to "weld" the coils of clay that formed the vessel wall by beating the exterior of the pot with the paddle. The potter's other hand was held against the inside of the wall to serve as an anvil. The pot was then fired, heated to a high temperature to bake the clay.

The Early Woodland Florence phase, dating between 500 and 300 B.C., has also been identified in the American Bottom. Archaeological investigations at the Florence Street site (Figure 4-1), where the phase was first identified, revealed many Early Woodland pits and an oval structure measuring 20 feet by 23 feet (6 m by 7 m). A hearth or fireplace was found near the center of the structure. The small diameter of the posts used to build this structure suggests that it may have resembled a wigwam. Most of the flaked stone artifacts were contracting-stemmed projectile points and knives (Fortier et al. 1984:66–76).

Florence phase pottery differs from Marion Thick ceramics. The former had a variety of surface decorations placed over the cordmarking. The outside of some pots had been pinched with the fingernails while the clay was still soft, creating a series of impressions on the upper part of the vessel. Other times, the soft clay was decorated using a stick or bone to make impressions or punctations. The clay used to make Florence phase pots was tempered with small pieces of baked or fired clay called grog.

Most of the bone recovered from the Florence Street site came from white-tailed deer, with lesser amounts from other mammals. Fish, turtle, and bird bone was also identified, with all identifiable bird bone being wild turkey. These kinds of animal remains suggest that the site was occupied during the late fall and winter (Kelly and Cross 1984:223).

Life at Carrier Mills during the Early Woodland Period

Although the Carrier Mills area was used by prehistoric people during the Early Woodland period, it is very difficult to find much evidence of their presence. Early Woodland life at Carrier Mills was probably similar to that observed in the American Bottom. Those differences that did exist were largely attributable to the different environments inhabited by these Early Woodland groups.

The best evidence for Early Woodland occupation of Carrier Mills comes from recent studies of Crab Orchard pottery recovered from the three sites. These studies have focused on examining the way in which Woodland pottery was made (technology) and decorated (style) to see if any consistent changes occurred through time. In many parts of the eastern United States, the ways in which pots were decorated changed through time at a relatively rapid rate. When specific decorations are linked to a certain time period using radiocarbon dating or some other dating technique, pottery having these decorations can be used to date the feature in which it was found. Unfortunately for the Carrier Mills archaeologists, the ways in which Crab Orchard pottery was decorated changed very slowly, too slowly to be used for this purpose.

Analysis of Woodland pottery from the lower Illinois River valley and Carrier Mills has shown that the way in which pots were made might serve the same purpose that stylistic characteristics have in other parts of the world. These studies revealed that during the

Woodland period, the walls or sides of the pots were made thinner, the size of the particles used to temper the clay became smaller, and different materials were used as temper. The shapes of the pots also changed, becoming more rounded, or globular, with time (Braun 1983; Hargrave 1981). These changes in the way pots were made, or what archaeologists call the ceramic technology, seem to be attempts on the part of Woodland potters to make their pots more efficient for cooking.

Changes in the technology may reflect changes in the kinds of food that were being cooked (Braun 1983). Much of the plant foods eaten during the earlier part of the Woodland period consisted of nuts and oily seeds that could be best prepared by simmering or stewing at low temperatures. The thick-walled pots made at that time were satisfactory for this type of cooking since they could be gradually heated and did not have to withstand very high temperatures. During the later part of the Woodland period, starchy seeds, such as goosefoot, maygrass, and knotweed, gradually became more important parts of the diet. In order to properly and efficiently cook these small, hard seeds, they must be brought to a rapid boil and cooked at a high temperature. The use of thick-walled vessels for this kind of cooking would result in cracking or breaking because of the unequal heating of different parts of the pot. To help overcome the problems associated with high-temperature cooking, Woodland potters began to make the sides of the pots thinner so that they would heat more evenly, reducing the possibility of damage. The smaller size of the temper particles and the change of the shape of cooking pots also served to reduce heat damage.

Of course, these changes occurred at a relatively slow rate over a long period of time. Archaeologists have measured the rate of technological change by using radiocarbon dating to assign pottery having a certain wall thickness to a specific time. Although the use of technological characteristics of pottery for dating purposes is still in an experimental stage, it may help to solve many of the dating problems that have plagued Illinois archaeology.

Archaeologists analyzed Crab Orchard pottery collected from pits at the Carrier Mills sites using the technological approach just discussed. They defined a trend of technological change utilizing pottery from pits that could be radiocarbon dated, then they projected the ages of the remaining pits by basing them on the technological characteristics of the pottery they contained. Although most of the Crab Orchard pottery at Carrier Mills appeared to be Middle Woodland, some very early Crab Orchard pottery was present. Crab Orchard pottery from several pits probably dates between 600 and 400 B.C. The vessel illustrated in Plate 4-1 is typical of early Crab Orchard vessels found in southern Illinois and was reconstructed from fragments found in a large pit feature at Area A. The vessel is a jar measuring 18.5 inches (47 cm) in height. The base or bottom of the jar is only 3 inches (8 cm) in diameter, so it is unlikely that it stood upright without some kind of external support. Some of these large, unstable vessels may have been kept in pits and used for food storage. The opening at the top of the jar is roughly 10 inches (25 cm) in diameter. The exterior is fabric impressed, a term that refers to the impressions made when the wall of the unfired vessel was struck with the edge of a cord-wrapped paddle, or more rarely, with an actual piece of fabric, during manufacture. The clay is tempered with fairly large pieces of crushed rock or grit. Fragments of vessels shown in Plate 4-2 (Row 1) have predicted dates of 620 B.C. and 440 B.C., respectively. Both of these early specimens were found in Area A Type 1 pits (Plate 4-3). Some of the Early Woodland Crab Orchard pottery had cord-marked exteriors, but fabric-impressed pottery was more common. None of the early Crab Orchard pottery from Carrier Mills had any kind of decoration other than the basic fabric-impressed or cordmarked surface treatment.

PLATE 4-1. Early Crab Orchard jar from Area A.

PLATE 4-2. Large rim sections of probable Early Woodland Crab Orchard pots.

PLATE 4-3. A large Area A Type 1 pit containing pieces of a Crab Orchard pot.

In most aspects, the life of the Carrier Mills Early Woodland people was probably quite similar to that of the Late Archaic period. Their diet consisted of a combination of plant and animal foods that were hunted and collected in the forests, grasslands, lakes, swamps, and streams of the Saline valley. Hickory nuts and acorns were probably very important plant foods, and white-tailed deer and wild turkey were the main sources of animal protein and fat. They also consumed fish, waterfowl, mammals, and reptiles that inhabited the lake-swamp area west of the Carrier Mills Archaeological District.

The Early Woodland inhabitants probably used a wide variety of flaked stone, groundstone, and bone tools to perform many different activities, but archaeologists are currently unable to distinguish most of these from those of earlier and later inhabitants. Nothing is known about the kinds of houses in which they lived, but they may have been similar to Early Woodland structures identified in the American Bottom.

They were probably a relatively mobile society, moving over the land to take advantage of the food sources that became available during the different seasons of the year. In some parts of the East and Midwest, Early Woodland peoples practiced complex mortuary customs involving exotic artifacts and burial mounds, which provided clues to their level of social organization. This burial ceremonialism is particularly well known in the Kentucky–Ohio–West Virginia area, where it has been given the name Adena. No burial practices of this nature are known for southern Illinois.

§ 200 B.C.–A.D. 400:
The Middle
Woodland Period

The Middle Woodland period in the Midwest was a time of major technological, social, and economic change. The period is marked by an increase in population, a decrease in the movement of groups over the landscape, greater differences in the social position or status of individuals, long-distance trade, and increased experimentation with growing plants.

Most Middle Woodland sites in southern Illinois contain Crab Orchard pottery.

These sites are generally small and reflect relatively short-term occupations. More permanent, longer-term occupations have been found, but they are confined to sites located along the floodplains of the major river valleys. Middle Woodland Crab Orchard sites are restricted to the part of southern Illinois dominated by deciduous forests; they do not usually occur in the prairie-dominated areas to the north.

Projectile points made by the Middle Woodland people of southern Illinois include the Snyders and Affinis Snyders corner-notched and the Lowe Flared-Base point types (Figure 1-3). The Snyders corner-notched and a local variant known as the Affinis Snyders corner-notched type are thought to have been manufactured during the early and middle parts of the period. The smaller Lowe Flared-Base point was produced toward the end of the period; archaeologists have linked the appearance of these smaller projectile points to the introduction of the bow and arrow into the region at about that time.

Crab Orchard pottery continued to be made throughout this period. Pots made during the early part of the period had either cordmarked or fabric-impressed exteriors. Those manufactured during the late Middle Woodland were almost exclusively cordmarked. Some Crab Orchard vessels were decorated using a variety of techniques, but they were still rather plain compared to pots made by people living in other parts of the eastern United States at this time.

The Middle Woodland diet does not seem to have differed significantly from that of earlier times. The most important foods came from naturally occurring plants and animals, although Middle Woodland people experimented with horticulture or gardening using both local and nonlocal plants. Hickory nuts and acorns were probably the most important plant foods, but a wide assortment of weed seeds, fruits, and roots also formed a significant part of the diet. The most important meat sources were the white-tailed deer and the wild turkey.

One of the most intensively studied aspects of Middle Woodland culture is the extensive trade network commonly referred to as the Hopewell Interaction Sphere (Brose and Greber 1979; Caldwell 1964). Although the way in which the exchange network operated is still unclear, it distributed a wide variety of raw materials and finished goods over a large part of the eastern United States. Material exchanged included an assortment of items made of copper, marine shell, mica, obsidian, and other nonlocal raw materials. Many of the objects made from these materials are often found with burials. Elaborate burial goods were reserved for relatively few individuals. This practice emphasized their high social position in the society and reflected the increasingly more complex way in which many prehistoric midwestern groups were organized. Most of these individuals were buried in specially prepared tombs in earthen burial mounds.

Hopewell artifacts have been found at several southern Illinois sites, but they are more the exception than the rule. Middle Woodland burial mounds are rare in southern Illinois. The closest to the Carrier Mills Archaeological District is the Rutherford Mound (Fowler 1957) located on a hilltop near the junction of the Saline and Ohio rivers (Figure 4-1). Many different kinds of Hopewell artifacts were associated with the burials in these mounds. The Wilson Mounds (Figure 4-1) and Hubele Village (Neumann and Fowler 1952), located on the lower Wabash River, contain mound burials and Hopewell artifacts with Crab Orchard pottery.

The Twenhafel site, located in the floodplain of the Mississippi River in extreme southwestern Illinois (Hofman 1980), is the largest and most complex Middle Woodland Crab Orchard site in the region (Figure 4-1). Over the years excavations have yielded typical Hopewell artifacts, such as clay figurines, mica, galena (lead) cubes, and objects made from marine shell and copper.

Once again, in order to put life at Carrier Mills during the Middle Woodland into proper perspective, we need to see what was occurring in other parts of Illinois. The most intensive studies of Middle Woodland lifeways have taken place in the lower Illinois River valley. Since the late 1950s, archaeologists Stuart Struever and James Brown and their associates at the Center of American Archeology have made a monumental effort to learn how the Middle Woodland inhabitants used the abundant resources found in the Illinois valley. Middle Woodland sites in this part of Illinois are recognized by the presence of Havana Series pottery and Snyders projectile points. Havana Series pottery is composed of a number of distinctive types based on the kind of decoration on the outside of the vessel. The most common types are called Havana Cordmarked and Havana Plain. The outside surfaces of Havana Cordmarked pots are covered with cord impressions from top to bottom and those of Havana Plain vessels are smooth. Other types of Havana pottery were decorated using incised or stamped lines that occur in bands or zones on the upper part of the pot (Griffin 1952:101–114). Havana pots were generally large, open-mouthed jars that were used for both cooking and food storage (Cantwell 1980:98).

Another kind of pottery found on some Middle Woodland sites is called Hopewell Ware. These small, finely made jars were probably used for ceremonial rather than utilitarian purposes and many have been found with burials. Clay used to make the jars was tempered with crushed limestone. The outside of the jars was highly polished and decorated by areas of incised lines or stamping that were often arranged to form a design (Griffin 1952:114–115).

Another artifact that is often found on Middle Woodland sites is called a prismatic blade. Prismatic blades (or simply blades) are a special kind of flake removed from a specially prepared core, often called a blade core. Blades are parallel-sided flakes that are at least twice as long as they are wide. Blade production more efficiently uses the raw material, in this case chert, by controlling the size and shape of the flake (blade) being removed.

Numerous Middle Woodland burial mounds are situated along the valley margins or on top of the bluffs that flank the Illinois River (Figure 4-1). These mounds contained the remains of individuals who occupied important positions in Middle Woodland society. Most mounds contained central submound tombs, and many burials were accompanied by a variety of exotic artifacts made of copper, mica, or other nonlocal materials.

Although hickory nuts remained an important plant food throughout the Middle Woodland period in the Illinois valley, many kinds of starchy weed seeds, such as goosefoot, maygrass, and knotweed, played an increasingly more significant role in the diet. Some of these plants were probably cultivated by Middle Woodland gardeners (Asch et al. 1979:83–84).

The Middle Woodland occupation in the American Bottom appears to share much in common with that of the preceding Early Woodland period. Middle Woodland settlements consisted of small, seasonally occupied sites located near river and creek channels in the floodplain (Figure 4-1). Features uncovered at these sites are widely scattered, perhaps indicating the presence of only a few family groups. The diet of these people primarily consisted of seasonally available plants and animals that lived in the wet areas of the bottom and in the adjacent uplands. Nuts were an important food source throughout the period (Fortier et al. 1984:80–103). By the end of the Middle Woodland, cultivated plants, largely represented by maygrass, knotweed, and goosefoot, were becoming an important part of the diet (Johannessen 1984:201–202).

Artifacts commonly found at Middle Woodland sites in this part of Illinois also include broad-bladed, corner-notched projectile points (Snyders-like), zoned or stamped pottery, and prismatic blades. Much of the American Bottom Middle Woodland pottery is similar to Havana pottery from the Illinois River valley (Fortier et al. 1984).

Life at Carrier Mills during the Middle Woodland Period

Unlike the preceding Early Woodland occupation, abundant evidence exists for a major Middle Woodland occupation at Carrier Mills. Most of the evidence occurs in the form of Crab Orchard pottery and corner-notched projectile points. Unfortunately, no undisturbed Middle Woodland occupation zone was preserved. Much of the material left behind by the Middle Woodland inhabitants was recovered from soil that had been disturbed by plowing. Most of what we know about their way of life is based on the study of material collected from the fill of large storage pits uncovered at several sites.

Archaeologists obtained three radiocarbon dates for the Carrier Mills Middle Woodland occupation. The earliest date of 230 B.C. ± 55 came from a circular, flat-bottomed storage pit at Sa-88. Pottery in the pit fill included fragments of both cordmarked and fabric-impressed Crab Orchard vessels. A date of A.D. 15 ± 60 was obtained from a kind of feature known as an earth oven that probably served as a Middle Woodland cooking facility. A final Middle Woodland date of A.D. 150 ± 105 came from a large Type 1 feature at Sa-86. More than 100 pieces of Crab Orchard pottery, including the bottoms of three jars (Plate 4-4), were found in the pit. Although the radiocarbon dates provide a range of 230 B.C. ± 55 to A.D. 150 ± 105 for the Middle Woodland occupation, the technological and decorative characteristics of the pottery indicate that people lived at Carrier Mills throughout the Middle Woodland period (200 B.C.–A.D. 400).

Middle Woodland artifacts were found at all of the activity areas in the District, but the kinds of activities conducted and the intensity of Middle Woodland occupation varied considerably. Michael Hargrave's analysis of Crab Orchard pottery found in Middle Woodland pits provides a means for studying the history of the Middle Woodland occupation. As we have seen, it is sometimes possible to determine the age of pottery found in a pit and approximate when the pit was used. As expected, few Woodland pits at Carrier Mills date prior to 350 B.C., the time at which pottery was just being introduced to the area. Numerous features were dated to the period between 350 B.C. and A.D. 1, indicating a time of intensive Middle Woodland activity. Hargrave noted a sharp decrease in the number of features dated to between A.D. 1 and A.D. 300, which is probably a result of fewer people living in the area. The remainder of the period is marked by a gradual increase in occupation.

Why did the population decrease between A.D. 1 and A.D. 300? In other parts of Illinois, particularly in the Illinois valley, the number of people living in the major river and tributary floodplains increased (Asch et al. 1979). Major Middle Woodland occupations in the Wabash, lower Saline, and Ohio River valleys dating to this time have been discovered. These include the Rutherford Mound site (Fowler 1957), the Hubele and Wilson Mounds sites (Neumann and Fowler 1952) (Figure 4-1), and the Mann site (Kellar 1979), located in southern Indiana. These large sites may have developed as Middle Woodland people moved out of interior drainages, like the Saline River, and into the larger floodplains. People living at these large sites were involved in long-distance exchange associated with the Hopewell Interaction Sphere. Even though a decrease in occupation at Carrier Mills may have taken place during the late Middle Woodland, the area continued to be occupied to some extent throughout the period. At Carrier Mills, some pottery dating to between A.D. 1 and A.D. 450 has Havana and Hopewell decorations, perhaps reflecting the ties of the Carrier Mills Middle Woodland people to those living in the larger floodplain sites.

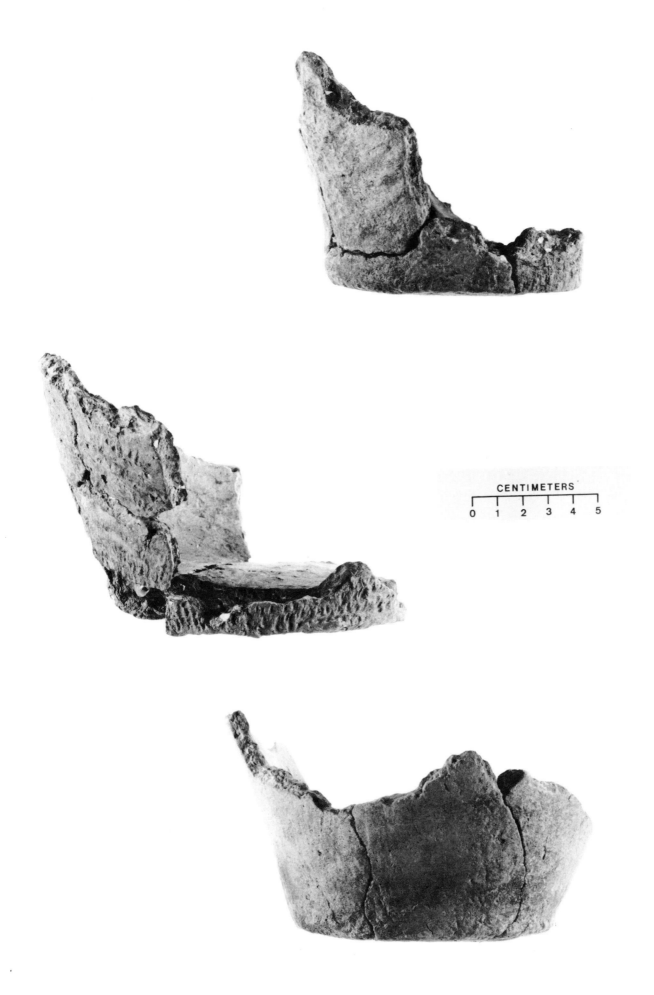

CENTIMETERS
0 1 2 3 4 5

PLATE 4-4. Crab Orchard vessel bases from Area 1.

Area A of Sa-87 and Area 1 of Sa-86 were the most intensively occupied portions of the District during the Middle Woodland period. An intermediate level of activity characterized Sa-88, while the remaining four activity areas contain relatively small amounts of Middle Woodland pottery and few features. The latter four areas appear to have been occupied on a very intermittent basis by small groups of people. Even though Area A and Area 1 appear to have experienced the most intensive Middle Woodland activity, the character of the two occupations differs to some extent. The density of Crab Orchard pottery per cubic meter of excavated midden is quite high at both sites, but a considerable difference is evident in the quantity and kinds of pit features.

The Area A Middle Woodland occupation covers approximately 3,650 square yards (3,000 m²). It overlays the late Middle Archaic occupation, and many of the Middle Woodland features intrude into the older zone (Plate 3-4). The soil in which the Middle Woodland artifacts were found appears to be the disturbed upper portion of the Middle Archaic midden zone. Middle Archaic artifacts were commonly found in the Middle Woodland pits, suggesting that some of the pit fill also may be recycled Middle Archaic midden.

Fieldworkers excavated about one-third of the central part of Area A during 1978 and 1979. They identified approximately 100 Middle Woodland pits within this area. If the frequency of pits was as high in the unexcavated part of the site as in the excavated portion, as many as 300 features might have been present. Additional features located outside the central area would have increased this total. Approximately 85 percent of the Area A Middle Woodland features were deep, cylindrical pits. The remaining were shallow, basin-shaped pits that have been referred to as Type 2 features. Type 1 features were probably used for underground food storage, and the predominance of them at Area A suggests that the inhabitants conducted many food processing and storage activities there.

The Middle Woodland occupation at Area 1 covered approximately 3,400 square yards (2,800 m²) along the ridge that ran through the center of the site. Fieldwork produced a relatively large amount of Crab Orchard pottery but only 30 Middle Woodland features. The small number of features is particularly surprising since the plowzone was removed from 100 percent of the site, permitting the identification of virtually all features. Area 1 Middle Woodland features were scattered throughout the site.

Shallow, basin-shaped Type 2 features were the most common, accounting for roughly 80 percent of all the Area 1 Middle Woodland pits. Type 1 features were rare, representing only 10 percent of the total. The remaining features consisted of pits containing evidence of burning; they may have served as roasting pits or earth ovens. The difference in the kinds of features used by the Middle Woodland people who lived at Area A and Area 1 probably reflect different kinds of activities that were carried out at the two sites.

Decorations on the Area A Crab Orchard pottery indicate that most of the activity in this part of the District took place during the early and middle portions of the Middle Woodland period. Little pottery made during the late Middle Woodland was found. In contrast, Area 1 and Sa-88 appear to have been occupied throughout the period. Area B of Sa-87 and Area 2 of Sa-86 were most intensively occupied during the late Middle Woodland.

The People and Their Possessions

Flaked Stone Tools. Middle Woodland utilitarian artifacts found at Carrier Mills largely consist of diagnostic flaked stone tools and pieces of Crab Orchard pots. Projectile points and tools made from broken and recycled projectile points represent the only parts of the Middle Woodland tool kit that are easily distinguished from implements associated with other occupations.

Projectile points made by the earliest Middle Woodland inhabitants of Carrier Mills were probably very similar to the straight- and contracting-stemmed forms that were common during the Late Archaic and Early Woodland times. The Cypress Constricting Stemmed points have been found with Middle Woodland Crab Orchard pottery at several Illinois archaeological sites. Sometime during the early portion of the Middle Woodland occupation, these points began to be replaced by the corner-notched points referred to as Snyders and Affinis Snyders points (Figure 1-3). Snyders projectile points are commonly associated with Havana phase sites in central Illinois, and while they did occur at Carrier Mills, the Affinis Snyders variety is much more common. The Affinis Snyders points appear to have been made from about 400 or 300 B.C. until around A.D. 400.

Snyders points are relatively large and may have been used as knives (Plate 4-5, Row 1, No. 1). The body of the point is triangular and quite broad, with some examples being almost oval in outline. Large, deep notches are present near the base, and barbs are created at the junction of the notch and the lateral edge or side of the point. These points are quite thin and exhibit a high degree of craftsmanship in their manufacture.

Affinis Snyders points (Plate 4-5, Row 2) are generally smaller than the Snyders, and the body is more triangular in outline, lacking the oval appearance common among Snyders points. Several examples of end scrapers and drills made from broken Affinis Snyders projectile points indicate that the Middle Woodland people recycled broken tools to fabricate new ones, but the incidence of Middle Woodland recycling was not nearly as common as during the Middle Archaic period (Plate 3-5, Row 5, No. 5).

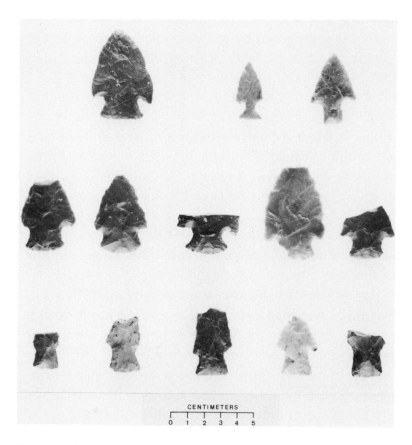

CENTIMETERS
0 1 2 3 4 5

PLATE 4-5. Woodland projectile points. Row 1, Number 1, Snyders; Numbers 2 and 3, Motley; Row 2, Affinis Snyders; Row 3, Lowe Flared Base.

Lowe Flared Base projectile points (Figure 1-3; Plate 4-5, Row 3) were produced during the late Middle Woodland and early Late Woodland period. Similar points were manufactured from A.D. 300 to 500 in the area formerly occupied by groups that made Havana pottery (Kline and Apfelstadt 1975). A relatively small number of these points were found at Carrier Mills, perhaps as a result of its considerable distance from groups that made Havana pottery. Most Lowe points have an elongated triangular body and an expanding stem that forms acute corners with the base. In many ways, their shape is similar to that of some of the expanding-stem Late Archaic points, but they are smaller than the older versions. Because of their relatively small size, they have often been linked to the introduction of the bow and arrow into this region.

Not surprisingly, cherts used to make Middle Woodland flaked stone implements came from the same sources used by earlier people. The major distinction between the chert used to make the Middle Woodland points and the tools of previous Carrier Mills residents is the increased importance of high-quality Cobden chert from the western Shawnee Hills and the decreased importance of chert from local eastern Shawnee Hills area. The percentage of Middle Woodland flaked stone tools made from Cobden chert is the highest of any of the occupations represented at Carrier Mills. The increasing importance of this source area to the Carrier Mills people can be traced to the Late Archaic and Early Woodland periods.

The Cobden chert quarries are located in Union County, approximately 40 miles southwest of Carrier Mills (Figure 3-1). Archaeological investigations in southwestern Illinois have shown that chert was taken from this source area throughout prehistory but that the quarries were most intensively exploited during the Middle Woodland period. In its unmodified form, Cobden chert occurs as round nodules and is commonly referred to as ball chert because of its spherical shape. The outside of the nodules are covered by a rough layer, the cortex, formed by weathering of the chert. The chert inside the nodule is a high-quality, smooth-grained, dense material that ranges in color from blue to gray to black. One of the most distinctive characteristics of Cobden chert is the presence of concentric rings or bands that are created during the formation of the nodule (Plate 3-6). Because of the very distinctive appearance of Cobden chert, it is easily recognized at archaeological sites.

Evidence from other parts of Illinois and adjacent areas of the Midwest indicate that Cobden chert was widely exchanged among Middle Woodland groups. It is often found on sites with Havana occupations in the Illinois River valley. The Middle Woodland groups living near the Cobden quarries manufactured discs or blanks from sections of Cobden nodules (Plate 3-6) and exchanged them with groups living in other areas. The Twenhafel site, the Middle Woodland mound center located near the junction of the Big Muddy and Mississippi rivers (Figure 4-1), may have played an instrumental role in this exchange network (Winters 1984).

Although much more common during the subsequent Late Woodland and Mississippian periods, another implement that may have seen limited use during the Middle Woodland period is the flaked stone hoe (Plate 4-6). No Middle Woodland hoes were found, but the distinctive flakes produced when hoes are repaired or resharpened were found in a number of Area A Middle Woodland features. Hoe flakes are a specialized type of debitage attributable to hoes or other kinds of digging implements because they have a distinctive glaze, called hoe polish, on the outer surface of the flake. The polish is created by the repeated abrasion of the soil on the surface of the hoe as it enters the ground. Flaked stone hoes associated with a Middle Woodland occupation at the Sugar Camp Hill site (Figure 4-1), Williamson County, Illinois, may have been used to dig storage and burial pits. The side

PLATE 4-6. Examples of large flaked stone hoes. Hoe polish is visible on several specimens.

walls of at least one pit showed indications of the use of these implements (Maxwell 1951:121). Hoes would have been quite useful for digging the numerous large Middle Woodland pits found at Area A.

Pottery. One of the major distinctions in the way of life of the Carrier Mills Middle Woodland people and the people who lived in the District during earlier times is the use of pottery. Even though pottery first appeared during the Early Woodland period, material that can be dated to that time is extremely rare. Pots made during the first half of the Middle Woodland period were probably not much different from Early Woodland vessels.

Middle Woodland pottery can generally be divided into two subdivisions based on the appearance of certain kinds of decoration during the second half of the period. Early Middle Woodland pots have thick walls, the clay is tempered with coarse particles of grit, and decoration is rare. During the last half of the period, pots have thinner walls, the clay is tempered with smaller particles, and the upper portions of the pots are often decorated. In spite of these long-term trends, the majority of the pieces of pottery fall into the gray area between these two extremes, creating problems in their assignment to a specific part of the Middle Woodland occupation.

Many of the vessels made by the early Middle Woodland people were probably quite similar to the jar shown in Plate 4-1. They were basically deep, thick-walled conoidal vessels with small, flattened bases. Many of the early jars resembled overgrown flowerpots. They were usually tempered with crushed rock (grit) or a mixture of grit and clay (grog). Grog temper eventually became more popular later in the Middle Woodland (Butler and Jefferies 1986). During the early Middle Woodland at Carrier Mills, approximately 70 percent of the pots had fabric-impressed exteriors; the remainder were cordmarked. By about A.D. 300 to 450, fabric-impressed pottery became less common, and by around A.D. 450 or shortly thereafter it accounted for less than 8 percent of the pottery.

Several examples of jar bottoms or bases were found in Middle Woodland Type 1 features. Three bases found in one of these large circular pits at Area 1 of Sa-86 are shown in Plate 4-4. All three bases are flat-bottomed and range from 3.5 inches to 5 inches (9 cm to 13 cm) in diameter; they appear to be parts of jars having shapes similar to the jar in Plate 4-1. A radiocarbon date obtained from this pit indicated that the jars date to about A.D. 150 ± 105, approximately 350 years younger than the estimated age of the jar in Plate 4-1.

Why were the three bases in this feature in the first place? It is possible that the feature served as a trash pit in which the jars were discarded when they were broken. A second possibility is that food was placed in the jars that were in turn placed in the pit and stored underground. The small bases would not have been large enough to keep the jars from overturning unless they were supported in some way, such as by placing them in a pit. All of the jars may have been broken when one of these large heavy containers was accidentally dropped while being removed or replaced in the pit (Hargrave 1982). Whatever the reason, they are some of the larger examples of early Middle Woodland vessels found at Carrier Mills.

During the second half of the Middle Woodland period, pots having cordmarked or plain exteriors became more common, as did pots having decorations on the upper parts of the vessel walls. Decorations were applied in bands or zones on the rim of the vessel, with each zone containing a specific kind of decoration. Tools used to decorate the unfired vessels include sharp edges for making incised lines or angular notches, objects of various design used to make stamped impressions, and dowels to make notches along the top of the rim. In some cases, nodes occur just below the top of the vessel. Nodes were formed by punching a small dowel partially through the vessel wall from the inside, leaving a circular raised area, or bump, on the outside. The earliest occurrence of nodes at Carrier Mills dates to A.D. 15 and they are common until about A.D. 440; they are also occasionally found on vessels made after this time. Pieces of Middle Woodland pottery decorated using these techniques are shown in Plates 4-7 and 4-8.

PLATE 4-7. Examples of Crab Orchard pottery with nodes.

PLATE 4-8. Examples of decorated Middle Woodland pottery.

Plate 4-7 (Row 1) shows sections of two late Middle Woodland vessels from Area 1. One example is a fabric-impressed jar with notches just below the top of the vessel and a row of nodes immediately below the notches (Plate 4-7, Row 1, No. 2). The shape of the vessel wall suggests that this jar had a similar conoidal shape as the earlier Middle Woodland jar shown in Plate 4-1, except that it was thinner and made better than the older specimen. A smaller portion of a second vessel was also found in this feature. It had a much more globular or round shape, suggesting that both conoidal and globular-shaped jars were made during the late Middle Woodland period. A second late Middle Woodland jar fragment from Area 1 (Plate 4-7, Row 1, No. 1) also has notches and nodes and appears to have been part of a globular vessel.

No Middle Woodland ornamental objects were identified among the thousands of artifacts found at Carrier Mills, but a clay figurine that could have been used ceremonially was recovered from the Area A midden. Surprisingly, the figurine was not found in a burial, in a pit, or in any context that would be interpreted as "ceremonial," but simply in the general midden soil. The apparently "unceremonial" nature of the disposal of this object raises many questions about its significance to the Middle Woodland people who lived at Area A. The figurine, very similar to others found at certain Middle Woodland sites throughout much of the eastern United States, is a representation of a male in a semireclined position (Figure 4-2; Plate 4-9). It is about 3 inches (8 cm) tall, 1.5 inches (3.6 cm) wide at the shoulders, and roughly .5 inch (1 cm) thick at the waist. The clay used to make the figurine was finely textured and light gray to buff in color. The surface is highly polished and the details were applied using a sharp object, such as a stylus. The facial details are very well formed. The eyes are deep, slanted, and almond shaped. Ears and nose have been molded by pinching clay from the head and details added using a stylus. The top and back of the head are flattened and the neck is quite short. Fine incised horizontal lines placed over both ears may represent hair. Clothing details are limited to a small breech cloth around the waist, and there is no evidence of ornaments or other kinds of personal adornment on the body.

PLATE 4-9. Hopewellian ceramic figurine from Area A.

Although clay figurines of this type are not commonly found, a number have been reported from Middle Woodland sites involved in the Hopewell Interaction Sphere. One of the largest figurine collections in the Midwest comes from the Mann site, located near the junction of the Wabash and Ohio rivers in southwest Indiana. More than 150 figurine fragments have been recovered from the site and many others exist in private collections (Kellar 1979). Some of the Mann site figurines have facial features that are very similar to those on the Carrier Mills man, presenting the possibility that it was made at the Mann site, then brought to Carrier Mills. With the exception of several pieces of pottery having Hopewellian or Havana-like decorations, the figurine is the only strong evidence for involvement of the Carrier Mills people with the Hopewell exchange network.

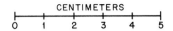

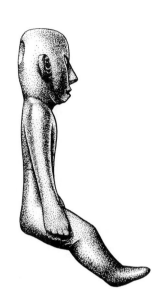

Figure 4-2. Hopewellian ceramic figurine.

Figurines also occurred at several other southern Illinois Middle Woodland sites. One specimen, described as a female with a pinched node for a nose and conical modeled and carved breasts, comes from the Sugar Camp Hill site located about 25 miles west of Carrier Mills (Maxwell 1951). One complete figurine and parts of 22 others are reported from the Twenhafel site, located in western Jackson County (Griffin et al. 1970) (Figure 4-1). Clay figurines, such as these from Illinois and Indiana, were probably manufactured during the last half of the Middle Woodland period.

Nonportable Equipment. Much of the nonportable equipment consisted of the various pits and hearths used for food preparation and storage. Most of the Middle Woodland features were assigned to one of three feature types. The majority were Type 1 features, most of which were found at Area A of Sa-87. The average diameter of these large circular pits was slightly more than 3 feet (1 m), and they averaged about 1.5 feet (.5 m) deep (Plate 4-10). The size and shape of the pits suggest that they were probably used for food storage. The approximately 100 Type 1 features at Area A indicate that food storage was a very important Middle Woodland activity in this part of the District. Excellent drainage characteristics make the Area A soil especially suitable for underground storage. Experiments conducted during the fall of 1978 showed that rainwater was not retained in Area A pits, quickly draining after the rain stopped. In contrast, deep pits dug at other sites often acted as wells, quickly filling with water and creating poor conditions for storage of perishable materials.

Type 2 features, shallow, basin-shaped depressions, compose the majority of Middle Woodland features at other sites. It seems likely that Type 2 features represent a very wide range of activities, many of which probably involved the processing or preparation of food. Type 2 features were generally much smaller than Type 1 features.

PLATE 4-10. Middle Woodland Type 1 features at Area A.

The third category of Middle Woodland features, Type 5, was found only at Area 1. Type 5 features, often called earth ovens, include all those showing clear evidence of heating, as indicated by a layer of red or orange burned clay on the interior of the pit (Plate 4-11). Some of these features contained large pieces of sandstone, perhaps intended to help retain the heat required for cooking (Plate 4-11). Several contained a thick layer of charcoal in the bottom, indicating that a fire was built in the pit. Others contained no charcoal, suggesting that the rocks may have been heated in a fire before they were placed in the pit. Once the temperature in the earth oven had reached the proper temperature, food was placed in the pit and the pit covered while the food cooked. This technique would have been useful in preparing many kinds of food.

PLATE 4-11. Lower portion of a Type 5 feature (earth oven) containing large sandstone rocks.

Food Habits

One of the research topics that most interested the Carrier Mills archaeologists concerned how the diet of the prehistoric people changed through time. The detailed study of Middle Archaic food remains provided an excellent foundation for such a study against which the food remains of later peoples could be compared and contrasted. The numerous Middle Woodland pits contained valuable information concerning the eating habits of these people.

Study of carbonized plant remains from 33 Middle Woodland pits, located at Areas 1 and 2 of Sa-86, Areas A and B of Sa-87, and Sa-88, showed that the relative importance of fruits and seeds increased from the Middle Archaic to the Middle Woodland periods. Compared to the Middle Archaic, the significance of nuts appears to decrease in Middle Woodland times. These trends basically conform with long-term dietary trends in other parts of Illinois and the Midwest at this time.

The most common fruits represented in Middle Woodland pits were persimmons, plums, and grapes. The increased abundance of fruits suggests that fields and open, disturbed woods were more prevalent in the Carrier Mills area, since the trees and vines that produce these fruits prefer these growing conditions. Open areas may have been created by the Middle Woodland residents while clearing land for garden spots.

The consumption of weed seeds also appears to have increased between the Middle Archaic and Middle Woodland periods. The ratio of weed seeds to nutshell in Middle Woodland features is nearly six times that found in Middle Archaic features. Most of the difference is due to the increased number of goosefoot and knotweed seeds. Pits also contain a much higher ratio of grass seeds, particularly maygrass, possibly reflecting the development of grass seed collection and/or cultivation practices by the start of the Middle Woodland period. Maygrass seeds in these features have added significance because Carrier Mills is north of the area where maygrass naturally grows. Humans were probably responsible for its presence, providing additional support for the theory that they had undertaken prehistoric gardening.

Wild beans were also consumed by the Middle Woodland people of Carrier Mills. The seeds and pods were probably a good source of food. Several carbonized roots, bulbs, and tubers were found in Middle Woodland pits, primarily at Area A. Identified specimens include wild onion or garlic, spring beauty, American lotus, and groundnut. These plant parts grow below ground and could have been collected from early spring through late fall. Groundnuts were found in at least two Area A Middle Woodland pits. Groundnut tubers are a very good source of protein and can be easily stored for later use.

Although the relative importance of fruits and various seed-bearing plants increased when compared to the Middle Archaic period, their significance in the diet of the Carrier Mills people was not as great as in many other parts of Illinois. Hickory nuts continued to be a major food source for the Carrier Mills Middle Woodland people, and to a lesser extent so did walnuts, hazelnuts, and acorns.

The increased consumption of seeds documented at Carrier Mills may be attributable to Middle Woodland gardeners who were growing more of their food. The midden soils in many parts of the District, enriched by previous human occupation, would have served as excellent garden spots. The presence of hoe flakes in Middle Woodland features suggests that gardening was an ongoing activity by this time.

The wide range of Middle Woodland plant remains indicates that people were living at Carrier Mills during most if not all of the year. Few indications of spring occupation were preserved, but the groundnut tubers are potentially available at this time. Maygrass seed matures between April and June, and its presence in Middle Woodland pits documents occupation of the District at that time. Wild beans and most fruits mature in mid-to-late summer, and nuts and certain fruits are available in the fall. Many of these foods can be dried and stored for later use, and the large number of deep circular pits at Area A were probably used for this purpose.

Study of animal bones collected from more than 80 Middle Woodland features at Area 1 of Sa-86, Area A of Sa-87, and Sa-88 showed that Middle Woodland people hunted and fished in the same areas as their Middle Archaic ancestors. Animals that commonly lived along the edge of forests contributed approximately 80 percent of the meat in the Middle Woodland diet. The white-tailed deer was the most important animal hunted in this area and accounted for more than three-quarters of all the meat consumed. Elk, woodchuck, rabbit, and wild turkey were sometimes found along the forest edge.

Roughly 10 percent of the meat eaten by Middle Woodland people came from lakes, rivers, swamps, or other wet areas. The beaver was the most important species, followed by mink and muskrat. A variety of ducks, geese, and swans was available on a seasonal basis, and some were year-round residents. Aquatic reptiles, amphibians, and fish probably account for about 3 percent of the meat in the diet. The importance of fish is probably underrepresented, since many of the small bones of the species commonly found in these waters would have passed through the one-quarter-inch wire mesh used to screen the pit fill.

The remaining meat in the Middle Woodland diet came from animals that lived in wooded areas. The raccoon was the most important, followed by the opossum, gray squirrel, gray fox, and the passenger pigeon. Besides serving as important sources of protein, many of these animals provided furs, skins, and bone to make an assortment of implements, clothing, ornamental items, and ceremonial objects.

Burial Customs

As previously discussed, some Illinois Middle Woodland sites contained burial mounds and the remains of high-status individuals. These burials were often placed in pits or tombs under the mound and were accompanied by a wide variety of exotic items made from nonlocal raw materials. Such was not the case at Carrier Mills. Although archaeologists found abundant evidence for intensive Middle Woodland occupation at several locations, very few of the nearly 500 burials recovered during 1978 and 1979 were Middle Woodland. Several burials at Sa-88 were tentatively classified as Middle Woodland based on the presence of artifacts found in the soil immediately surrounding the skeleton, but even these few are questionable and provide little information about the burial customs of these people. Carrier Mills Middle Woodland burials appeared to contain individuals of relatively low social position who possessed few, if any, social distinctions. None was accompanied by artifacts associated with the Hopewell Interaction Sphere. If high-status individuals lived at Carrier Mills, apparently they were buried outside the District. No Middle Woodland burial mounds have been reported along the South Fork of the Saline River; perhaps certain ceremonial activities, such as burial of high-status people, occurred at larger sites located along the Wabash and Ohio river valleys.

Trade with Local and Distant Groups

In many parts of the eastern United States, the Middle Woodland period is characterized by the long-distance exchange of "exotic" raw materials (copper, obsidian, mica, marine shell, and so on) and a diverse selection of objects made from these materials. Archaeological investigation at Carrier Mills produced little evidence to show that Middle

Woodland residents were very deeply involved in long-distance exchange.

The best examples of trade are the clay figurine found at Area A and isolated pieces of pottery resembling Havana Series pottery from the lower Illinois and Wabash valleys. The Area A figurine is quite similar to some of the many specimens found at the Mann site, located roughly 43 miles east of Carrier Mills. It seems likely that the figurine was manufactured at the Mann site, then traded to someone who brought it to Carrier Mills. The discovery of other figurines in southern Illinois similar to those at Mann indicates that exchange between Middle Woodland people living in southern Illinois and southern Indiana was not uncommon.

Pieces of Middle Woodland pots having decorations similar to those on Havana Series pottery occasionally turned up at Carrier Mills. Most of the time, the Havana decorations were applied to Crab Orchard pottery that was locally produced in the Carrier Mills area. In a few cases, however, actual trade vessels from the lower Illinois or Wabash river valleys may be represented. These pieces are more finely crafted than most examples found at Carrier Mills. Some are tempered with pieces of finely crushed limestone and have a highly polished outside surface. Decorations on the outsides of the vessels include various kinds of incising and stamping frequently found on Hopewellian jars from Middle Woodland sites in the major river valleys of the Midwest.

A final possible indication of Middle Woodland exchange is the relative increase in tools made from nonlocal Cobden chert. The presence of Cobden chert at Middle Woodland sites in the lower Illinois River valley shows that this material was involved in long-distance exchange. Although Carrier Mills is only about 40 miles away from the Cobden chert quarries and the quarries could have been visited by people from Carrier Mills, all things considered, exchange of chert is probably a more likely possibility than direct access to the source area.

Summary

Despite the fact that few undisturbed Middle Woodland deposits were found at Carrier Mills, much has been learned about how these people lived by studying the artifacts and other material they left behind. A number of different activities have been identified, including hunting, nut and seed collecting and processing, food storage, and possibly gardening.

Hunting is indicated by the numerous projectile points and knives found at most of the Carrier Mills sites. Bone from a diverse assortment of land and aquatic mammals collected from Middle Woodland features shows that hunters visited many different habitats to obtain game. The animals killed by Middle Woodland hunters and the relative importance of the different species in their diet is very similar to that of the Middle Archaic people. The recovery of fish bone shows that fishing continued to provide a certain amount of food. The kinds of fish represented indicate that conditions in the river and lake were basically unchanged from those during the Middle Archaic period.

Nut collecting and processing activities are reflected by the large amount of carbonized nutshell in Middle Woodland features. Implements used to perform these tasks are probably present, but they cannot be distinguished from tools serving the same functions during other periods of site use. The hickory was the most intensively used of the nut-producing trees. Compared to the Middle Archaic period, nuts appear to have been slightly less important in the Middle Woodland diet.

The collecting and processing of weed seeds and fruits are also indicated by their carbonized remains in Middle Woodland pits. The wide variety of seeds found suggests that many different environmental zones were frequented to collect plant foods. A comparison of fruit and weed seeds with the amount of nutshell shows that they form a larger part of the diet than during the Middle Archaic period. Maygrass seeds were found in some Middle Woodland features. Some archaeologists think that this seed-bearing plant was cultivated during the Middle Woodland period. If it had been grown at Carrier Mills, still another activity would be indicated: gardening. Hoe flakes found in several Middle Woodland features provide additional support for gardening during this time, particularly at Area A.

Apparently, many of the plant foods that were collected or grown by the Middle Woodland people were stored for later use. Evidence of food storage at Area A is indicated by the numerous large, deep, cylindrical pits. The increased evidence for food storage during this time suggests that a larger portion of the Middle Woodland diet was composed of plant foods than during earlier times, many of which could be processed and stored.

Diagnostic flaked stone tools and pottery provide information on a few additional Middle Woodland tasks. End scrapers and drills made from recycled broken corner-notched projectile points show that manufacturing and repairing flaked stone tools took place. Hafted end-scrapers were probably used for preparing hides, and the drills were probably associated with a variety of manufacturing activities.

The thousands of pieces of Crab Orchard pottery and the large size and weight of the vessels suggest that Middle Woodland pots were probably locally manufactured. The weight of vessels similar to the one shown in Plate 4-1 probably approached 13 pounds (6,000 g) when empty and considerably more when full. Carrying these large, cumbersome pots very far would have been difficult.

Pots are also associated with food processing and storage. The thick-walled Crab Orchard vessels produced at Carrier Mills during most of the Middle Woodland period would have been useful for preparing foods that could be slowly cooked at relatively low temperatures, such as nuts and oily seeds. The persistence in making thick-walled vessels in this part of southern Illinois is paralleled by the continued importance of nuts as a food source.

§ A.D. 400–1000: The Late Woodland Period

In many ways, the Late Woodland period in southern Illinois was a continuation of Middle Woodland trends. The number of sites and the large size of many argue for a continued increase in population for the southern Illinois area. The food remains found at some of these sites indicate that the Late Woodland people selected from a wide variety of resources. In contrast to the Middle Woodland period, long-distance trade and exchange between people in different parts of the eastern United States declined during the Late Woodland. Instead, greater cooperation and exchange of ideas took place among groups living in the same region, and they tended to rely more on resources found locally.

Houses made by the Late Woodland people were somewhat different from those of earlier times. Smaller structures designed to house smaller family groups—probably consisting of parents and children—replaced the larger ones built during the Middle Woodland period. Changes in house size may mean a basic restructuring in the way Late Woodland societies were organized. Late Woodland houses were often arranged in a cluster to form a village. Gardening continued to become more important, providing a significant part of the Late Woodland diet. Crops grown included a number of native weeds with which earlier gardeners had experimented, as well as plants introduced from outside the Midwest.

Late Woodland cooking pots are thinner-walled, have a finer temper, and are more globular in shape than Middle Woodland vessels. Lowe projectile points were commonly made during the early portion of the Late Woodland period (Figure 1-3). These were replaced by smaller triangular-shaped varieties during the last half of the Late Woodland.

By the second half of the period, three regions of Late Woodland development can be identified for southern Illinois. One is centered in the American Bottom and extends east through the Kaskaskia River valley to about the Carlyle Reservoir; a second covers the northern Shawnee Hills, the Big Muddy and Saline River valleys, and portions of the Mississippi River valley; and a third extends south of the Shawnee Hills along the Ohio River valley. Additional Late Woodland phases have been identified in the Wabash River valley along the eastern border of Illinois. The Carrier Mills Archaeological District is located in the Big Muddy–Saline River area but decoration on some of the pottery suggests that residents maintained ties with Late Woodland groups in adjacent portions of Illinois and Indiana.

Late Woodland period archaeology in the American Bottom has received considerable attention because of the construction of Interstate Highway 270 (I-270) around East St. Louis. Archaeologists have documented three distinct phases (Rosewood, Mund, and Patrick) for that area, based on differences in pottery. Changes also occurred in flaked stone tools, features, structures (houses and other kinds of buildings), community organization, and diet (Kelly et al. 1984).

Studies of plant and animal remains from Late Woodland features indicate that inhabitants obtained most of their food from within about one mile of the site. They ate a wide assortment of natural foods as well as a number of cultivated plants. Foods native to the area include various nuts, fruits, berries, and tubers; domesticated plants consisted of squash, marsh elder, sunflower, and maize.

Considerable change also occurred in the places people choose to live. During the early part of the Late Woodland, most sites were located in the uplands and relatively few in the bottom area. By the end of the period, substantial communities consisting of numerous houses and other structures were built in the American Bottom. Houses were smaller and shaped differently than earlier ones. A gradual increase in the population of the American Bottom also took place during this time (Kelly et al. 1984).

Archaeologists have identified two periods of Late Woodland occupation in the Big Muddy–Saline River area based on differences in local pottery. The earliest period dates from about A.D. 400 to 700 or 800. Archaeologists call pottery manufactured by the early Late Woodland people Raymond ceramics; pottery made during the last half of the period is called Dillinger pottery. The name is taken from the Dillinger family who owned the land near the Big Muddy River, where a large Late Woodland site (the Dillinger site) is located. Excavated by Moreau Maxwell in 1940, it produced important information about Late Woodland life in southern Illinois. Radiocarbon dates indicate that Dillinger pottery was made between A.D. 900 and 1000.

We do not know very much about the size and distribution of Late Woodland sites in the Big Muddy–Saline River area, but it appears that the population density in this part of southern Illinois was somewhat lower than that in other river valleys. Raymond phase sites have not been identified in the Mississippi River valley, but large Dillinger phase villages were built on elevated parts of the floodplains and on the bluffs overlooking locations where tributary streams entered the Mississippi River floodplain.

Stone forts—stone walls or enclosures on bluff tops in the Shawnee Hills—were probably built by Late Woodland people (Brieschke and Rackerby 1973). To date, 11 of these forts have been identified (Figure 4-1). Although several have been studied by archaeologists, their purpose is still unclear. Some people have speculated that they were ceremonial enclosures, while others maintain that they functioned as corrals for holding animals or as defensive fortifications. Pottery found in two forts resembles early Late Woodland material like that made in the Ohio valley.

The Late Woodland Lewis phase has been defined for the area south of the Shawnee Hills along the Ohio River. Pottery from this part of southern Illinois was similar to that made in the Big Muddy–Saline River area, except that Lewis vessels were tempered with clay instead of crushed rock. Lewis sites are generally small and are found on elevated areas in the floodplain. Most of what is known about the Lewis phase is based on archaeological work done in the Black Bottom by the University of Chicago in the 1930s and by Southern Illinois University at Carbondale in the 1960s and 1970s.

Although relatively little archaeological work has been done in the Wabash River valley, Howard Winters's survey, conducted in the mid-1960s, identified three Late Woodland cultures (Winters 1967). One of these, the Duffy-Yankeetown complex, dating to the last part of the Late Woodland period, has been found as far south as the Saline River valley. Pottery associated with this occupation consists of clay-tempered vessels decorated with incising and stamping.

Many questions remain unanswered concerning the lifeways of the Late Woodland people of southern Illinois. The work at Carrier Mills produced new information that will eventually help answer these questions.

Life at Carrier Mills during the Late Woodland Period

Archaeologists found evidence of Late Woodland occupation at all seven activity areas in the Carrier Mills Archaeological District. Although the three radiocarbon dates for this period span only from A.D. 685 ± 60 to 955 ± 65, the Carrier Mills area was occupied, at least to some extent, throughout the entire Late Woodland period. The number of people living at each site varied, as did the time of the most intensive occupations. Evidence of Late Woodland activity included projectile points, pottery, and features. Archaeologists recovered most of the Late Woodland artifacts from plow-disturbed soil. The only relatively undisturbed Late Woodland material came from the roughly 170 pit features excavated during the two field seasons.

We can trace Late Woodland population trends at Carrier Mills by comparing the relative amounts of pottery made during the first and second halves of the period. Raymond pots, manufactured during the early Late Woodland, have cordmarked exteriors but were generally undecorated. In contrast, the later Late Woodland Duffy and Yankeetown vessels lack cordmarking but were decorated with stamping and incising.

Archaeologists found very little evidence of an early Late Woodland occupation (ca. A.D. 450–650) at Carrier Mills. Raymond pottery and Lowe Flared Base projectile points were scarce. Perhaps early Late Woodland people in southeast Illinois preferred to live in the major river valleys (Wabash and Ohio) rather than in the upper reaches of tributary drainages, like the South Fork of the Saline River.

In contrast, activity picked up at Carrier Mills during the remainder of the Late Woodland period (A.D. 650–1000). The large number of terminal Late Woodland (ca. A.D. 900–1000) artifacts found in some areas indicate that a substantial number of people lived at Carrier Mills at that time.

Area B of Sa-87 showed signs of the most intensive Late Woodland occupation, covering in excess of 16,000 square yards (14,000 m²) (Figure 2-2). Excavation of the central part of the site yielded more than 25,000 pieces of Late Woodland pottery and over 300 small triangular projectile points.

A second intensive, although smaller, Late Woodland occupation occurred at Area 1 of Sa-86. The distribution of Late Woodland pottery on the surface of the site indicates that the occupation covered about 13,000 square yards (11,000 m²). Because the Area 1 midden deposit was much shallower than at Area B, Late Woodland pits extended into the light-colored subsoil and were visible when the plowzone was removed from the site. Ninety-two features, consisting of cylindrical storage pits, basin-shaped pits, and earth ovens, were identified and provided important information about Late Woodland eating habits and pottery. Less intensive Late Woodland occupations were encountered at Area 2 of Sa-86, Area A of Sa-87, and Sa-88, but even these yielded many Late Woodland ceramics and features. The two remaining activity areas (Area 4 of Sa-86 and Area C of Sa-87) contained no Late Woodland features and few artifacts.

The decoration on pottery found at these sites helps archaeologists determine during which part of the Late Woodland period a site was occupied. The high percentage of Duffy and Yankeetown pottery indicates that Area B was most frequently used during the last half of the Late Woodland period. Much of the Area 1 Late Woodland occupation also appears to have taken place toward the end of the Late Woodland. In contrast, Sa-88 seems to have been more commonly occupied during the first half of the period.

If the quantity of pottery and projectile points accurately reflects the number of people living at Carrier Mills, then there clearly was an increase in population during the Late Woodland period. We should keep a few points in mind, however. As the use of pottery became more common during the Woodland period, the number and kinds of pots used by each household probably increased. Also, the small triangular projectile points used by Late Woodland hunters were part of the bow and arrow technology; hunting with a bow and arrow probably required more arrows, hence more points, than previously used hunting techniques. The larger quantity of Late Woodland pottery and projectile points, compared to the Middle Woodland period, may be partially due to these technological changes and not totally the result of an increase in population. The Late Woodland population of Carrier Mills probably was greater than during the Middle Woodland period, but the size of the increase is uncertain.

The People and Their Possessions

Flaked Stone Tools. Although the people living at Carrier Mills during the Late Woodland period conducted many activities that required a wide assortment of implements and raw materials, most of what we know about their way of life is derived from study of the diagnostic flaked stone tools and pottery. The two most common kinds of Late Woodland flaked stone tools found at Carrier Mills were projectile points and hoe flakes produced by resharpening and repairing flaked stone hoes.

Late Woodland people appear to have made fewer formal flaked stone tools than in earlier times; instead, they relied on tools made from amorphously shaped chert flakes. Many of these informal flake tools were made simply by sharpening the edge of a flake. The emphasis on flake tools represents a more economical use of chert.

Relatively few examples of tools manufactured from recycled broken projectile points were found, but those that were identified were made into drills, perforators, or hafted end-scrapers. Most Late Woodland projectile points were too small for recycling into other kinds of tools.

Late Woodland projectile points found at Carrier Mills include the Lowe Flared Base point and a variety of small triangular-shaped points known as Madison or Scully points. The Lowe Flared Base points (Plate 4-5, Row 3) were relatively rare at Carrier Mills, representing only about 5 percent of all the Late Woodland projectile points.

The small Madison points were the most prevalent of the Late Woodland projectile points (Plate 4-12, Rows 1 and 2, Nos. 1–7). Although Madison points were also made

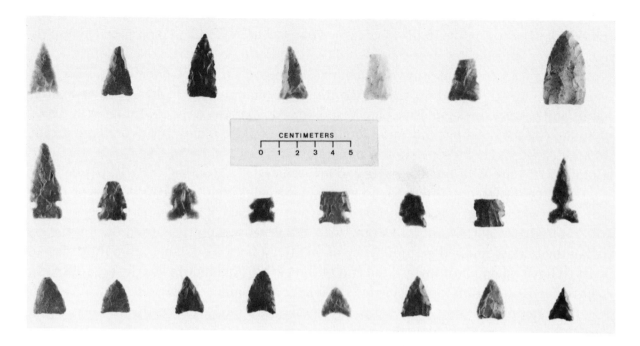

PLATE 4-12. Late Woodland/Mississippian triangular projectile points. Row 1, Madison—Stemless variant (last specimen is robust form); Row 2, Madison—Notched variant (last specimen is Cahokia Notched type, Mississippian period); Row 3, Scully.

during the subsequent Mississippian period (A.D. 1000–1600), the absence of a major Mississippian occupation at Carrier Mills suggests that most were made and used by Late Woodland hunters. Two varieties of Madison points were found at Carrier Mills, stemless and notched. Madison points are generally no longer than 1.6 inches (4 cm) and no wider than .6 inch (1.5 cm). The decrease in size and change in shape of these points, compared to earlier varieties, resulted from a shift in hafting techniques linked to the introduction of the bow and arrow.

Madison stemless points (Plate 4-12, Row 1) have a flat, thin triangular body. The sides are straight, but the base may be slightly concave. Most of these points are manufactured from flakes that were knocked off chert cores. Some of these small points were shaped simply by removing small flakes from the edge of the larger flake, leaving much of the original flake surface unmodified. Production of these points appears to have been much more economical in terms of raw material use, time, and energy compared to the manufacture of earlier point types.

Madison notched points (Plate 4-12, Row 2, Nos. 1–7) are very similar to the stemless variety, except for the addition of small notches just above the base. The notched variety was relatively uncommon at Carrier Mills, representing about 2 percent of the Madison points.

Another variety of small triangular point, the Scully, was also made by the Late Woodland hunters (Plate 4-12, Row 3). Scully points average about .8 inch (2 cm) long and about .4 inch (1 cm) wide, being somewhat shorter than the Madison points. The sides are convex and the base is concave, presenting a rather heart-shaped appearance. Scully points were relatively rare, compared to the Madison stemless points.

Chert used by Late Woodland hunters to make their projectile points differed to some extent from that used during the Middle Woodland period. Middle Woodland people had a strong preference for the high-quality cherts found in the western Shawnee Hills, particularly the Cobden chert (Figure 3-1). By Late Woodland times, a marked shift can be seen toward the increasing use of cherts found in the local area. At Carrier Mills, nearly 75 percent of the Late Woodland projectile points were made from chert that could be found in the nearby eastern Shawnee Hills. The increased emphasis of local cherts during the Late Woodland period indicates a greater use of local resources brought about by a more sedentary lifestyle.

Although there was a decrease in the use of western Shawnee Hills chert to make projectile points, other cherts from that part of southern Illinois were used to make flaked stone hoes. Unfortunately, few complete examples of these tools were found at Carrier Mills, but the recovery of many hoe flakes from Late Woodland features and from sites having intensive Late Woodland occupations shows that these implements were used by the Late Woodland people.

Flaked stone hoes are commonly found on Late Woodland and Mississippian sites in Illinois and other parts of the Midwest (Plate 4-6). These implements vary in size, depending on the size of the piece of chert selected to make the hoe and the number of times it was resharpened. Continued resharpening reduced the size of the hoe until, eventually, it was no longer usable and was discarded, or more likely, used to make another kind of tool. Several examples of scrapers made from broken or discarded hoes were found at Carrier Mills.

Late Woodland hoes were usually made from Mill Creek or Kaolin chert because they could be easily flaked from the lens-shaped nodules. Approximately 75 percent of the Carrier Mills hoe flakes were Mill Creek and about 10 percent were Kaolin. Since the Late Woodland people were much more sedentary than earlier groups who lived at Carrier Mills, and since the sources of the preferred cherts were located some distance away in the western Shawnee Hills, they may have obtained the material through some kind of special exchange system. It is possible that Late Woodland groups living in the vicinity of the Mill Creek quarries restricted access to them in order to control the distribution of this desired material.

Hoe flakes were especially common at Area 1 of Sa-86 and Area B of Sa-87, the location of the two most intensive Late Woodland occupations, but they also occurred at the other activity areas as well. Archaeologists expect hoe flakes to be found at habitation sites where hoes were resharpened by people who tended the gardens and in areas that were used as gardens. Areas of rich midden soil found at some of the Carrier Mills sites probably served as gardens during the Late Woodland and Mississippian periods. These soils contain exceptionally high concentrations of many of the chemicals required for good plant growth. Archaeological work at other sites in Illinois has uncovered evidence of Mississippian farmers planting their gardens on preexisting midden deposits (Fowler 1969), so it would have been reasonable for the Late Woodland people at Carrier Mills to farm these extremely rich soils. Hundreds of years later, these prehistoric sites were recognized by early American farmers as good spots for their gardens.

Pottery. During the Late Woodland period, pottery vessels continued to assume an increasingly important role in the lives of the Carrier Mills people. Many more vessels were used by Late Woodland households than during the Middle Woodland period, and by the end of the Late Woodland, an assortment of bowls, jars, and platters were being produced. Vessel walls continued to be made thinner throughout the period, and fine clay particles gradually replaced grit as the preferred kind of material with which to temper the clay. Both of these changes in the way pots were made were probably in response to changes in the kinds of foods prepared by the Late Woodland people. The thinner walls, finer temper, and changes in the shape of cooking pots helped the vessels to withstand the higher temperatures required to cook the starchy seeds that were a popular source of food.

Most of what is known about Late Woodland pottery at Carrier Mills comes from features excavated at Sa-86 and Sa-88. Pottery found in features tends to be larger and less disturbed than material from the plowzone. Occasionally, pieces of the same pot are found which can be pieced together, providing the archaeologist with a better idea of the vessel's original size and shape. Radiocarbon dates are sometimes obtained from these features, tying together a particular style of vessel with a specific point in time.

The Carrier Mills Late Woodland pottery falls into several categories or types. Raymond and Dillinger pottery, commonly found on Late Woodland sites in interior southern Illinois, are present. Relatively few examples of the early Late Woodland Raymond pottery were found, but late Late Woodland Dillinger pottery was very common. Raymond pottery occurs as both straight-sided bowls with rounded bottoms and small constricted-neck jars. Clay used to make these pots was tempered with crushed rock, and the outsides of the vessels were cordmarked (Maxwell 1951). Dillinger pottery was made in a wider variety of vessel shapes, including globular and straight-sided jars, large shallow bowls or platters, and small bowls. The clay was tempered with crushed rock or clay, the latter becoming more common toward the end of the period. Vessel exteriors were either cordmarked or plain. Dillinger pots were sometimes decorated with incising, nodes, or notches along the rim (Maxwell 1951). Vessels made at the end of the Late Woodland period were very thin-walled and were tempered with small particles of clay.

Several other kinds of pottery, commonly found on Late Woodland sites along the lower Wabash River in extreme southeastern Illinois, were also present at Carrier Mills. Duffy pottery is identified by the distinctive vertical lines, or bar stamps, that decorate the upper portion of bowls and jars. The lower parts of these vessels are undecorated. Yankeetown pottery, more commonly found in southwest Indiana, is also present. Most of the Yankeetown vessels have plain exteriors, but cordmarking is present on some. Both the Duffy and Yankeetown pottery were manufactured around A.D. 900 and 1000. The presence of substantial amounts of this material at Carrier Mills suggests that some kind of social ties were maintained with people living farther to the southeast, along the lower Wabash River, during the last part of the Late Woodland period.

The only example of an early Late Woodland Raymond pot was found accompanying a burial at Area A. It was the only pot found with any of the Carrier Mills burials. The vessel probably contained food or some other substance when it was placed in the grave. Approximately one-half of the vessel could be reconstructed, revealing a rounded-bottom jar with straight sides (Plate 4-13). Its exterior was cordmarked, and the clay was tempered with particles of crushed rock. Before breaking, the jar was roughly 8 inches (20 cm) tall and about 7 inches (18 cm) in diameter.

An assortment of partially reconstructed vessels provided archaeologist Michael Hargrave with considerable information on the kinds of pots made during the last half of the Late Woodland period. One Late Woodland feature at Area 1, radiocarbon dated to A.D. 955 ± 65, contained over 1,600 pieces of pottery representing more than 70 different vessels. Included in this collection were a wide assortment of jars, as well as a few bowls and platters. Some of the jars had round or globular bodies, and others had straight sides that tapered toward rounded or slightly flattened bottoms.

Plate 4-14 shows the upper portion of a Late Woodland, Dillinger-like cordmarked jar. The lower portion of the vessel was not found in the pit. The opening, or mouth, of this jar was about 12 inches (30 cm) in diameter. A smaller, more globular, Dillinger-like cordmarked jar is shown in Plate 4-15. The opening of this vessel was only about 8 inches (20 cm) in diameter. Several of the Late Woodland jars have lugs along the rim of the open-

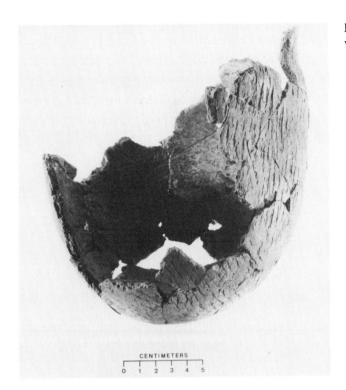

PLATE 4-13. Early Late Woodland vessel associated with an Area A burial.

PLATE 4-14. Upper portion of a Late Woodland Dillinger jar from Area 1.

PLATE 4-15. Late Woodland Dillinger jar from Sa-88.

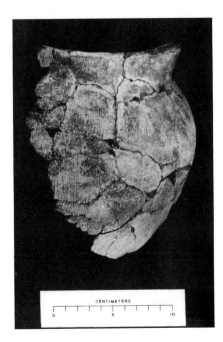

ing. Lugs are small projections extending from the rim for carrying the vessel. The shape and orientation of the lugs vary. Most are triangular-shaped and extend vertically above the rim, but a few extend in a horizontal direction. On rare occasions, lugs were made in the shape of an animal head. Two examples of animal effigy lugs were found at Carrier Mills. One appears to be a reptile of some type, perhaps a turtle; the second resembles a dog or a bear (Figure 4-3).

Figure 4-3. Late Woodland rim effigies.

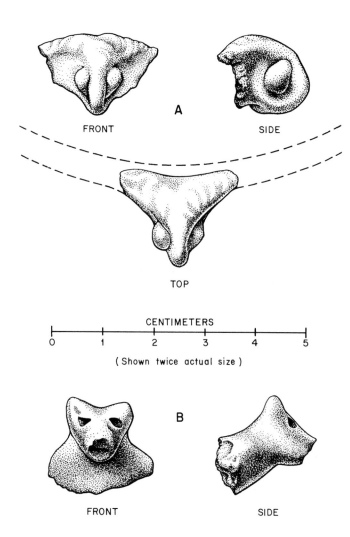

The upper portion of the cordmarked jar shown in Plate 4-16 is decorated with a series of curved lines that were drawn below the rim while the clay was still soft. Shallow notches are also visible along the top of the rim. The unbroken vessel would have been about 12 inches (30 cm) in diameter; the vessel opening was about 6 inches (15 cm) in diameter. The vessel is probably a type of pottery known as Dillinger Decorated.

An example of a Duffy Bar-Stamped jar was found at Area B of Sa-87 (Plate 4-17, Row 1, No. 1). These vessels were usually clay tempered and had plain exteriors. The term "bar-stamped" refers to the vertical lines found on the outside of jars and the inside of bowls. The Carrier Mills vessel had a globular body with a single row of bar stamps placed below the mouth.

Very few Late Woodland bowls were found at Carrier Mills, which might be partially due to the difficulty of distinguishing small fragments of bowls from those of jars. When

PLATE 4-16. Section of a Late Woodland Dillinger vessel from Area 1.

bowls were found in features, they were associated with jars made very late in the Late Woodland period, which suggests that bowls were not produced until the end of the period.

Archaeologists found several reconstructable sections of shallow platters. One specimen was about 16 inches (40 cm) in diameter and roughly 2.5 inches (6 cm) deep. It had a

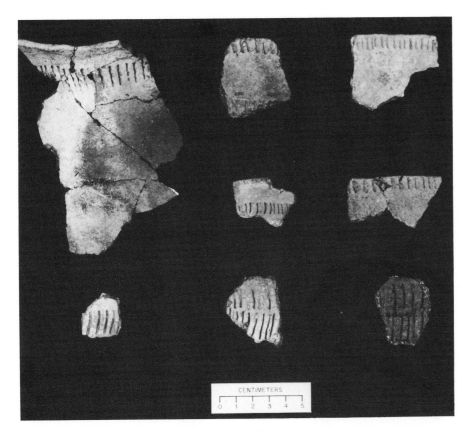

PLATE 4-17. Examples of Late Woodland Duffy Bar-Stamped pottery. Large piece in Row 1 (Number 1) is from Area B.

cordmarked exterior and a plain interior. A second platter, measuring about 20 inches (50 cm) in diameter and 2 to 3 inches (6 to 8 cm) deep, was also recovered.

In most cases, determining the exact purpose, or purposes, for which a pottery vessel was used is a very difficult task. The various kinds of bowls, jars, and platters made by Late Woodland people at Carrier Mills were an important part of many of their activities. Bowls could be used for cooking as well as for serving and storing food. Globular jars would have been suitable for storing food or liquids. Platters were probably used for preparing and serving food. Ongoing research by archaeologists interested in how pottery containers were made and used promises to answer some of the questions about the role of ceramic vessels in prehistoric societies.

Despite the large quantity of Late Woodland artifacts and features found at Carrier Mills, no examples of ornamental or ceremonial objects were recovered. The absence of these artifacts is not surprising since they are usually discovered with burials, of which very few Late Woodland ones were identified at Carrier Mills.

Nonportable Equipment. Most of the 170 Late Woodland features were deep, cylindrical pits (Type 1), shallow, basin-shaped pits (Type 2), or earth ovens (Type 5). The large, deep Type 1 pits commonly used by the Middle Woodland residents of the District occurred much less frequently during the Late Woodland period. The only site where the Type 1 features represented a majority of Late Woodland features was Area A, but only six pits were identified compared to the 118 Middle Woodland ones found there. Late Woodland Type 1 pits were only about one-half the size of the Middle Woodland ones. The decrease in the number of these probable storage pits may suggest a change in the way food was being stored or possibly a decrease in the importance of foods that were stored in this manner.

The shallow, basin-shaped Type 2 pits account for about 75 percent of all Late Woodland features, most of which were found at Area 1 of Sa-86 or at Sa-88 (Plate 4-18). Only four were found at Area B of Sa-87, but in view of the intense Late Woodland occupation, many more were probably hidden in the dark midden soil. The large number of Type 2 pits uncovered at these sites indicates that activities associated with the processing of food and other resources were often performed there.

PLATE 4-18. Lower portion of a Late Woodland Type 2 feature at Sa-86 containing pieces of pottery.

Large earth ovens were constructed by Late Woodland people living at Area 1 of Sa-86. These deep, circular cooking facilities often contained large blocks of sandstone and a thick layer of charcoal on the bottom of the pit. Like Middle Woodland earth ovens, some Late Woodland ovens were heated by first building a fire in the pit, then placing sandstone rocks on the fire. When the fire went out, the rocks remained very hot, and the food could be cooked by placing it on the hot rocks and covering the pit. Earth ovens having no charcoal on the pit bottom could have operated using rocks heated in a fire built outside the pit, the rocks being placed in the oven when they were hot. Either technique would have produced abundant heat for cooking a wide assortment of foods.

Although it may not commonly be thought of as equipment, a very essential part of survival is some kind of shelter. Numerous Late Woodland houses must have been built at Carrier Mills, but in spite of the extensive fieldwork, none were identified. Archaeologists observed and mapped numerous postmolds, but very few formed patterns resembling a house or structure. Several possible postmold alignments were mapped during the excavation of Area 1, but investigators could not determine if they were part of an actual house outline or simply an alignment of isolated postmolds.

Food Habits

Many of the gradual changes in eating habits that first occurred during the last part of the Archaic and earlier portions of the Woodland period, like gardening and the consumption of starchy seeds, were greatly accelerated during the Late Woodland. By around A.D. 700, people living in many parts of the lower Illinois River valley were beginning to grow maize; by the end of the Late Woodland period, they largely replaced cultivated seeds with maize as a major source of food. The inhabitants began to use the bow and arrow about this time, which provided a much more efficient means of hunting. The combined effects of these changes allowed more people to live in the uplands for longer periods, although the largest sites were still located near the major rivers (Asch et al. 1979).

Plant remains from Late Woodland sites in the American Bottom contain additional varieties of cultivated plants and more evidence for gardening than during the Middle Woodland period. The inhabitants consumed fewer nuts and the larger quantities of starchy seed crops, mostly maygrass, knotweed, and goosefoot. They also grew squash, gourds, marsh elder, and tobacco. Archaeologists have thus far found very little evidence of maize at American Bottom Late Woodland sites (Johannessen 1984).

These changes in the eating habits of Late Woodland groups in other parts of Illinois also occurred at Carrier Mills, but at a much slower rate. By comparing the amounts of nutshell and seeds collected from Late Woodland features, archaeologists found that the use of fruits and seeds greatly increased during this time—the use of fruit was nearly 4 times that of the Middle Woodland period and the use of weed seeds was about 74 times greater than during Middle Woodland times. They ate an assortment of fruit, including persimmons, plums, and grapes, and seeds from goosefoot, knotweed, and maygrass.

Nuts continued to be a major source of food. The same varieties that were popular during earlier times were also collected during the Late Woodland. Hickory nuts continued to be the most intensively collected variety, but they were not as important as before. The significance of acorns is difficult to assess because the shell does not preserve very well; however, it appears that they were more important than during the Middle Woodland period. Walnut and hazelnut collection also seems to have increased relative to hickory nut.

Archaeologists uncovered small amounts of maize in a number of Late Woodland features, most of it from one pit at Sa-86. Small fragments of squash or gourd rind were also collected from several Late Woodland pits. The scattered occurrence of small quantities of these plants indicates that, although they were cultivated by Late Woodland gardeners, the food they produced represented only a minor part of the diet.

The Late Woodland inhabitants probably lived at Carrier Mills the year round. Plant remains from Late Woodland features indicate that occupation took place at least from spring through late fall. Maygrass becomes available in the late spring and early summer. Maize, grape, squash/gourd, and a number of other plants point to a midsummer presence. A fall occupation is reflected by a variety of seeds and nutshells. The presence of Late Woodland storage pits and the storage potential of much of the food would have made the winter and early spring seasons survivable.

Jonathan Bloom's and Emanuel Breitburg's studies (Jefferies and Butler 1982) of animal bone contained in Late Woodland feature fill showed that most of the meat in the diet came from animals that lived near the forest edge. Not surprisingly, approximately three-fourths of all the meat came from deer or elk. The remainder came from a wide assortment of small mammals, birds, waterfowl, reptiles, and fish that lived in the forests, rivers, lakes, and swamps found in the surrounding area. The Late Woodland pattern of animal use was very similar to that of earlier Archaic and Woodland peoples living at Carrier Mills. This continuity implies that environmental conditions in the Carrier Mills area were generally stable during most of the prehistoric period.

Burial Customs

Archaeologists found very few human burials that could be dated to the Late Woodland period. No doubt some of the many burials excavated at Area A and Sa-88 containing no diagnostic artifacts were Late Woodland, but these cannot be distinguished from burials dating to other periods of occupation. The best example of a Late Woodland burial was that of a juvenile interred on the north slope of Area A. This person was placed in an extended position and was accompanied by the early Late Woodland vessel shown in Plate 4-13, indicating that burial occurred between A.D. 400 and 700 or 800.

Another example of a Late Woodland burial was found in a large storage pit at Sa-88 (Plate 4-19). The burial was that of a young adult male, about 22 years old, who had been placed in the pit in a flexed position. Archaeologists dated the remains based on the Late Woodland pottery found in the pit fill. At least 18 other burials found at Sa-88 also dated to the Late Woodland period. These individuals were classified as Late Woodland because of the kind of pottery found in the fill of the burial pit. Bodies were placed in both extended and flexed positions.

In addition to the humans buried in the District, a number of dogs were interred. All of the examples were found in the upper levels of the Area A midden deposit and, based on their shallow depth, probably dated to the Woodland period. Archaeologists also found isolated dog bones in Archaic and Woodland pits.

The best example of a dog burial, Dog Burial 2, was that of a mature animal of indeterminate sex (Plate 4-20). The positioning of the bones indicates that the dog was intentionally buried shortly after death. No artifacts were associated with the burial. The bones do not show signs of cut marks—which usually indicate butchering—suggesting that these dogs were not used as a meat source; skeletal material from other Midwest Woodland and Archaic sites indicates that dogs occasionally may have been eaten (Parmalee 1965; Parmalee et al. 1972). Although the significance of burying these animals is not known, it suggests that dogs occupied a special position in the lives of the Carrier Mills people. Dog burials are also known for other Archaic and Woodland sites in the Southeast and Midwest.

PLATE 4-19. Flexed burial in a Late Woodland storage pit (Type 1 feature) at Sa-88.

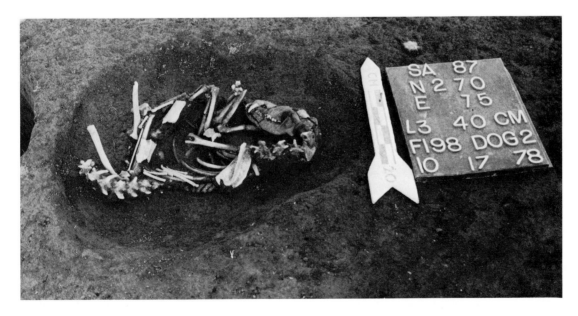

PLATE 4-20. Dog burial at Area A.

Summary

In many ways, Late Woodland life closely resembled that during the Middle Woodland period. Many of the differences that did exist were related to changes in the kinds of foods the people were eating and the ways in which they obtained and prepared them.

Archaeologists have identified many different activities performed by the Late Woodland people based on the artifacts and food remains found in Late Woodland features (Figure 4-4). These include hunting, nut and seed collecting and processing, and gardening. Hunting is indicated by the projectile points and animal bones found in Late Woodland features. Late Woodland triangular projectile points are much smaller than earlier ones; they were probably used as arrow tips. Even though the means of hunting, and perhaps the way hunting groups were organized, had changed, the kinds of animals that were hunted were the same as during the Middle Woodland period. The Late Woodland people continued to supplement their diet by fishing and hunting waterfowl.

They collected and processed nuts and seeds, as indicated by the abundance of carbonized nutshell and seeds in feature fill. The Late Woodland inhabitants still preferred hickory nuts over all others, but they consumed more acorns, walnuts, and hazelnuts than before—perhaps as a result of increasing demand on the food sources by the larger population living in the area.

The Late Woodland inhabitants left behind numerous hoe flakes, indicating gardening. The plants they cultivated probably included a variety of native, seed-bearing plants, as well as squash and gourds. They also experimented with growing maize.

Changes in the way they made cooking pots could reflect differences in the kinds of food the inhabitants prepared. Archaeologists have linked the differences in vessel wall thickness, temper, and shape to the increased consumption of starchy seeds. The large, deep, circular pits found at some of the Carrier Mills sites were probably used for food storage.

Figure 4-4. This reconstruction of Late Woodland life at Carrier Mills shows a number of traits introduced to the area during the Woodland period. Hunters in the background are returning with game that they killed using a bow and arrow. Women in the foreground are preparing food using ceramic cooking pots. Some of the plant foods may have been grown in nearby garden plots.

5 Mississippian Farmsteaders: A.D. 1000–1600

The final 600 years of midwestern prehistory are known as the Mississippian period. Archaeologists coined the term Mississippian because some of the first sites investigated by archaeologists dating to this period were located along the Mississippi River. Although numerous large Mississippian sites are located in that river valley, many others have been found along the floodplains of other major rivers throughout the Midwest and Southeast. Smaller Mississippian sites occur along tributary rivers and streams that drain the interiors of these regions.

During the Mississippian period, native Americans grew maize as a major source of their food, organized their society in complex ways, developed large communities, and exchanged goods made from exotic raw materials over long distances. The widespread cultivation of maize introduced from Mexico first took place during the Late Woodland period, but it was not until the Mississippian period that the crop became a significant source of food. Other introduced plants, such as beans, squash, and pumpkins, were also grown by Mississippian farmers. The rich alluvial soil found in the floodplain was excellent for growing maize and other crops. Even though gardening produced a major part of their diet, the Mississippian inhabitants continued to hunt and collect the wild animals and native plants they found in the area.

Mississippian communities tended to be large and complex, usually consisting of a number of towns, villages, and farmsteads joined together by social, political, and economic ties. These sites were often organized in a hierarchy, with one large ceremonial/political center linked with a series of smaller towns. Each town, in turn, was linked with a number of smaller villages, and each village was tied to a series of farmsteads. Farmsteads generally consisted of several structures that were occupied by a family. Much of the food eaten by people living in the large settlements was probably produced by those who lived and tended gardens at the farmsteads.

Mississippian societies were highly structured compared to those of the preceding Archaic and Woodland periods. In some areas, societies were organized into chiefdoms that were ruled by a chief or priest and the members of his family. The ruling group occupied a very high position in the society, and all other families and individuals held social positions below those of the ruling group. The chief lived at a ceremonial/administrative center. Large, flat-topped earth mounds that served as substructures for public buildings were common features at these large sites. Often, the mounds were arranged around a large, vacant public area called a plaza.

When a high-status person died, his or her body was often placed in a tomb constructed in, or under, an earthen burial mound. Many grave goods were interred with the deceased. These objects were often made of materials not locally available, such as copper, mica, or marine shell.

Items manufactured using these nonlocal materials also serve as evidence for the reestablishment of long-distance trade during the Mississippian period. Flaked stone hoes made of Mill Creek chert from southern Illinois were often traded during this time. Archaeologists have found Mill Creek hoes on Mississippian sites as far away as southern Wisconsin, northern Mississippi, eastern Ohio, and eastern Oklahoma (Winters 1981).

One of the most diagnostic characteristics of the Mississippian period is the production of shell-tempered pottery. The use of crushed mussel shells as temper enabled Mississippian cooking vessels to withstand the stresses of heating and cooking better than the grit- and clay-tempered Woodland pots. Mississippian potters made their vessels in a wide variety of shapes that included various sizes of bowls and jars, bottles, plates, and pans. They decorated the rims of some bowls with animal effigy heads and occasionally made bottles in the shapes of animals. They incised, stamped, engraved, or painted some pottery vessels and left others undecorated. The Mississippian people probably used highly decorated vessels for special or ceremonial occasions and undecorated ones for domestic purposes.

Mississippian projectile points were small, triangular-shaped points similar to those manufactured during the last half of the Late Woodland period. In many cases, archaeologists cannot distinguish Late Woodland varieties from those dating to the Mississippian period. Small notches occur on the base and sides of some Mississippian triangular points found in the American Bottom and, occasionally, in parts of southern and central Illinois.

Archaeologists have been intensively studying Mississippian life in the American Bottom of west-central Illinois for many years. Much of their work has focused on the Mississippian ceremonial center of Cahokia (Figure 5-1). The site covers approximately 3,700 acres and originally contained more than 100 earth mounds. The largest of these, Monks Mound, measures approximately 1,000 feet north-south and 800 feet east-west and is 100 feet high. The mound was built in a number of construction stages between ca. A.D. 900 and 1200. At various points in time, large buildings or enclosures were constructed on top of the mound. The central part of the Cahokia site was enclosed by a large stockade made of logs placed upright in a deep trench. Watchtowers and gates were placed at regular intervals along the wall. Evidence of rebuilding suggests that the stockade was replaced several times (Fowler 1977, 1978; Reed 1977).

Many other Mississippian sites have also been identified in the American Bottom (Figure 5-1), ranging in size and complexity from relatively large sites with mounds and plazas to small farmsteads. It seems likely that during much of the Mississippian period the people who lived at these settlements were closely tied to events at Cahokia.

Recent work conducted in connection with the I-270 highway construction project has provided significant new information about Mississippian life in the American Bottom. Most of this research focused on the excavation of sites without mounds located in the floodplain surrounding the larger mound sites. Some of the most useful information concerns the size and organization of Mississippian communities and households. Most

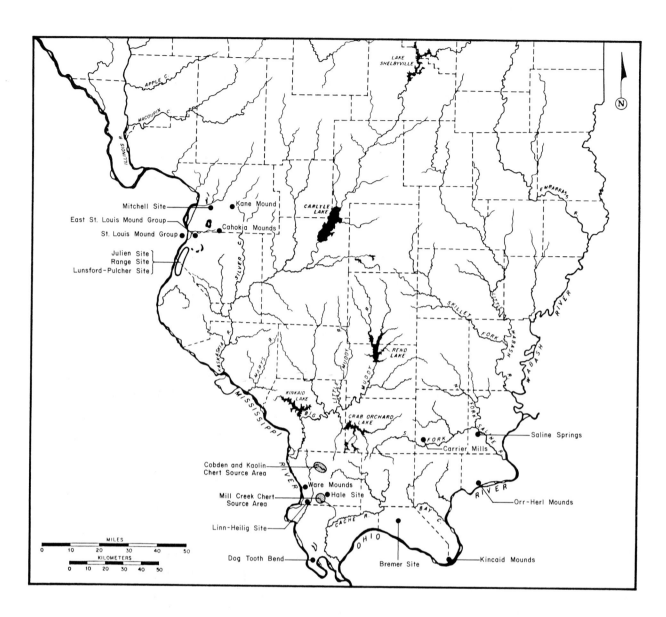

Figure 5-1. Major Mississippian sites in southern and south-central Illinois.

outlying communities consisted of scattered households occupied by small groups of closely related individuals on a year-round basis. In the early part of the period, they made their rectangular-shaped houses by placing wall posts in individual postholes. During this period, there was a gradual shift toward building larger, rectangular houses for which the wall posts were set in long, narrow trenches instead of individual postholes. These structures, known as "wall-trench" houses, are commonly found on Mississippian sites in many parts of the Midwest. Household features consisted of one or two structures and associated pits and hearths (Milner et al. 1984).

Study of plant and animal remains from household sites indicates that Mississippian people obtained much of their food close to home. Most of the meat they ate came from white-tailed deer, ducks, and geese. They also consumed many different kinds of fish. Garden plots, placed near their houses, supplied maize, gourds, and squash, while starchy seeds, such as maygrass, knotweed, and goosefoot, continued to form a significant part of their diet. They also collected acorns and hickory nuts along the bluffs that line the eastern edge of the American Bottom (Milner et al. 1984).

Although they concentrated food-getting activities on the ridges, lakes, and swamps near the households, the Mississippians maintained ties with people in faraway parts of the Midwest and Southeast. They enjoyed a long-distance exchange network that provided them with exotic goods. Much of this trade may have been conducted or controlled by people living at the large mound centers (Milner et al. 1984).

A second area of Illinois in which Mississippian period settlement has been intensively studied is the Black Bottom area of the Ohio River floodplain in southeast Illinois. Archaeologists from the University of Chicago conducted initial work there in the 1930s and 1940s, with subsequent investigations carried out in the 1960s and 1970s by professionals from Southern Illinois University at Carbondale. Much of the research has focused on the Kincaid site (Muller 1978) (Figure 5-1). The site is a large palisaded mound center covering about 175 acres. The mound complex consists of five mounds situated around a plaza and five additional mounds located east of the first group. Smaller mound centers occurred in the area surrounding Kincaid, including the Orr-Herl site near Rosiclaire (Figure 5-1), the Bremer site in the Cache River valley (Figure 5-1), and several sites across the Ohio River in Kentucky. Archaeologists have found numerous small farmsteads and hamlets (consisting of several farmsteads) in the Black Bottom. Many of these small settlements appear to be parts of dispersed villages.

The earliest Mississippian occupation at Kincaid dates to around A.D. 900 or 1000. Occupation appears to have reached its peak about A.D. 1200 to 1300, followed by a gradual reduction or dispersal of the population in the 1300s. By A.D. 1400, Kincaid was probably no longer a major center, although some archaeologists contend that the site was an important center in the Black Bottom until just before European contact.

In recent years, Mississippian period archaeological investigation in the southern Illinois area has centered on the Great Salt Spring (Saline Springs) site, located on the lower Saline River in Gallatin County (Figure 5-1). Artifacts and features found in the deep midden deposit indicate that salt production was the major activity at the spring during the Mississippian period. Pieces of salt pans—large, shallow clay pans in which the silty brine from the springs was placed and allowed to evaporate—were found throughout the site. Fired, clay-lined basins with a flue or trough extending to the north or northwest were also common. These special features were probably used to heat the brine-filled salt pans directly or to heat rocks that were placed in the brine to speed up evaporation of the water. When evaporation was complete, a thin layer of salt was deposited on the bottom of the pan (Muller 1984).

Other large Mississippian sites have been identified in the Mississippi River floodplain of southern Illinois. Among these are the Ware, Linn-Heilig, and Dogtooth Bend mounds (Figure 5-1), and some of the mounds at Twenhafel (Figure 4-1).

Mill Creek chert, used to make flaked stone hoes, comes from the extreme western portion of the Shawnee Hills. The Hale site (Figure 5-1), the only known mound center in this part of the Shawnee Hills, is located adjacent to the source area of Mill Creek chert. The Mississippian people living at the Hale site may have governed access to the chert, controlling its distribution during much of the Mississippian period.

The large, intensively occupied Mississippian sites occur in the floodplains of many major midwestern rivers. Occupation in the uplands, on the other hand, was generally sparse, consisting largely of isolated homesteads or small groups of homesteads. Mississippian settlements in the upper reaches of the Saline River valley were similar to those found in other parts of interior southern Illinois. Thus far, archaeologists have not yet found Mis-

§ Mississippian Life at Carrier Mills

sissippian mounds along the Saline River floodplain. The largest known Mississippian site in the valley is the one at the Great Salt Spring, but this site is not characteristic of others along the Saline. Archaeological survey of the North Fork of the Saline River identified virtually no Mississippian sites in that area.

Habitation of the Carrier Mills area during the Mississippian period was minimal. Archaeologists found fewer than 40 pieces of shell-tempered pottery during the surface collection or while excavating the hundreds of units they placed throughout the District. No doubt some of the small, triangular Madison projectile points and hoe flakes are attributable to the Mississippian occupation, but these cannot be distinguished from most points made during Late Woodland times. Only four diagnostic Mississippian points were recovered during the nine months of fieldwork.

Archaeologists found the most convincing evidence for a Mississippian occupation at Area 1 of Sa-86, where they uncovered two rectangular, wall-trench houses while removing the plowzone. More than 200 pieces of shell-tempered pottery were recovered from the interior of the two structures, and a section of a globular shell-tempered jar was found in one. Charcoal samples collected from the burned timbers of the two houses provided radiocarbon dates of A.D. 1130 ± 50 and A.D. 1375 ± 60, indicating that the two houses were not occupied at the same time.

Why did so few people live at Carrier Mills during this period? Much of the reason may be the Mississippians' reliance on floodplain agriculture. The ability to grow maize was the foundation of the Mississippian way of life. With the exception of the midden areas, there was very little good farmland at Carrier Mills. The Mississippian occupation of the Carrier Mills area represents a definite backwoods way of life compared to that of the large mound centers and towns of the floodplains.

The People and Their Possessions

Personal Equipment

Except for the relatively few pieces of shell-tempered pottery and four diagnostic projectile points, archaeologists did not find Mississippian utilitarian, ornamental, or ceremonial objects at Carrier Mills. The largest concentration of pottery was found in Structure 2, much of which belonged to a large, shell-tempered vessel. Some of the pieces could be refitted, forming the upper portion of a very large globular jar (Plate 5-1). Before being broken, the mouth of the jar was about 12 inches (20 cm) in diameter, but the maximum diameter of the vessel was considerably larger, based on the shape of the wall of the reconstructed section. Jars of this type were probably used for both food storage and cooking.

The four Mississippian projectile points are a type of small triangular point known as a Cahokia point. These points usually have three notches, one along the edge of the base and one on each side, just above the base (Plate 4-12, Row 2, No. 8). Like the other small, triangular Late Woodland-Mississippian points, Cahokia points were also made to go on the tips of arrows. These points commonly occur on Mississippian sites in the American Bottom.

Nonportable Equipment

Although no Mississippian pits or hearths were found during the many months of fieldwork at Carrier Mills, the two wall-trench houses exposed at Area 1 provided a con-

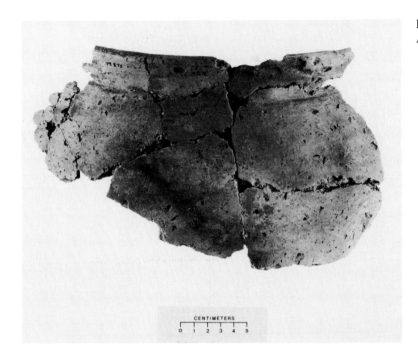

PLATE 5-1. Mississippian jar from Area 1, Structure 2.

siderable amount of information about Mississippian life. The first of these houses, Structure 1, was situated at the extreme western edge of Area 1. The dimensions of the rectangular house were about 14 feet by 18 feet (4.1 m by 5.4 m), with the long walls oriented in a roughly north-south direction (Figure 5-2). The floor area was about 237 square feet (22 m²) and was defined by the four wall trenches that marked the locations of the former walls (Plate 5-2). The actual floor surface used by the inhabitants had been destroyed by plowing.

The Mississippians constructed houses like Structure 1 by first digging the wall trenches that would hold the vertical wall posts. The maximum depth of the Structure 1

PLATE 5-2. The outline of Structure 1 is marked by the excavated wall trenches that once supported the structure's wall posts.

trenches ranged from 13 inches to 18 inches (33 cm to 45 cm), but they were originally somewhat deeper since the upper portions were destroyed by plowing. The four wall trenches were separated by 4 inches to 8 inches (10 cm to 20 cm) at the corners. Based on the width of the trenches, the diameter of the wall posts ranged from 4 inches to 8 inches (10 cm to 20 cm). Once they placed wall posts in the trenches, they wove smaller sticks and vines in between the posts, then plastered them over with clay or mud. This building technique is known as wattle and daub construction. The roof was supported by a series of beams that, in turn, were supported by internal posts set into the floor of the house. Some of the postmolds shown in Figure 5-2 may mark the location of roof support posts. They

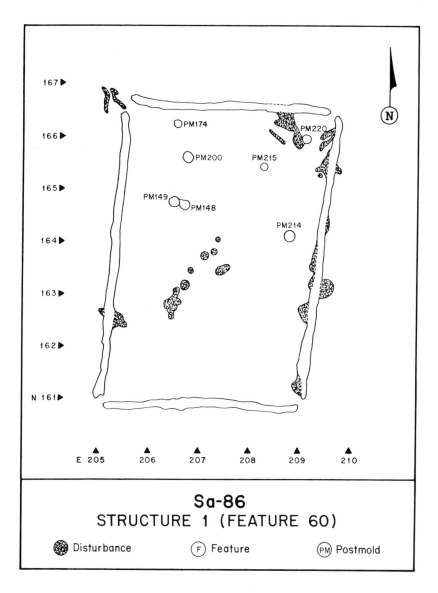

Figure 5-2. Structure 1 floor plan.

probably covered the frame of the roof with a thick layer of thatch for protection from the elements. Because of problems like rotting timbers and vermin, houses like Structure 1 could be used for only a few years before they had to be repaired or replaced. The finished house may have looked something like the one shown in Figure 5-3.

Large areas of burned soil and masses of charcoal located within the house indicate that the structure burned down. Since no evidence of burning was observed outside the house, it appears that the walls collapsed inward as the house burned.

The second Mississippian house was located about 66 feet (20 m) southeast of Structure 1. This house, known as Structure 2, was also rectangular, but it had only three wall trenches. The fourth side appears to have been constructed with the posts set in individual holes instead of in a trench. Charcoal from a burned timber yielded a date of A.D. 1375 ± 60, indicating that this house was about 250 years younger than Structure 1.

Figure 5-3. This reconstruction of Mississippian life at Carrier Mills illustrates what the structures represented by the wall trenches at Area 1 may have looked like. Garden plots containing maize are visible in the background. The women on the left are processing corn, while the man at the far right is repairing a flaked stone hoe.

The floor area of Structure 2 was about 269 square feet (25 m²), slightly larger than Structure 1. The house measured 17 feet by 14 feet (5.2 m by 4.2 m), the longest walls being on the northwest and southeast sides. The southwest wall was marked by a series of six evenly spaced postmolds. The wall trenches for the other three walls ranged from 10 inches to 16 inches (24 cm to 40 cm) deep, but like those of Structure 1 they were cut through by plowing. The northeast wall trench was particularly interesting because it showed how the wall posts were placed in the trench. Eight individual postmolds were visible along the outer edge of the trench (Plate 5-3; Figure 5-4). The postmolds were about 3 inches (8 cm) in diameter and ranged from 1 inch to 5 inches (3 cm to 12 cm) deep. Based on the distance between some of the postmolds, it appears that the wall posts were spaced about 2 inches (5 cm) apart. The positioning of the posts along the outer edge of the wall trench suggests that a log may have been placed in the trench behind the posts for added support. Several additional postmolds visible on the house floor may mark the former locations of roof support posts.

With the exception of the southwest side of Structure 2, construction of the house was probably very similar to Structure 1. Structure 2 also appears to have burned down, as indicated by areas of burned clay, charcoal, and burned timbers. Archaeologists located several pit features in the floor area but could not determine if they were dug by the house's inhabitants or if they predated the Mississippian period. Most of the artifacts recovered from the floor area predate the Mississippian occupation. The major exceptions were pieces of the shell-tempered jar collected from the southern and eastern sections of the house floor.

Excavation in and around the houses revealed little about the activities of the people

PLATE 5-3. East wall trench of Structure 2 showing individual postmolds, marked by flags, along trench bottom.

who lived in them. House size and method of construction suggest that these structures were built fairly well and were designed to last for more than one season. In contrast, neither had recognizable hearths, and the southwest wall of Structure 2 appeared to be open, or at least not very substantial. Early historical records left by Spanish, French, and English explorers indicate that Indians residing in the southeastern United States lived in a variety of structures. During the warm summer months, they may have lived under simple ramadas, structures that consisted of a roof supported by a post at each of the four corners. This kind of shelter would have been sufficient to keep off the rain and dew. Other kinds of warm-weather structures were more substantial. Winter houses were sometimes smaller than summer ones and were usually built in a pit or basin to conserve heat. A basic requirement for a winter house would have been a hearth or fireplace to keep the inhabitants warm (Swanton 1946:386–420).

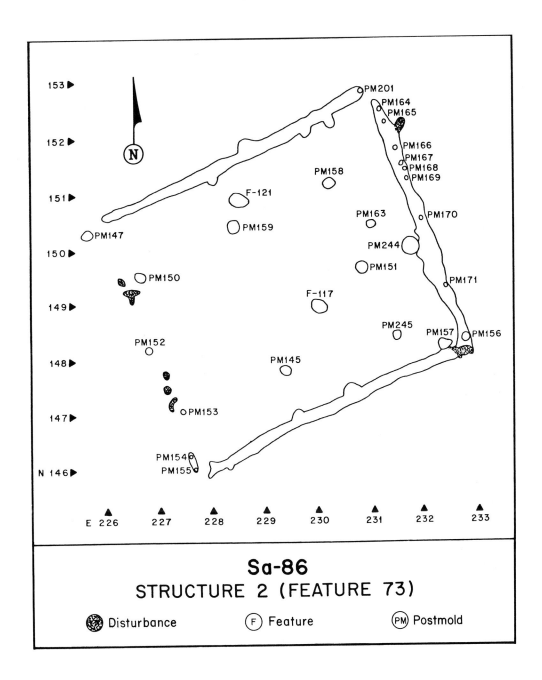

Figure 5-4. Structure 2 floor plan.

The two Carrier Mills houses are obviously much more substantial than would be expected for summer houses, but they lack many of the characteristics associated with winter houses. Based on the small amount of Mississippian material found near the structures and the proximity of the rich midden deposit located in the center of Area 1, perhaps they were occupied for a short time by Mississippian farmers who grew their crops in the nearby midden areas. Very little good farmland was present in the Carrier Mills area before the shallow lake was drained in the early twentieth century. The best farmland available to the Mississippian farmers was located along the low upland ridges, like those in the District. The rich midden soils found on the Carrier Mills sites would have served as excellent garden spots.

Small fragments of carbonized maize contained in soil collected from the floor and wall trenches of Structures 1 and 2 serve as additional evidence for Mississippian gardening at Carrier Mills. Hoe flakes and fragments found in the upper portion of the midden also suggest that these areas were used as gardens during the late prehistoric times.

Isolated Mississippian farmsteads with middens from earlier periods have also been discovered in other parts of Illinois, particularly in the Big Muddy and Kaskaskia drainages (Fowler 1969). Prehistoric gardeners probably made it a common practice to farm old middens in the smaller river valleys and tributary drainages where good bottomland soil was relatively scarce. Along the major river drainages, such as the Mississippi and the Ohio rivers, farmsteads were more numerous and were usually clustered around the larger settlements. Very little is known about the way of life of the Mississippian people living along the smaller rivers that drain the vast interior of southern Illinois.

§ Mississippian Postscript

Little is known about the Indians who lived near Carrier Mills following the Mississippian period. Archaeologists did not find any evidence of Indian activity following A.D. 1500, but no doubt hunting parties periodically visited the area in search of the abundant wildlife that continued to inhabit the swamp, riverine, and upland habitats.

Archaeological evidence from the major river valleys of the Midwest and Southeast points to a general abandonment of the large mound centers, like Cahokia. Spanish and French explorers who first encountered these sites in the sixteenth and seventeenth centuries reported that they were inhabited by only a few people who knew little about the origin or purpose of the mounds. The major changes in the Indian societies and the distribution of the people over the landscape are probably related to many environmental and social factors. For example, diseases introduced by the early explorers, including smallpox, influenza, and measles, rapidly decimated the Indian populations, adding to the disruption of their societies.

French explorers passing through the Ohio valley in the seventeenth century reported that the only resident Indians were scattered groups of Shawnee and Piankashaw who had been in the area for only a short time. These groups probably came from the east, having moved west to escape the hostile Iroquois Indians. The Shawnee inhabited a village near the location of Old Shawneetown from 1746 to 1748 (Temple 1966). In 1759, 40 lodges of Shawnee were reported to be camped near the mouth of the Saline River. Although local tradition suggests that the Black Earth site was once occupied by the Shawnee, there is little evidence to suggest that they ever spent much time in what is now Saline County. By 1825, the remnants of the Shawnee were removed from southern Illinois and were resettled in Oklahoma and Kansas.

6 Lakeview: A Nineteenth-Century Black Community

All of the archaeological materials discussed up to this point were left behind by the prehistoric people who spent at least part of their lives at Carrier Mills. In this chapter, we shall explore the activities of newcomers who lived along the South Fork of the Saline River beginning in the early nineteenth century. The descendants of some of these early settlers continue to live in the Carrier Mills vicinity today.

The Historic period in southern Illinois began with the arrival of the first French explorers in the mid-seventeenth century. French settlement was generally limited to a few areas along the Mississippi and Ohio rivers. Immigrants of English extraction were responsible for large-scale settlement of the region.

The first Anglo-American settlement in southern Illinois was established around 1800 at Shawneetown on the Ohio River. The number of settlers rose sharply following the War of 1812. Many of these early residents settled along the lower Saline River, near the large saline springs in what is now Gallatin County. Like their Indian predecessors, the American settlers used the brine from the springs to make salt, thereby establishing the first industry in southern Illinois. The federal government purchased the springs in 1802, then leased them to private companies. Black slaves and indentured workers composed part of the work force at the springs.

One of the earliest Historic occupations in what is modern Saline County was the Lakeview community, a small settlement of black freedmen located in and adjacent to the Carrier Mills Archaeological District. Brian Butler and Don Merritt's study (Jefferies and Butler 1982) of Lakeview and its residents involved a detailed analysis of both the archaeological and historical records. In this case, the archaeological record consisted of the personal and household possessions of former Lakeview residents recovered during the surface collection and excavation of the three Carrier Mills sites. Most of the artifacts were found in a few large, trash-filled pits that were the subsurface remains of a cistern, a privy, and several other underground facilities. The historical record was composed of an assortment of documents, such as census returns and land transaction records, as well as a number of nineteenth- and early twentieth-century maps.

To understand the status of Lakeview in nineteenth-century southern Illinois, we must first examine the social environment of the South and Midwest during the pre–Civil War era. Most blacks living in the South were slaves. A small number of black freedmen also existed, some of whom crossed the Ohio River to seek a better life in states like Illinois, where slavery was illegal. Although slavery had been outlawed in the state since 1818, many early white settlers held anti-black sentiments, so southern Illinois remained a socially and economically hostile area for blacks.

Illinois, like other midwestern border states, passed the Black Laws devised to maintain tight control of blacks and to discourage their immigration to Illinois. A free black could not reside in the state unless he or she registered and furnished proof of freedom. Many local white residents did not view blacks favorably, and these feelings surfaced from time to time. Gangs of vigilantes and thieves continually tormented black residents without fear of being captured or punished. Blacks were often kidnapped, taken over the state line, and sold back into slavery. In spite of the many risks, small groups of black immigrants continued to cross the Ohio River to southern Illinois. Some of these individuals and families making the dangerous trip north eventually settled in what is now Saline County, becoming the first residents of Lakeview.

§ A Historical Sketch

The Lakeview community, originally known as the Pond Settlement, was centered on an area of low uplands just north of the South Fork of the Saline River and south of the present town of Carrier Mills (Figure 6-1). The settlement covered approximately four square miles, but some of this area contained parts of the swamps and lakes that nearly encircle the uplands. The names "Lakeview" and "Pond" were given to the community because of its close proximity to the wetlands. The southwestern portion of Lakeview lies within the boundary of the Carrier Mills Archaeological District.

Lakeview was never a formal community or village, like many of the early white settlements of southern Illinois. Instead, it was made up of a series of small farms or farmsteads that were scattered over this isolated section of the Saline River valley. In view of the feelings of the time, the isolation of the Lakeview area may have been an important factor for black settlement in this vicinity.

According to local tradition, Lakeview was established by a group of black freedmen who immigrated from North Carolina after the War of 1812. Their actual arrival probably dates to shortly after 1820. The 1830 census records reveal that the first Lakeview residents included the Taborn, Mitchell, and Evans families. County records show that Zachariah Taborn and his wife Lydia originally came from Wake County, North Carolina, between 1820 and 1826. The families of Joseph and Abel Cole may have been part of this early group, but the first official indication of their presence appears in the 1840 census records.

Despite the fact that the nearby Saline salt works employed many blacks as laborers, very few of the people living at Lakeview, or in other parts of southern Illinois for that matter, were ever part of that group. When the work force at the salt springs was reduced in size in the 1820s because of decreasing profits, most of the slaves and indentured workers (a distinction of little significance when it came to blacks) were returned to their original owners in Kentucky.

The earliest Lakeview residents were self-sufficient. They depended on a mixture of hunting and farming for their food. In many ways, their diet may not have been substantially different from that of the Mississippian people who built their houses in the same lo-

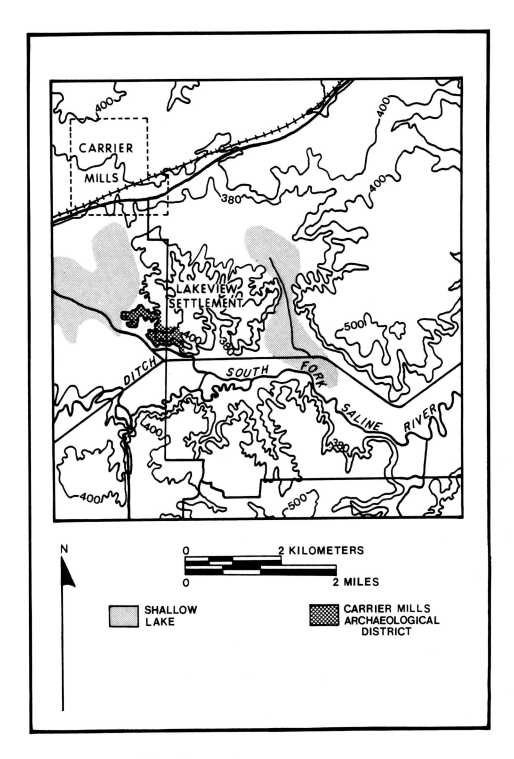

Figure 6-1. Location of the Lakeview settlement.

cation some 500 years earlier. Through the years, some of the Lakeview people obtained work as day laborers or servants.

Information collected from census and land transaction records provides a general picture of the growth of Lakeview during the mid-to-late nineteenth century. Unfortunately, many of the most informative records are incomplete; other records are missing altogether. Problems with the census records may reflect a lack of effort on the part of the census takers to track down residents living on the isolated farms. On the other hand, some blacks may have intentionally avoided the census takers, fearing problems with their legal status. Difficulties with land transaction records stem from a lack of adequate records, problems with squatters living on land they did not own, and distinguishing between landowners and tenants.

Census records show that approximately 24 people, residing in four households, lived at Lakeview in 1830. The number of households and individuals grew slowly during the pre–Civil War period, but a more rapid increase in both is evident following the end of the war. Before 1870, most of the growth was due to individuals and families moving to the community from North Carolina, Kentucky, Tennessee, and occasionally Georgia and Alabama. Population growth slowed after 1870, with most of the increase coming from births within the community. By 1880, Lakeview contained 128 people living in 31 households. By 1900, the population and number of households had reached a point where it was no longer possible to geographically distinguish Lakeview from surrounding communities (although the sociological distinction remained very sharp).

Dates of some of the earliest land transactions (1847 to 1860) and the areas affected are shown in Figure 6-2. The Taborn and Cole families seem to have had major land holdings during the pre–Civil War era. Zachariah and Kimber Taborn owned considerable

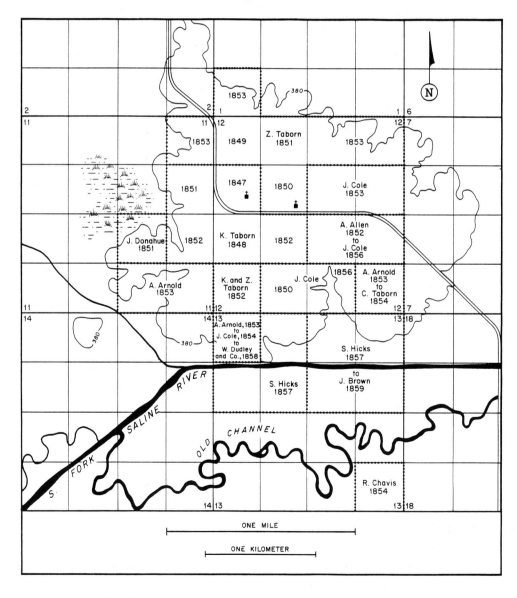

Figure 6-2. Initial land transactions in the Lakeview area (1847–1860).

acreage in the northwest portion of Lakeview. Joseph Cole owned more than 240 acres east and south of Kimber Taborn's land.

By 1856, all of the central and northern parts of the uplands that formed the core of Lakeview were owned by blacks, most of it by the three individuals just mentioned. The remainder of the uplands to the west and south were either unpurchased or owned by whites living outside the community. The preference for the northern and eastern areas is not surprising since much of the land to the south and west was unsuitable for farming.

White settlement in this part of Saline County increased during the 1860s. In 1865, George W. Carrier, the first resident of Morrillsville, later known as Carriers Mills, then Carrier Mills, purchased land. By 1870, whites were living within or adjacent to the core area of Lakeview, largely because of the breakup of Kimber Taborn's landholdings and the purchase by whites of land owned by Joseph Cole. Whites continued to buy land around Lakeview during the remainder of the nineteenth century, resulting in the breakup of large land holdings. Blacks still owned most of the main portion of Lakeview, but their property no longer consisted of the large tracts that characterized land ownership earlier in the nineteenth century.

The first Lakeview school was a log structure built before the Civil War on land donated by Zachariah Taborn (Hancock 1947:167). The log schoolhouse was used until it burned in 1896. A frame building, known as the Lakeview School, was constructed around 1900 to replace the log structure and continued to be used until 1950.

The first Lakeview church, the Union Community Church, was probably built around 1879, the year recorded for a land transfer from Zachariah and Catherine Taborn to the Union Church (Cofield 1976). The site of this church is presently occupied by the Mt. Zion Missionary Baptist Church.

Before 1900, bad roads isolated Lakeview from the surrounding communities. The roads that did exist were dirt and largely concentrated in the central part of the community. In the early 1900s, a north-south county road was constructed through Lakeview, connecting the community with major east-west highways and improving the quality of transportation and communication with the outside world.

Little is known about the typical Lakeview family before the 1870s. Various records suggest that by 1880 the households generally consisted of parents and their children. Occasionally, extra individuals were included, such as older unmarried relatives, a newly married couple (often an older son and his wife), or adolescents identified as farmhands or servants. This last group often included nieces or nephews of the parents. The average Lakeview household contained 5 or 6 individuals, but occasionally up to 10 people might reside in a single household.

During the early days at Lakeview, marriage partners often came from relatively distant locations, largely because of the small number of potential spouses living in the immediate vicinity. As the Lakeview population grew, people more commonly selected their partners within the community. This trend eventually created a situation where most people were related either by blood or by marriage.

Historical records contribute considerable information about the general pattern of settlement and land use during the early Lakeview days, but they provide relatively few insights into the daily lives and activities of its residents. For these details, archaeologists Brian Butler and Don Merritt relied on the artifacts recovered from the home sites and the abandoned wells, privies, and pits these people used for trash disposal.

§ The People and Their Possessions

Historic-period occupants within the Carrier Mills Archaeological District settled in the same spots selected for habitation by the prehistoric peoples. The favorable physiographic aspects of these locations (elevation above water, drainage, soil type, and so on) made them desirable for habitation through the ages. Also, like their prehistoric Mississippian predecessors, the early Historic settlers may have recognized the high agricultural potential of the rich Archaic and Woodland midden deposits.

Artifacts left behind by the nineteenth-century Lakeview residents included broken pottery (stoneware and refined earthenware), glass (bottle glass and flat window glass), bricks, and a wide assortment of metal objects. Stoneware was usually gray or buff-colored and coated with lead-based or salt glazes. Stoneware vessels were generally used for food storage. The earthenware category includes an assortment of ironstone, pearlware, and whiteware plates, cups, platters, bowls, and other vessels used for serving food. Many earthenware items used by the Lakeview residents were manufactured in the upper Ohio River valley, but a few ironstone vessels had markings indicating they were made in Great Britain.

Most of the glass fragments found at Carrier Mills are from bottles or other kinds of containers. Markings on some of the larger fragments show that most of the patent medicines and other liquids they once contained were manufactured in Ohio and Pennsylvania. The presence of these bottles in this part of Illinois underscores the importance of the Ohio River trade route during the mid- and late nineteenth century. Most of the larger pieces of glass and pottery came from the few, large, trash-filled pits excavated in 1978. Most artifacts recovered from plow-disturbed deposits were difficult to identify because of their small size or poor state of preservation.

Many of the metal objects found in the Historic pits were utilitarian implements, such as eating utensils, tools or tool parts, nails, and even a cow bell. One of the more intriguing metal artifacts found during the 1978 field season was a badly worn United States silver three-cent piece. The date on the coin was not legible, but these coins were minted only from 1851 to 1873.

A final category of Historic materials found during the fieldwork was coal and cinders. Coal had been used as a household fuel. The mineral was first mined in this part of southern Illinois in the 1870s, and a small mine that operated in the late nineteenth or early twentieth century is situated just south of Sa-86.

The best information concerning Historic use of the Carrier Mills area came from Sa-86. The oldest artifacts dating to this period, recovered from the central part of Area 1, may date to as early as the 1830s. Two large pit features, Features 109 and 231 (Figure 6-3), were associated with this artifact scatter. The scatter covered about 1,800 square yards (1,500 m²) and was probably associated with a house that existed in that spot until it was destroyed or dismantled in the 1860s.

Feature 109 was a deep, circular pit that probably functioned as a cistern to hold rainwater that ran off the roof of the nearby house. The pit was approximately 9 feet (2.7 m) in diameter and 8 feet (2.5 m) deep (Plate 6-1). It had been filled over a short period of time with artifacts dating from the 1840s to sometime in the 1860s. Much of the contents appeared to be the remains of the house that probably stood nearby. Some of the more interesting objects contained in the cistern are shown in Plate 6-2 and include decorated pearlware ceramics (A, C-E), plain and decorated whiteware ceramics (B, F, H-J), pieces of eating utensils (P-S), buttons (L-O), decorated yellowware (G), fragments of stoneware and earthenware smoking pipes (K), and a small spoked wheel, perhaps from a toy (T). The silver three-cent piece also came from this feature, as did several bottle fragments (Plate 6-3). Some were hand blown, but most were made using bottle molds. Many of the

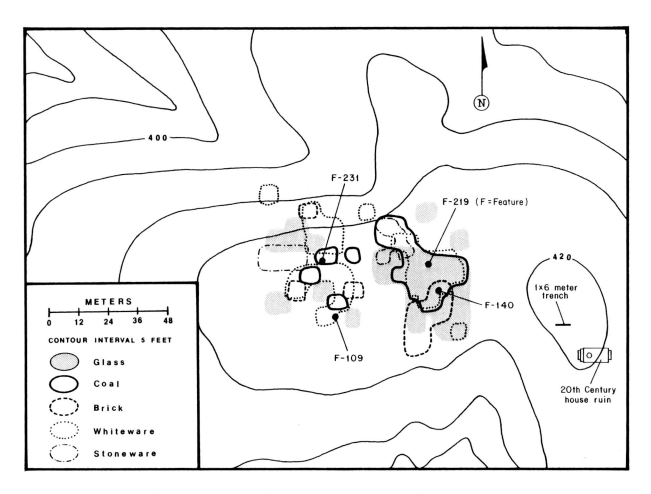

Figure 6-3. Distribution of Historic artifacts and location of various features at Sa-86.

PLATE 6-1. Early stage of excavation of Sa-86 Feature 109.

specimens once contained patent medicines. One of the bottles contained "Dr. D. Jayne' Liniment" (Plate 6-3, *A*), manufactured in Philadelphia in the 1860s. A second fragment had the words "Keller Drug C - Evansville" (Plate 6-3, *J*), and a third fragment showed that the specimen came from Cincinnati, Ohio (Plate 6-3, *B*). Two fragments of what is com-

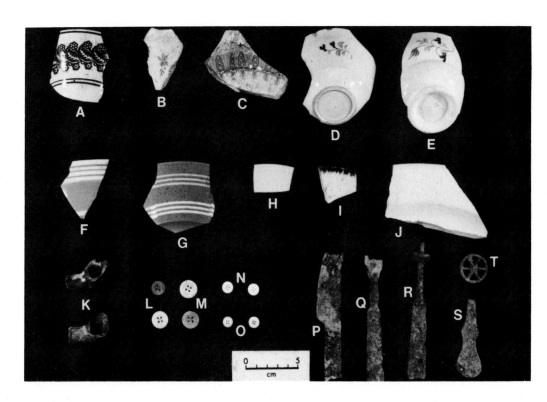

PLATE 6-2. Ceramics and miscellaneous objects recovered from the nineteenth-century cistern (Feature 109) at Sa-86.

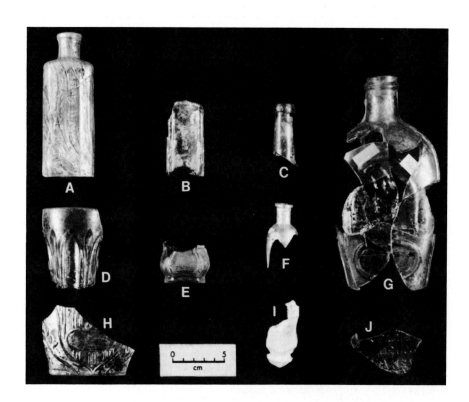

PLATE 6-3. Fragments of glass bottles and other miscellaneous glass objects found in the cistern (Feature 109) at Sa-86.

monly referred to as an eagle flask were also recovered from the abandoned cistern (Plate 6-3, *G* and *H*), along with parts of a perfume bottle (Plate 6-3, *E*), a goblet (Plate 6-3, *D*), and a milk glass candleholder (Plate 6-3, *I*).

Most of the Feature 109 artifacts date from about 1840 to sometime in the 1860s and represent virtually every aspect of mid-nineteenth-century domestic life. What is unusual is that such a diverse assortment of objects would occur in a pit that was filled during an apparently short time. One explanation for their cooccurrence is that they were discarded or lost around and under the nearby house over a period of many years. When the structure was destroyed, its remains, along with the material on the ground around it, were used to fill the abandoned cistern.

Following the abandonment of the first structure, a second one was built a short distance to the east. Its artifact scatter is about the same size as the earlier one, but it contains more material. The greater number of artifacts may be associated with the occupants' increased ability to purchase consumer goods. A second deep circular pit (Feature 219) was exposed near this scatter, and excavation showed that it served as a privy, not a cistern (Figure 6-3). The lower portion of the pit fill, attributable to the initial purpose for which the 7 foot (2 m) deep pit was dug, contained no artifacts. A second zone of relatively sterile fill was deposited over the lower zone. No doubt this layer of soil was placed in the privy to reduce the offensive odors. A third soil zone appeared to be deposited over a much longer time and contained the vast majority of the artifacts. A wide range of domestic activities also are represented by these artifacts. The privy was capped by a layer of sterile clay. An assortment of glass and ceramic objects from Feature 219 are shown in Plate 6-4. Analysis of these and other artifacts indicated that the privy was much younger than Feature 109, the majority of the artifacts dating to the 1890s.

Archaeologists located a third concentration of Historic artifacts and the remains of an early twentieth-century house about 66 yards (60 m) east of the second scatter, adjacent to the county road constructed early in the twentieth century (Figure 6-3). The filling of the privy in the 1890s may mark the construction date of this most recent house, since the distance from the privy to the new house would have made future use inconvenient.

PLATE 6-4. Ceramic and glass items found in the late nineteenth-century privy (Feature 219) at Sa-86.

A trench excavated near the road produced abundant artifacts dating to the 1940s and 1950s, although a few may be somewhat older. Most of these items, including Karo Syrup, Clorox, Pepsi Cola, and Jergens Lotion bottles, Mason jars, and even an ice skate, were recovered from an abandoned root cellar associated with the final Historic occupation at Sa-86.

It is difficult to identify the specific families that lived in the houses that once stood at Sa-86. Records of land transactions are highly fragmentary, and the site is located on the boundary between Township Sections 11 and 14. The earliest recorded transaction for this part of Section 14 dates to 1884 and involves the sale of the land to Davis Maghee by J. H. Maghee for $5.00—probably a token payment between family members. Census records show that the Maghee family did not reside in the immediate Carrier Mills area. In 1889, Josiah and Daw Taborn acquired the land, and in 1893 Josiah apparently sold his portion to Daw. The adjacent part of Section 11 was acquired by Aaron Arnold in 1853, but like the Maghees he did not live in the area. No other records for this tract exist until 1873, when Bird Taborn leased the mineral rights to two individuals named Clark and Glass. The occupation associated with the earliest artifact scatter probably predates the 1853 land transaction. The acquisitions of part of Section 14 by the Taborns may be associated with the occupation responsible for the second artifact scatter.

Archaeologists identified a second area of Historic activity at Sa-88, in the western part of the District. Most of the Historic material was associated with a small farmstead, consisting of a house, a tool shed, an outhouse, a root/storm cellar, an animal coop, a wagon shed, and a barn, situated at the extreme western end of the site (Figure 6-4). The original house was a 23 foot by 15 foot rectangular, square-notched log cabin. An 8 foot by 15 foot frame addition was constructed at a later date, and eventually the log exterior of the original cabin was sided-over (Plates 6-5 and 6-6). The year in which the cabin was built is difficult to determine, but a late nineteenth-century construction date seems likely. The cabin may have been built on another site and then later moved to the ridge top at Sa-88. The present roof supports, siding, and front porch probably date to about 1935. This date is based on the publication dates found on all the newspapers that were placed under wallpaper on the interior walls and the assumption that interior and exterior renovations were done at the same time. Most of the outbuildings date from the 1930s to the 1950s. The cabin itself was occupied until the 1960s.

As at Sa-86, it was difficult to locate information about the ownership of this property. This small area is the only part of a 40-acre tract that was not low or swampy and was, consequently, the only suitable area for a house site. The land was sold in 1856 to James Swan under the provisions of the Swampland Act. Later, in 1888, Priscilla Taborn sold the land to L. D. (Daw?) Taborn. In 1890, George W. Carrier sold land to Andrew Chavers (Chavis?) that included this 40-acre tract, and this may mark the beginning of the use of this area as a farmstead. A concrete well cap located near the house bears the name Chavous (Chavers?), and the inscription indicates that the well was first walled with rock in 1890. The land in question was still owned by a Chavous in 1978.

A dirt road was built along the property line east of the house around 1900, and it is shown on a 1925 USGS map of this area. The road was later abandoned, but a metal frame bridge over a small drainage ditch south of the cabin was still standing in 1978.

Additional scatters of Historic artifacts were identified at Sa-88 marking the former location of structures. One of these was probably associated with a house, but the origin of the others is unclear. Some of the artifacts collected from these scatters date to the mid-nineteenth century. Additional Historic artifact scatters were identified at Areas A and B of Sa-87.

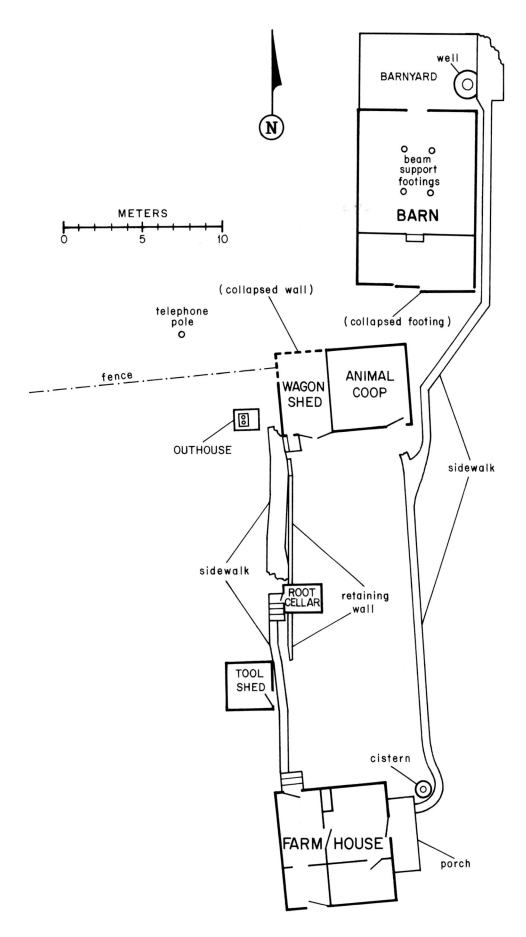

Figure 6-4. Plan view of farmstead complex at Sa-88.

PLATE 6-5. Front view of sided-over log cabin at west end of Sa-88.

PLATE 6-6. Side view of cabin at Sa-88. Logs are visible at bottom center of wall.

Archaeologists located a number of surface artifact scatters, as well as several large trash-filled pits, that produced the bulk of the archaeological data on Historic use of the area. Several of these scatters at Sa-86 and Sa-88 contained items dating from 1840 to 1870. Other scatters contained more modern artifacts dating from the 1880s to the early 1900s. The oldest scatters are characterized by a high percentage of refined earthenware pottery (pearlware, yellowware, whiteware, and so on) and small amounts of glass and brick. Later artifact scatters have a lower percentage of whiteware and a higher percentage of bottle glass.

A major problem in studying the Historic occupation of Carrier Mills was the lack of actual remains of the houses and other buildings. Without them, it is difficult to be sure of a building's former location. This problem is made more complicated by the practice of families dumping their refuse a considerable distance from their houses. Without structural remains, it is difficult to distinguish trash disposal areas from actual house sites, especially after years of plowing.

Most of the Historic material at Carrier Mills indicates that Lakeview residents were at the low end of the economic scale. Very few expensive or high-quality objects were found among the refuse, suggesting that the families owned few such items. What they did own they probably passed from one generation to the next. These items would have been used only on special occasions, further reducing the chance of their breakage and discard. Manufactured items, primarily bottles, indicate that major economic ties were with the cities of the Ohio valley and the Northeast such as Pittsburg, Philadelphia, Cincinnati, and Evansville.

The portion of the Lakeview community that was in the Carrier Mills Archaeological District included a number of farmsteads and their associated structural and artifactual remains. The archaeological data recovered from various parts of the District have provided a glimpse of both the sequence of occupation and the range of activities associated with the farmsteads. Even though the study of the Historic materials was restricted to this small part of Lakeview, it has provided us with a picture of what life was like during the nineteenth century in this small, isolated southern Illinois community.

7 A Retrospective Look

The landscape of the Carrier Mills Archaeological District looks quite different now than it did on that cold, snowy Christmas Eve of 1977 when Southern Illinois University archaeologists completed test excavations at the Black Earth site. The low ridges where Middle Archaic hunters and gatherers and Mississippian gardeners once lived are now part of the new Peabody Coal Company mine that supplies coal to power companies and other industries throughout the Midwest. Even though the sites are now gone, the extensive archaeological program conducted by Southern Illinois University preserved much of the information contained in these sites for future generations. The Carrier Mills archaeologists are confident that they have a good understanding of the way of life of the people living along the Saline River during much of the past 10,000 years.

The artifacts and other cultural materials produced by the Carrier Mills work are stored or curated at Southern Illinois University where they can be studied by archaeologists in the years to come. The Carrier Mills Archaeological Project is officially completed, but the potential to learn much more still exists.

The successful completion of the Carrier Mills Archaeological Project demonstrates the benefits of cooperation between those groups favoring the preservation of significant cultural resources, represented by Southern Illinois University, and those favoring economic and industrial development, represented by Peabody Coal Company. The spirit of cooperation that developed between these two organizations prevented an issue that could have grown into a major source of disagreement and discontent from ever developing. Instead, the agreement that was reached served the interests of both parties and provided the archaeological community and the general public with a much better understanding of how southern Illinois' past inhabitants lived.

New information about life along the Saline River during the prehistoric and early Historic periods was obtained by using modern scientific techniques in the field and laboratory and employing highly trained specialists to analyze the data and interpret the results. All of the research was conducted within the framework of a well-conceived research plan that targeted those aspects of prehistoric life to be investigated and specified how to collect the required data. Good archaeological research requires a lot of time, patience, attention to detail, and hard work, but the benefits are obvious.

Unfortunately, many southern Illinois archaeological sites are "excavated" by people who have not received the necessary training to do the job properly. Some of these people dig at archaeological sites just to add to their personal artifact collections; others loot sites to obtain artifacts that they can sell to other collectors. Some artifact collectors are unaware of the damage they do or the amount of information they destroy by pursuing their avocation; others, motivated by monetary gain, simply do not care.

Those who are seriously interested in learning more about the prehistoric people of southern Illinois can do so by taking archaeology classes offered by universities and community colleges or by enrolling in an archaeological field school where they can learn about proper field and laboratory techniques from trained instructors. People who dig archaeological sites just to get the artifacts destroy information that might tell an archaeologist something new and interesting about southern Illinois' past.

Archaeologists are often asked about the "best" or "most significant" thing they find during the excavation of a site. Many times, the thing the person asking the question regards as significant or best is quite different from that identified by the archaeologist. For most archaeologists, the most important part of a project is usually not the most beautiful or most exotic artifact recovered but the information that reveals something new about the diet, technology, health, or social organization of a sites' past inhabitants.

The work at Carrier Mills revealed many new facts about prehistoric life in southern Illinois. One of the most significant aspects of the project was the thick Middle Archaic midden deposit found at Area A of the Black Earth site. Its significance is based on several factors. First, the meter-thick deposit was largely undisturbed by plowing or other modern activities because it was protected by overlying deposits. With the exception of artifacts from intrusive pits dug by Woodland period inhabitants, all of the artifacts from the midden zone were attributable to Middle Archaic activities. This enabled archaeologists to study many aspects of Middle Archaic life that could not be investigated at sites with mixed cultural deposits.

Second, because the midden zone was deposited over a nearly 1,000-year period, archaeologists could study how the lives of the Middle Archaic inhabitants changed through time by comparing the contents of the lower, older deposits with those of the more recent, upper midden levels.

The third factor adding to the significance of the midden was the excellent quality of bone preservation attributable to the extremely alkaline soils. Among the different categories of skeletal material recovered were the bones of animals killed by Middle Archaic hunters, bone tools and ornaments and the by-products of their manufacture, and human skeletal remains from the more than 150 Middle Archaic burials. Since bone preservation is very poor at most southern Illinois archaeological sites, very little was known about the parts of Middle Archaic life represented by these remains.

The study of the bones of the various mammals, birds, fish, and reptiles provided archaeologists with new information about the importance of different animals in the Middle Archaic diet and the extent to which the various natural habitats surrounding the Black Earth site were exploited by Middle Archaic hunters, trappers, and fishermen. The more than 2,000 bone artifacts found at the Black Earth site, representing an assortment of manufacturing, maintenance, and ceremonial activities, constitute one of the largest collections from the Midwest. Very little information existed about this component of Middle Archaic technology prior to the Carrier Mills work. Analysis of the elaborately carved and engraved bone pins provided archaeologists with new insights into the organization of Middle Archaic societies in the Midwest.

The recovery of well-preserved Middle Archaic burials enabled project archaeologists to study the biological characteristics of the inhabitants, as well as to investigate the various diseases and injuries from which they suffered. Analysis of the mortuary program yielded new information about how Middle Archaic society was organized. Collectively, the information recovered from the midden zone provided Carrier Mills archaeologists with an excellent picture of what life was like along the banks of the Saline River 5,000 to 6,000 years ago.

Although the new information about Middle Archaic life was very significant, the project also yielded important findings about the other prehistoric and Historic occupations represented in the District. Analysis of the Carrier Mills Woodland pottery gave archaeologists new insights into changes in the way pottery was made and why these changes occurred. The study of plant remains from Archaic, Woodland, and Mississippian midden deposits and features provided significant new information about how prehistoric people used southern Illinois' native plants and how their way of life was altered by the introduction of nonlocal plants.

Excavation of the two Mississippian structures and their limited contents gave archaeologists a glimpse of what life was like at Carrier Mills only a few centuries before European contact. These findings were made more significant because of the relatively little known about Mississippian lifeways in interior southern Illinois compared to what is known about Mississippian people living on the Ohio River and Mississippi River floodplains.

Finally, the study of the Lakeview community demonstrated the value of using archaeological and archival materials to investigate the history of this early black settlement and its relationships with other nineteenth- and early twentieth-century southern Illinois communities.

The only way we can learn more about the cultures of the people who inhabited southern Illinois during the millennia that preceded Euro-American settlement is through archaeology. These people had no written language and left no records to provide answers to our questions. The Indians inhabiting the region when the first settlers came to southern Illinois were different in many ways from those who lived here thousands, or even hundreds, of years earlier. Accounts and descriptions made by the settlers of the way of life of the Indians they encountered provide few hints about the prehistoric inhabitants.

The Carrier Mills Archaeological Project exemplifies the benefits to professional archaeologists and to the general public of a well-planned, scientifically oriented archaeological research project. The technical reports produced by the project archaeologists contain the detailed information required to interpret past human behavior at Carrier Mills. Archaeologists can compare what was found at Carrier Mills with that from other archaeological sites in the region to investigate similarities and differences among prehistoric groups. Unfortunately, these reports have a limited distribution and are usually found only in university libraries or in archaeological laboratories. Most people seldom have an opportunity to read these reports, and even if they did they would find much of the detailed information irrelevant to their interests. In many cases, the public is unaware that the work has ever been done.

This book represents the combined efforts of Peabody Coal Company and the archaeologists at Southern Illinois University to make the public aware of the results of this important archaeological project. Hopefully, it demonstrates how archaeology produces information about the past and provides the readers with a better understanding of how southern Illinois' past inhabitants lived.

References

Index

References

ARMELAGOS, GEORGE J.
1969 Disease in Ancient Nubia. *Science* 163:255–259.

ASCH, DAVID L., and NANCY B. ASCH
1982 A Chronology for the Development of Prehistoric Horticulture in Westcentral Illinois. Paper presented at the Forty-seventh Annual Meeting of the Society for American Archaeology, Minneapolis.

ASCH, DAVID L., KENNETH B. FARNSWORTH, and NANCY B. ASCH
1979 Woodland Subsistence and Settlement in West Central Illinois. In *Hopewell Archaeology*, edited by David S. Brose and N'omi Greber, pp. 80–85. Kent State University Press, Kent, Ohio.

BLAKELY, R. L.
1971 Comparison of the Mortality Profiles of Archaic, Middle Woodland, and Middle Mississippian Skeletal Populations. *American Journal of Physical Anthropology* 34:43–54.

BRAUN, DAVID P.
1983 Pots as Tools. In *Archaeological Hammers and Theories*, edited by James A. Moore and Arthur S. Keene, pp. 107–134. Academic Press, New York.

BRIESCHKE, WALTER L., and FRANK RACKERBY
1973 The "Stone Forts" of Illinois. *Outdoor Illinois* 12:19–26.

BROSE, DAVID S., and N'OMI GREBER (editors)
1979 *Hopewell Archaeology: The Chillicothe Conference*. Kent State University Press, Kent, Ohio.

BROWN, JAMES A., and ROBERT K. VIERRA
1983 What Happened in the Middle Archaic? Introduction to an Ecological Approach to Koster Site Archaeology. In *Archaic Hunters and Gatherers in the American Midwest*, edited by James L. Phillips and James A. Brown, pp. 165–195. Academic Press, New York.

BUTLER, BRIAN M., and RICHARD W. JEFFERIES
1986 Crab Orchard and Early Woodland Cultures in the Middle South. In *The Kampsville Conference on Early Woodland*, edited by Kenneth B. Farnsworth and Thomas E. Emerson, Center for American Archeology, Kampsville, in press.

CALDWELL, JOSEPH R.
1964 Interaction Spheres in Prehistory. In *Hopewellian Studies*, edited by Joseph Caldwell and Robert Hall, pp. 133–143. Scientific Papers No. 12. Illinois State Museum, Springfield.

CANTWELL, ANNE-MARIE
1980 *Dickson Camp and Pond: Two Early Havana Tradition Sites in the Central Illinois Valley*. Reports of Investigations, No. 36. Illinois State Museum, Springfield.

COFIELD, JEWELL
1976 *Memories of Lakeview*. Privately published.

COOK, S. F., and R. F. HEIZER
1965 *Studies on the Chemical Analysis of Archaeological Sites*. University of California Press, Berkeley and Los Angeles.

COOK, THOMAS G.

1976 *Koster: An Artifact Analysis of Two Archaic Phases in West Central Illinois*. Koster Research Reports No. 3, Northwestern University Archaeological Program Prehistoric Records No. 1.

CRAWFORD, GARY W.

1982 Late Archaic Plant Remains from West-Central Kentucky: A Summary. *Mid-Continental Journal of Archaeology* 7:205–224.

DANIELS, S. G. H.

1972 Research Design Models. In *Models in Archaeology*, edited by David L. Clarke, pp. 201–229. Methuen, London.

DEEVEY, EDWARD S., and RICHARD F. FLINT

1957 Postglacial Hypsithermal Interval. *Science* 125:182–184.

FORTIER, ANDREW C., THOMAS E. EMERSON, and FRED A. FINNEY

1984 Early Woodland and Middle Woodland Periods. In *American Bottom Archaeology*, edited by Charles J. Bareis and James W. Porter, pp. 59–103. University of Illinois Press, Urbana and Chicago.

FOWLER, MELVIN C.

1957 *Rutherford Mound, Hardin County, Illinois*. Scientific Papers No. 7(1). Illinois State Museum, Springfield.

1959 *Summary Report of Modoc Rock Shelter: 1952, 1953, 1955, 1956*. Illinois State Museum Reports of Investigations No. 8.

1969 Middle Mississippian Agricultural Fields. *American Antiquity* 34:365–375.

1977 The Cahokia Site. In *Explorations into Cahokia Archaeology*, edited by Melvin L. Fowler, pp. 1–30. Bulletin No. 7. Illinois Archaeological Survey, Urbana.

1978 Cahokia and the American Bottom: Settlement Archeology. In *Mississippian Settlement Patterns*, edited by Bruce D. Smith, pp. 455–478. Academic Press, New York.

FOWLER, MELVIN L., and ROBERT L. HALL

1978 Late Prehistory of the Illinois Area. In *Northeast,* edited by Bruce G. Trigger, pp. 560–568. Handbook of North American Indians, vol. 15, William G. Sturtevant, general editor. Smithsonian Institution, Washington, D.C.

FRYE, JOHN C., A. B. LEONARD, H. B. WILLMAN, and H. D. GLASS

1972 *Geology and Paleontology of Late Pleistocene Lake Saline, Southeastern Illinois*. Illinois State Geological Survey Circular No. 471.

GRIFFIN, JAMES B.

1952 Some Early and Middle Woodland Pottery Types in Illinois. In *Hopewellian Communities in Illinois*, edited by Thorne Deuel, pp. 93–129. Scientific Papers No. 5. Illinois State Museum, Springfield.

GRIFFIN, JAMES B. (editor)

1961 *Lake Superior Copper and the Indians: Miscellaneous Studies of Great Lakes Prehistory*. Anthropological Papers No. 17. Museum of Anthropology, University of Michigan, Ann Arbor.

GRIFFIN, J. B., R. E. FLANDERS, and P. F. TITTERINGTON

1970 *The Burial Complexes of the Knight and Norton Mounds in Illinois and Michigan*. University of Michigan Museum of Anthropology Memoir No. 2.

GRUGER, EBERHARD

1972 Late Quaternary Vegetation Development in South-central Illinois. *Quaternary Research* 2:217–231.

HANCOCK, FLORENCE L.

1947 Schools of Saline County. In *Saline County: A Century of History*, edited by S. Thompson, Z. Sloan, and A. Shestak, pp. 147–168. Saline County Historical Society, Harrisburg, Illinois.

HARGRAVE, MICHAEL L.

1981 *Woodland Ceramic Chronometry and Occupational Intensity at the Carrier Mills Archaeological District, Saline County, Illinois*. Unpublished M.A. thesis, Department of Anthropology, Southern Illinois University at Carbondale.

1982 Woodland Ceramic Decoration, Form, and Chronometry in the Carrier Mills Archaeological District. In *The Carrier Mills Archaeological Project: Human Adaptation in the Saline Valley, Illinois*, edited by Richard W. Jefferies and Brian M. Butler, pp. 1233–1288. Research Paper No. 33. Center for Archaeological Investigations, Southern Illinois University at Carbondale.

HOFMAN, J. L.

1980 Twenhafel Archaeology: The Southeastern Connection. *Tennessee Anthropologist* 5:185–201.

ILLINOIS GENERAL LAND OFFICE

1844 Transcription of Illinois Field Notes: Books 60–65. National Archives vols. 85, 107, and 113.

ILLINOIS STATE WATER SURVEY
1958 *Water Resources and Climate*. Atlas of Illinois Resources Section No. 1.

JANZEN, D. E.
1977 An Examination of Late Archaic Development in the Falls of the Ohio River Area. In *For the Director: Research Essays in Honor of James B. Griffin,* edited by C. E. Cleland, pp. 123–143. University of Michigan Museum of Anthropology Anthropological Papers No. 61.

JEFFERIES, RICHARD W., and BRIAN M. BUTLER (editors)
1982 *The Carrier Mills Archaeological Project: Human Adaptation in the Saline Valley, Illinois*. Research Paper No. 33. Center for Archaeological Investigations, Southern Illinois University at Carbondale.

JOHANNESSEN, SISSEL
1984 Paleoethnobotany. In *American Bottom Archaeology*, edited by Charles J. Bareis and James W. Porter, pp. 197–214. University of Illinois Press, Urbana and Chicago.

KELLAR, JAMES H.
1979 The Mann Site and "Hopewell" in the Lower Wabash-Ohio Valley. In *Hopewell Archaeology*, edited by David S. Brose and N'omi Greber, pp. 100–107. Kent State University Press, Kent, Ohio.

KELLY, JOHN E., FRED A. FINNEY, DALE L. McELRATH, and STEVEN OZUK
1984 Late Woodland Period. In *American Bottom Archaeology*, edited by Charles J. Bareis and James W. Porter, pp. 104–127. University of Illinois Press, Urbana and Chicago.

KELLY, LUCRETIA S., and PAULA G. CROSS
1984 Zooarchaeology. In *American Bottom Archaeology*, edited by Charles J. Bareis and James W. Porter, pp. 215–232. University of Illinois Press, Urbana and Chicago.

KING, JAMES E., and WILLIAM H. ALLEN, JR.
1977 A Holocene Vegetation Record from the Mississippi River Valley, Southeastern Missouri. *Quaternary Research* 8:307–323.

KING, THOMAS F., PATRICIA PARKER HICKMAN, and GARY BERG
1977 *Anthropology in Historic Preservation: Caring for Culture's Clutter*. Academic Press, New York.

KLINE, GERALD W., and GARY A. APFELSTADT
1975 Notes on the Lowe Flared Base Projectile Point. *Proceedings of the Indiana Academy of Sciences* 84:57–64.

LINDSEY, MARY NORMAN
1947 Coal Mines in Saline County. In *Saline County: A Century of History*, edited by S. Thompson, Z. Sloan, and A. Shestak, pp. 201–222. Saline County Historical Society, Harrisburg, Illinois.

LOPINOT, NEAL H.
1982 Plant Macroremains and Paleoethnobotanical Implications. In *The Carrier Mills Archaeological Project: Human Adaptation in the Saline Valley, Illinois*, edited by Richard W. Jefferies and Brian M. Butler, pp. 671–860. Research Paper No. 33. Center for Archaeological Investigations, Southern Illinois University at Carbondale.
1984 *Archaeobotanical Formation Processes and Late Middle Archaic Human-Plant Interrelationships in the Midcontinental U.S.A.* Unpublished Ph.D. dissertation, Department of Anthropology, Southern Illinois University at Carbondale.

MAXWELL, MOREAU S.
1951 *The Woodland Cultures in Southern Illinois: Archaeological Excavations in the Carbondale Area*. Logan Museum Publications in Anthropology Bulletin No. 7.

McELRATH, DALE L., THOMAS E. EMERSON, ANDREW C. FORTIER, and JAMES L. PHILLIPS
1984 Late Archaic Period. In *American Bottom Archaeology*, edited by Charles J. Bareis and James W. Porter, pp. 34–58. University of Illinois Press, Urbana and Chicago.

McNERNEY, MICHAEL J. (editor)
1975 *Archaeological Investigations in the Cedar Creek Reservoir, Jackson County, Illinois*. Southern Illinois Studies Research Records No. 12. Southern Illinois University Museum at Carbondale.

MILES, CLIFFORD, and BENNY WEISS
1978 *Soil Survey of Saline County, Illinois*. U.S. Department of Agriculture, Soil Conservation Service and Forest Service, in cooperation with Illinois Agricultural Experiment Station.

MILNER, GEORGE R., THOMAS E. EMERSON, MARK W. MEHRER, JOYCE A. WILLIAMS, and DUANE ESAREY
1984 Mississippian and Oneota Period. In *American Bottom Archaeology*, edited by Charles J. Bareis and James W. Porter, pp. 158–186. University of Illinois Press, Urbana and Chicago.

MULLER, JON

1978 The Kincaid System: Mississippian Settlement in the Environs of a Large Site. In *Mississippian Settlement Patterns*, edited by Bruce D. Smith, pp. 269–292. Academic Press, New York.

1984 Mississippian Specialization and Salt. *American Antiquity* 49:489–507.

MULLER, JON D., and DOUGLAS M. DAVY

1977 *Cultural Resources of the Ohio River Floodplain in Illinois*. Huntington District Corps of Engineers, Request No. DACW 59-77-Q-0053.

NEUMANN, GEORG K., and MELVIN L. FOWLER

1952 Hopewellian Sites in the Lower Wabash Valley. In *Hopewellian Communities in Illinois*, edited by Thorne Deuel, pp. 175–248. Scientific Papers No. 5. Illinois State Museum, Springfield.

PARMALEE, PAUL W.

1965 The Food Economy of Archaic and Woodland Peoples at Tick Creek Cave Site, Missouri. *Missouri Archaeologist* 24(1):1–34.

PARMALEE, PAUL W., ANDREAS A. PALOUMPIS, and NANCY WILSON

1972 *Animals Utilized by Woodland Peoples Occupying the Apple Creek Site, Illinois*. Reports of Investigations No. 23. Illinois State Museum, Springfield.

REED, NELSON A.

1977 Monks and Other Mississippian Mounds. In *Explorations into Cahokia Archaeology*, edited by Melvin L. Fowler, pp. 31–42. Bulletin No. 7. Illinois Archaeological Survey, Urbana.

RITZENTHALER, R. E., et al.

1957 Reigh Site Report No. 3. *Wisconsin Archaeologist* 38(4):278–310.

ROBISON, CATHY A., and BRIAN M. BUTLER

1981 Archaeological Summary of the Southern Illinois Region. Ms. on file, Center for Archaeological Investigations, Southern Illinois University at Carbondale.

ROSSO, WEYMAR A.

1975 *The Ecology of the South Fork of the Saline River as Affected by Surface Mine Wastes*. Ph.D. dissertation, Southern Illinois University at Carbondale. University Microfilms 76-13283, Ann Arbor.

SCHWEGMAN, JOHN

1975 The Natural Divisions of Illinois. In *Guide to Vascular Flora of Illinois*, by Robert H. Mohlenbrock, pp. 1–47. Southern Illinois University Press, Carbondale and Edwardsville.

SMITH, JOHN

1966 *The General Historie of Virginia, New England, and the Summer Isles*. Originally published 1624, London. University Microfilms, Ann Arbor.

STYLES, B. W., M. L. FOWLER, S. R. AHLER, F. B. KING, and T. R. STYLES

1981 *Modoc Rock Shelter Archaeological Project, Randolph County, Illinois, 1980–1981*. Completion report to the Department of the Interior, Heritage Conservation and Recreation Service and the Illinois Department of Conservation. Illinois State Museum and University of Wisconsin, Milwaukee.

SWANTON, JOHN R.

1946 *The Indians of the Southeastern United States*. Bureau of American Ethnology Bulletin No. 137.

TEMPLE, W. C.

1966 *Indian Villages of the Illinois Country*. Scientific Papers No. 2 (P. 2). Illinois State Museum, Springfield.

URBANEK, RICKARD P.

1976 *Vertebrate and Floral Diversity on Strip-mined Land in Williamson and Saline Counties, Illinois*. Unpublished M. A. thesis, Southern Illinois University at Carbondale.

WEBB, WILLIAM S.

1974 *Indian Knoll*. University of Tennessee Press, Knoxville. Originally published 1946, University of Kentucky, Lexington.

WILLEY, GORDON R., and PHILIP PHILLIPS

1958 *Method and Theory in American Archaeology*. University of Chicago Press, Chicago.

WINTERS, HOWARD D.

1967 *An Archaeological Survey of the Wabash Valley in Illinois*. Reports of Investigations No. 10. Illinois State Museum, Springfield.

1968 Value Systems and Trade Cycles of the Late Archaic in the Midwest. In *New Perspectives in Archaeology*, edited by S. R. Binford and L. R. Binford, pp. 175–221. Aldine, Chicago.

1969 *The Riverton Culture*. Illinois State Museum Reports of Investigations No. 13 and Illinois Archaeological Survey Monograph No. 1.

1981 Excavating in Museums: Notes on Mississippian Hoes and Middle Woodland Copper Gouges and Celts. In *The Research Potential of Anthropological Museum Collections*, edited by Anne-Marie E. Cantwell, James B. Griffin, and Nan A. Rothschild, pp. 17–34. Annals of the New York Academy of Sciences No. 376.

1984 The Significance of Chert Procurement and Exchange in the Middle Woodland Traditions of the Illinois Area. In *Prehistoric Chert Exploitation: Studies from the Midcontinent*, edited by Brian M. Butler and Ernest E. May, pp. 3–21. Occasional Paper No. 2. Center for Archaeological Investigations, Southern Illinois University at Carbondale.

Index

Abraders, 50, 51, 55
Absolute dating, 40. *See also* Radiocarbon dating
Acorns: Archaic use of, 68, 82, 89; Mississippian use of, 130; Woodland use of, 95, 96, 109, 123
Adaptation, human ability for, 29–30
Adena culture, 95
Adena-Cypress point type, 86, 88, 101, *Plate 3-35*
Adzes, 52, *Plate 3-10*
Affinis Snyders point type, 96, 101, *Plate 4-5*
American Bottom: Archaic occupation of, 85, 89; Mississippian occupation of, 129–30, 132; Woodland occupation of, 91–92, 97, 113, 123
American lotus, 109
American plum, 68, 109, 123
Anglo-American settlement, 16, 138, 139. *See also* Lakeview community
Antler implements: from the Black Earth site, 44; in burials, 73; Middle Archaic, 54, 57, 63, 65, 73, *Plates 3-15, 3-16*; for percussion flaking, 46, 57, *Plate 3-15. See also names of individual tool types*
Archaeological evidence, nature of, 3
Archaeological sites. *See* Sites, archaeological
Archaeological survey. *See* Survey, archaeological
Archaic period (8000–1000 B.C.): burials, 14, 35, 36, 37, 43, 61–62, 65, 70–75, 82, 83, 153–54, *Fig. 3-5, Plates 3-25–3-30*; diet, 36, 66–70, 76, 83, 89; Early (8000–6000 B.C.), 31–34; environment during, 31–32; culture history of, 14; Late (3000–1000 B.C.), 83–89; lifeways during, 34, 35, 36–37, 81–83, 85–86; Middle (6000–3000 B.C.), 35–83; radiocarbon dates for, 41
Architecture: Archaic, 66, *Plate 3-24*; Historic, 148–51, 154, *Fig. 6-4, Plates 6-5, 6-6*; Mississippian, 130, 132–38, *Fig. 5-2, Plates 5-2–5-4*; Woodland, 95, 112, 123
Arnold, Aaron, 148
Arnold Research Cave, 60
Arrowpoints, 16. *See also* Projectile points
Arthritis, 77, 78
Atlatl hooks, antler, 57, *Plate 3-16*
Atlatl weights, 50, 52–53, *Plate 3-11*
Awls, bone and antler, 55, 57, 62, 63, 73, *Plate 3-12*
Axes, Middle Archaic, 42, 50, 51–52, 73, *Plate 3-10*; miniature, 43, 61–62

Bannerstones. *See* Atlatl weights
Baskets, poor preservation of, 42
Beads, bone, 43, 59, 60, *Plate 3-13*
Beads, shell, 60–61, *Plate 3-18*
Beans: domesticated, 16, 128; wild, 68, 69, 109, 110

Beaver, 55, 69, 110
Bedstraw, 68, 69
Bifacial tools, 45, 73
Big Creek Coals, Inc., 6
Big Sandy point type, 37
Birds: Archaic use of, 55, 89; Woodland use of, 92, 95, 124
Bitternuts. *See* Hickory nuts
Blackberries, 68
Black Bottom, 114, 131
Black Earth site (Sa-87): Archaic occupation of, 37–40, *Fig. 3-6*; burial at, 74, *Plates 3-28, 3-29*; description of, 19–22; Historic occupation of, 148; middens at, 19–22, 153, *Fig. 2-3*; naming of, 4; preservation at, 44; radiocarbon dates for, 41; Shawnee Indians at, 138; Woodland occupations at, 98, 100, 114–15, 117
Black Laws, 140
Black raspberries, 68
Blades, 97
Blanks, making of, 46
Bloom, Jonathan, 124
Bobcat, 55, 69
Bobrowsky, Peter, 12
Bone, human. *See* Burials
Bone artifacts: abrading of, 51, 55; Archaic, 59–60, 73, *Plate 3-17*; from Black Earth site, 44; poor preservation of, 42. *See also names of individual tool types*
Bottles, patent medicine, 145
Bow and arrow, 15, 102, 115, 123
Bowfin. *See* Fish
Bowls, turtle shell, 55–57
Box turtles. *See* Turtles
Braun, David, 7
Breitburg, Emanuel, 12, 55, 69, 124
Bremer site, 131
Bricks, Historic, 144
Brown, James, 97
Broyles, Bettye, 5
Burial 137 (shaman), 61–62, 74
Burial 182, 71–72, *Fig. 3-5*
Burial 190A and 190B, 63, *Fig. 3-4, Plate 3-23*
Burials: Archaic, 14, 35, 36, 37, 43, 61–62, 65, 70–75, 82, 83, 153–54, *Fig. 3-5, Plates 3-25–3-30*; artifacts in, 43, 59, 61–62, 65, 73–74, *Plates 3-19–3-22*; clay caps in, 75; in features, 10; Mississippian, 129; in mounds, 3, 15, 95, 96, 97, 110, 129; multiple, 75, *Plate 3-30*; orientation of, 71; position of, 71–72; pottery in, 118, 124; preservation of, 39–40, 70; recording, 71;

Sites, archaeological: Archaic, 35, 82, 88, 89; condition of, 3; defined, 3; difficulty of identifying Paleoindian, 31; federal protection of, 6, 7; finding, 4, 5; location of, 4; Mississippian, 128, 131–32; size of, 3–4; Woodland, 92, 95–96, 97, 100, 109–10, 112, 113–14, 123–24
Site Sa-86, 19, 98, 100, 114–15, 117, 132, 144, 148
Site Sa-87. *See* Black Earth site
Site Sa-88, 22, 98, 115, 148
Skunks, 69
Slate, from artifact cache, 62
Snakes, 69
Snyders-like point type, 97
Snyders point type, 96, 97, 101, *Plate 4-5*
Social organization: Archaic, 14, 15, 70, 75, 83; inferred from burials, 14, 15, 70, 75, 83, 110; Mississippian, 16, 128–29, 131–32; Woodland, 15, 95, 110
"Soft hammer" percussion flaking, 46
Soils. *See* Middens; Soil samples
Soil samples, 10–11, 82
Somerset, Historic settlement at, 17
Southern Illinois University, Center for Archaeological Investigations, 7–8, 152, 154
Southern Illinois University Museum, 5
Southern Till Plain, 23, 28
South Fork of the Saline River, 4, 24, 27, 28
Spring beauty, 109
Squash: Archaic introduction of, 83; Mississippian cultivation of, 16, 128, 130; Woodland cultivation of, 15, 113, 123–24
Squirrel, 55, 69, 110
Stone, B. F., 28
Stone forts, 3, 113
Stone tools, 42. *See also names of individual tool types;* Chert, sources of
Struever, Stuart, 97
Subsistence: Archaic, 66–70, 76, 83, 89; and dental problems, 78–79; and disease and injury, 76; Historic, 140; Mississippian, 128, 130, 137; and nutritional stress, 76; Woodland, 93, 95, 96, 97, 109–10, 111–12, 123–24. *See also names of individual plants and animals;* Horticulture; Hunters and gatherers
Sugar Camp Hill site, 102–3, 107
Sumpweed, cultivation of, 83
Sunflowers, 15, 68, 69, 83, 113
Surface collection, controlled, 9
Survey, archaeological, 5
Swampland Act, 148
Swans, James, 148
Swans, 69, 110

Taborn, Bird, 148
Taborn, Catherine, 143
Taborn, Josiah and Daw, 148

Taborn, Kimber, 142–43
Taborn, L. D. (Daw?), 148
Taborn, Priscilla, 148
Taborn, Zachariah and Lydia, 140, 142–43
Thebes Notched point type, 32, *Plate 3-2*
Thinning flakes, 45, 46
Tick trefoil, 68
Timbering, in southern Illinois, 17
Titterington phase (Late Archaic), 85
Tobacco, cultivation of, 17, 123
Toolmaking: of bone tools, 59–60; of chert tools, 44–45, 46–47, *Plate 3-6;* of copper tools, 63; of groundstone tools, 50, 53; tools used in, 46, 55, 57
Tools, nonportable. *See* Features
Tools, portable. *See names of individual tool types;* Antler implements; Bone artifacts; Chert, implements of; Groundstone implements
Trade. *See* Exchange and trade
Trees, GLO surveyors' records of, 28
Trimble point type, 85, 88
Turkey: Archaic use of, 14, 46, 55, 69, 82, 89; Woodland use of, 95, 96, 110
Turtles: Archaic use of, 55, 63, 69, *Plate 3-14;* Woodland use of, 92
Twenhafel site, 96, 102, 107, 131

Unifacial tools, making of, 45
Unity Community Church, 143
Utilitarian equipment, 43. *See also names of individual tool types*

Wabash Border Division, 23, 28
Walnuts, 68, 69, 109, 123
Ware site, 131
Wedge, copper, 63, *Fig. 3-4, Plate 3-23*
Will Scarlet mine, 7
Wilson Mounds, 96, 98
Winters, Howard D., 63, 85
Woodchuck, 55, 69, 110
Wood cording, in southern Illinois, 17
Wooden implements, 42, 44
Woodland period (1000 B.C.–A.D. 1000): burials, 15, 95, 96, 97, 110, 124, *Plates 4-19, 4-20;* culture history of, 14–15; diet, 93, 95, 96, 97, 109–10, 111–12, 123–24; Early (1000–200 B.C.), 90–95; Late (A.D. 400–1000), 90, 112–26; lifeways during, 92, 95–96, 97, 100, 109–10, 112, 113–14, *Fig. 4-4;* Middle (200 B.C.–A.D. 400), 90, 95–112; radiocarbon dates for, 98, 104, 114, 118. *See also* Pottery, Woodland
Woods, William, 12, 38
Woodworking: edge-wear evidence of, 48; tools for, 52

Yankeetown ceramics, 115, 118. *See also* Duffy ceramics

Richard W. Jefferies received his Ph.D. from the University of Georgia in 1978. He was Director of the Carrier Mills Archaeological Project and co-editor of *The Carrier Mills Archaeological Project: Human Adaptation in the Saline Valley, Illinois.* His research interests include prehistoric cultures in the Southwest and Midwest; Woodland settlement and subsistence systems; lithic analysis; cultural ecology; and environmental adaptation. He is currently the Director of the Program for Cultural Resource Assessment and Adjunct Assistant Professor at the University of Kentucky.